CUBAN SLAVERY FROM THE INSIDE OUT

CARIBBEAN
STUDIES
SERIES

ANTON L. ALLAHAR AND NATASHA BARNES
Series Editors

CUBAN SLAVERY FROM THE INSIDE OUT

NONFICTION NARRATIVES OF CUBAN SLAVERY BY CUBAN AND US WRITERS

JULIA C. PAULK

UNIVERSITY PRESS OF MISSISSIPPI / JACKSON

The University Press of Mississippi is the scholarly publishing agency of
the Mississippi Institutions of Higher Learning: Alcorn State University,
Delta State University, Jackson State University, Mississippi State University,
Mississippi University for Women, Mississippi Valley State University,
University of Mississippi, and University of Southern Mississippi.

www.upress.state.ms.us

The University Press of Mississippi is a member
of the Association of University Presses.

Copyright © 2026 by University Press of Mississippi
All rights reserved
Manufactured in the United States of America
∞

Publisher: University Press of Mississippi, Jackson, USA
Authorised GPSR Safety Representative: Easy Access System Europe - Mustamäe tee 50, 10621 Tallinn, Estonia, gpsr.requests@easproject.com

Library of Congress Cataloging-in-Publication Data

Names: Paulk, Julia C. author
Title: Cuban slavery from the inside out : nonfiction narratives of Cuban slavery
   by Cuban and US writers / Julia C. Paulk.
Other titles: Caribbean studies series.
Description: Jackson : University Press of Mississippi, [2026] |
   Series: Caribbean studies series | Includes bibliographical references and index.
Identifiers: LCCN 2025041650 (print) | LCCN 2025041651 (ebook) |
   ISBN 9781496861498 hardback | ISBN 9781496861504 trade paperback |
   ISBN 9781496861511 epub | ISBN 9781496861528 epub |
   ISBN 9781496861535 pdf | ISBN 9781496861542 pdf
Subjects: LCSH: Manzano, Juan Francisco, 1797-1854 | Slavery—Cuba—History—
   19th century | Slavery—Cuba | Enslaved persons—Cuba—History—19th century |
   Plantation life—Cuba—History—19th century | Cuba—19th century
Classification: LCC HT1076 .P38 2026 (print) | LCC HT1076 (ebook)
LC record available at https://lccn.loc.gov/2025041650
LC ebook record available at https://lccn.loc.gov/2025041651

British Library Cataloging-in-Publication Data available

This book is dedicated to my North Stars, Sumit, Suvali, and Sachi, who have inspired and supported me every step of the way.

CONTENTS

Acknowledgments ix
Introduction: Writing About Cuban Slavery 3

PART I: WRITING FROM INSIDE CUBA
Chapter One: The Many Discourses of Juan Francisco Manzano:
   Disruptions to Coloniality in *Autobiografía del esclavo poeta* 31
Chapter Two: *Costumbrismo criollo*:
   Enlightenment Ideals and the Discourse of Coloniality 53
Chapter Three: The Tyrannies of Liberty and Equality:
   The Condesa de Merlin's Colonialist Travels. 77

PART II: WRITING FROM OUTSIDE CUBA
Chapter Four: Manifest Coloniality:
   Maturin Murray Ballou and the "Africanization" of Cuba 99
Chapter Five: Blackface, Plantations, and Tropical Spaces:
   Julia Ward Howe's *A Trip to Cuba*. 120
Chapter Six: La Guerra de los Diez Años and the Lost Cause:
   Eliza Ripley's Desengaño. 141

Conclusion and an Epilogue:
   Legacies of Nineteenth-Century Coloniality 162

Notes 171
Works Cited 181
Index 195

ACKNOWLEDGMENTS

I want to thank my academic friends and colleagues, especially those at Marquette University, for their years of support, intellectual companionship, and advice. This book has been a long time in development, and I could not have gotten to this point without the support of my professional and personal networks. The anonymous reviewers provided invaluable feedback that helped make the manuscript into a much stronger and more cohesive work, and I am grateful for their contributions. I would also like to offer my most sincere thanks to my editor, Lisa McMurtray, and to the University Press of Mississippi for their support of my work and the guidance that they have provided.

CUBAN SLAVERY FROM THE INSIDE OUT

INTRODUCTION

WRITING ABOUT CUBAN SLAVERY

Famously separated by a mere ninety miles, Cuba and the United States share a long history of conflicting interests, similar concerns, and mutual influence. Despite becoming independent nations more than a century apart, Cuba and the US are alike in having maintained the colonial institution of enslavement for the larger part of the nineteenth century. Likewise, both countries today continue to reckon with this history and with the racialized thought that justified the institution of enslavement. Cuba struggled through much of the nineteenth century to end its colonial status, yet largely denied inclusion into national identity for the island's majority Afro-descendant population. In the meantime, the US exponentially expanded its territorial footprint through the continued process of settler colonialism and debated with increasing intensity over whether enslavement would also be permitted to spread. The Civil War achieved emancipation in the US, but only briefly interrupted efforts at increasing the country's influence and did not halt the ideological battles over national identity and belonging. Throughout the century, Cuba attracted the attention of those in the US who were interested in southward expansion.

As is reflected in nonfiction narratives from both places, Cuban enslavement and the Afro-descendant population that was both exploited by and resistant to the institution were at the center of Cuban debates over reform and independence and also were important in domestic US contentions over enslavement and annexation. Finding themselves in the minority in the early decades of the nineteenth century, the members of Cuba's elite *sacarocracia* ("sugar aristocracy") proposed an incipient Cuban national identity that was understood to be racially and culturally white, similar to that of European Spain. In *Papeles sobre Cuba* (*Papers about Cuba*), for example, Antonio

3

Saco writes, "[The] Cuban nationality of which I have spoken, and the only one that should concern all sensible men, is that formed by the white race" (cited in Pérez, *On Becoming Cuban* 90; Gott 55). Saco and Domingo del Monte, both of whom were influential *criollo* intellectuals, promoted an ideological program of erasure of African identity, *blanqueamiento*, in their efforts to move the island towards their conception of modern nationhood, but stopped short of supporting immediate emancipation. By the final third of the century, however, *criollo* freedom fighters became convinced of the need to incorporate Cuba's populations of color into the struggle against Spain if they were to succeed.

Cuba was a potential acquisition of great interest to the US throughout the century, and the institution of enslavement, its reliance on Afro-descendant laborers, and Cuba's overall racial identity were often at the center of contention over potential annexation. The earliest US statesmen to express interest in Cuba did not identify enslavement as an obstacle to overtaking the island. For example, in 1823, Thomas Jefferson wrote the following to President James Monroe: "I candidly confess, that I have ever looked on Cuba as the most interesting addition which could ever be made to our system of States" (cited in Gott 58). At mid-century, enslavement on the island was an inducement for proslavery factions in the US looking to strengthen the institution domestically. Even for those opposed to enslavement, Hispanophobic perceptions of Cuba's population as nonwhite and incapable of self-governance supported the view that the island would eventually fall under US control. When the violence of the US Civil War ended, participants from both sides of the US conflict projected the ongoing domestic ideological fight over racial equality and abolition onto Cuba's wars of independence. Cuba was seen as an instrument to expand their international and domestic agendas by both pro- and antislavery factions. After almost a century of speculation over Cuba, the US occupied the island in 1898.

Enslavement in the American Hemisphere existed as an instrument of empire building and was justified by the discourse of coloniality as theorized by Aníbal Quijano and Walter D. Mignolo, which continues to shape attitudes towards racial equality and to affect material conditions.[1] As such, nonfiction narratives about enslavement in Cuba by authors from both countries offer the opportunity to further understand the operations of coloniality in the Caribbean and the US, yet they have remained largely unstudied. While Latin American theories of decoloniality from Andean perspectives have found increased prominence over the last several decades, the implications of this school of thought for the Caribbean, the site of modernity/coloniality's "big bang," have not been sufficiently explored (Maldonado-Torres 561).

Further, because they are largely trained in North Atlantic empirical frameworks, critics of US literature have not fully recognized the continuity and evolution of the original European discourse of coloniality in expressions of racial identity and expansionism in US narratives. I argue that the study of narratives about Cuban enslavement demonstrates that the original Spanish discourse of coloniality is contemporaneous with the Hispanophobic discourse of coloniality in nineteenth-century perspectives on colonial Cuba from both within and beyond the island. Further, following Mignolo, my analysis of nineteenth-century US narratives about Cuban enslavement illustrates the evolution of the original European discourse of coloniality into the Hispanophobia expressed in US discourse of the era, but which remains unrecognized as such in North American literary criticism. The Islamophobia, antisemitism, and anti-Black language of the Reconquista and the Conquista also appear in US narratives about Cuba. Finally, while coloniality is reinscribed in various forms in the narratives studied here, constant and effective resistance to oppressive ideologies presents itself in each of these works and points to pathways towards international solidarity.

While nineteenth-century authors from both Cuba and the US devoted a considerable amount of ink to the problems of race-based enslavement and issues of racial identity, contemporary scholars have typically approached such literature through academic disciplines delineated by language and nationality, resulting in a number of gaps in criticism and in comparative study in this area. There are remarkably few truly comparative studies of nineteenth-century literature focusing on race and enslavement, despite the importance of the topic throughout the hemisphere and ongoing interest in understanding the operations of coloniality in literature. This work is the first book-length analysis of nonfiction accounts of Cuban enslavement by authors from both Cuba and the US. Miguel A. Cabañas's *The Cultural "Other" in Nineteenth-Century Travel Narratives: How the United States and Latin America Described Each Other* appears to be the closest comparable text in terms of hemispheric scope. However, Cabañas's text is more widely focused on Latin America and does not study narratives about Cuba or Cuban enslavement. In Hispanic studies, there are a number of academic books and articles dedicated to Cuban novels about enslavement, yet Cuban nonfiction writing on this topic has received limited attention.[2] Rafael Ocasio's *Afro-Cuban Costumbrismo* is the only scholarly book that begins the important work of analyzing this particular nonfiction genre's approach to race and identity, yet many *artículos* and other types of nonfiction narratives focusing on Cuban enslavement remain understudied. In US literature, a large body of published works relevant to this topic remains significantly understudied: more than two hundred travel narratives about Cuba were published in English in the US in the nineteenth century.[3] The limited attention that these narratives have received has largely come from Cuban studies rather than US literature scholars.[4] One can only conclude that the critical neglect in scholarship on US literature of these Cuba narratives is a result of the longstanding ideology of US exceptionalism. The continued growth in hemispheric and transnational American studies indicates some change in this arena, yet current disciplinary training does not always prepare scholars fully for this undertaking. The present text intends to close some critical gaps through the analysis of literature about Cuban enslavement in a critical framework that is informed by Cuban perspectives, history, and cultural production while also considering US representations of racialized forced labor and discourse of empire building in order to better illustrate the operations of and resistance to coloniality in such narratives in a more hemispheric context.

DECOLONIZING AND RESISTANT METHODOLOGIES

This book presents a study of literature about the exploitation of racialized labor in Cuba that seeks to understand how this power dynamic is inscribed into literary nonfiction, with the hope that better comprehension of these structures can lead to different, more equitable ways of thinking in the future. I seek to employ methodologies for analyzing these narratives that do not commit epistemological injustice or reinscribe colonializing ideologies in scholarship.[5] My discussion of methodology begins with the concept of decoloniality because of its emphasis on pathways to overcoming the limitations of theoretical approaches that reproduce the inequities of coloniality. In *On Decoloniality: Concepts, Analytics, Praxis*, Walter D. Mignolo and Catherine E. Walsh explain that decoloniality "endeavors to delink from the theoretical tenets and conceptual instruments of Western thought" (7). To explain how one might go about detaching from Western or Eurocentric thought when already immersed in it, Mignolo and Walsh borrow powerful terminology from Audre Lorde, Lewis Gordon, and Jane Anna Gordon when describing this process: they refer to the implements of Western scholarship as "the master's tools" (7). Where Lorde argues that they "will never dismantle the master's house," Gordon and Gordon point out that the master's tools can be used to build one's own house, eventually transcending the master's edifice as more new houses are constructed (cited in Mignolo and Walsh 7). In other words, while dismantling old paradigms within the discourse of Western scholarship may be difficult, such paradigms can be transcended by building new frameworks. In a book about nineteenth-century writing on Cuban enslavement, calling the instruments of literary criticism "the master's tools" has particular resonance, and this expression is not used lightly here. A goal of this text is to challenge some of the precepts of Western and Northern white-centric thought as it is manifested in texts about Cuban enslavement while also exploring how literary criticism can aid in transcending rather than reiterating coloniality.

Scholars committed to decolonizing academic work often begin with acknowledgements of their own loci of enunciation as a strategy to avoid the universalizing tendencies of Western and Northern academic thought. In Global South studies, for example, Alfred J. López clarifies that the locus of enunciation is a positioning of the self and one's thought with relation to discourses and other structures of power with the intention to advocate for "knowledge production from geographical and epistemic positions historically viewed as marginal" (A. López 500). Epistemic location can refer not only to geographic location but also to "the scholar's disciplinary identifications and positions (departmental affiliations, access to research materials, travel funding, etc.) within or beyond the academy" (500). To this end, I begin by recognizing my academic training in Spanish American and comparative literature and my current employment in the US university system. Additionally, however, as Mignolo and Walsh state, "We are where we think, and our thinking is provoked by the history of the Americas (including the United States) and the Caribbean since the sixteenth century, when the very inception of modern/colonial patterns (i.e., coloniality) began to emerge" (2). My thinking has been provoked by the shared inheritance of racial ideologies and coloniality in both Cuba and the US that supported enslavement, that continues to have serious material and psychological repercussions, and that affects international relations. The fact that these are shared, although not identical, legacies indicates that there is also the opportunity to form relationships of solidarity among those marginalized by coloniality despite the contentious nature of official interactions between the two nations.

Contemporary literary and cultural criticism continues to move towards transnational and post-national frameworks that transcend the disciplinary and departmental structures within which US academics are trained and employed. Because these remain marginal fields in what continues to be a largely monolingual and monocultural US academy, however, I conceive of the present work as participating in Cuban studies and Latin American studies, in addition to contributing to Hemispheric and African diaspora studies. Although the nation-state is part of the apparatus of modernity/coloniality, the concept of national literatures and cultures has also served in less powerful countries as organizing forces for resistance to colonizing power. As other scholars have recognized, there is additionally the danger of subsuming literary traditions external to the US under a framework that presents itself as transnational and/or hemispheric, yet in practice reinscribes US exceptionalism.[6] For this reason, attention to the locus of textual production, to authorial self-identification, and to articulations of national identity remains important. A conceptual map of this study would place the micronarrative of enslavement in nineteenth-century Cuba at the center while also considering the macronarrative of colonialist power operating across the globe from Europe to Africa, to the American Hemisphere, and to Asia during the century when Spain's imperial power was coming to an end and the US was becoming part of the Global North.[7]

Observing the rise, development, and predominance of postcolonial theory in Western scholarship in the latter half of the twentieth century, Latin American and Latin Americanist theorists of decoloniality have been inspired by key developments, such as the publication of seminal texts by Frantz Fanon and Edward Said. However, they have also responded critically to the fact that this largely North Atlantic body of thought fails to consider Spanish and Portuguese colonization in the American Hemisphere and other parts of the globe. Iberian expansion on this side of the Atlantic began significantly earlier than British and French colonization in Africa and Asia, and did not necessarily take the same form as the latter types. The first model of European colonization challenges the framework in which North Atlantic postcolonial thought posits a number of concepts, among which modernity is of central importance. Whereas North Atlantic postcolonial theory dates modernity from the era of Enlightenment, theorists of coloniality/decoloniality argue that modernity necessarily begins with the Renaissance-era encounter with the American Hemisphere (Salvatore, "The Postcolonial in Latin America" 334–37).[8] The discourse of the conquest of Latin America, informed by that of the Christian Reconquista of Spain, initiated dialogues of European imperialism and Eurocentrism, as well as critiques of those phenomena that have continued to today (336–37). Despite the volume and quality of texts produced over the centuries, the creative and theoretical work of Latin Americans and the particularities of the region and its history have not been taken into consideration in the development of North Atlantic postcolonial thought. As Ricardo D. Salvatore summarizes, "At stake is the question of epistemic privilege and an aura of theories enunciated from Euro-North American universities" (335). The models of colonial economic dependence both on the metropolis and also on the subjugation of a large, racialized workforce in commodity production began when Cristóbal Colón first arrived in the Caribbean and promptly enslaved Indigenous people.[9] The African diaspora in the American Hemisphere began with the first permanent Spanish settlements in the Caribbean.[10] As historians Alex Borucki, David Eltis, and David Wheat describe, "Both the first and the last slave voyages to cross the Atlantic disembarked not very far from each other, in the Spanish colonies of Hispaniola (1505) and Cuba (1867)" (433).[11] Other European powers that came to occupy territory in the American Hemisphere followed the model of racialized enslavement first instituted by the Spanish empire.

Following the work of Aníbal Quijano, Mignolo argues that modernity and colonialism are inseparable concepts, and he proposes instead the compound term *modernity/coloniality* to explain the embedded and ongoing nature of coloniality in global systems of power that maintain inequality.[12] As Santiago Castro-Gómez summarizes this concept, "the modern world-system begins with the simultaneous synthesis of Spain as a 'center' and Hispanic America as its 'periphery.' There is no modernity without colonialism and no colonialism without modernity" (272).[13] Likewise, in *Coloniality at Large*, Mabel Moraña, Enrique Dussel, and Carlos A. Jáuregui define coloniality as a "term that encompasses the transhistoric expansion of colonial domination and the perpetuation of its effects in contemporary times" (2). Critics theorizing coloniality identify the patterns, structures, and discourse of empire building that began with Spanish colonization but that continue to operate in Latin America and the world at large. As Mignolo proposes, "Coloniality [is] the darker side of Western modernity" (*On Decoloniality* 106). On the heels of the Christian unification of Spain, the Spaniards who colonized much of the American Hemisphere framed conquest and settlement within narratives of the "salvation and civilization" of the purportedly godless Indigenous populations (106). These "narratives of modernity—salvation, progress, development" justified actions and behaviors that Indigenous and subjugated populations viewed as criminal (106). Although official processes of decolonization have occurred in much of the hemisphere, the power structures of coloniality that allow the accumulation of capital in limited places and the dehumanizing racialization of labor sources are still in operation and permeate Western/Northern thought. The wealthiest and most powerful countries in today's world are those that "manage and control the colonial matrix of power (CMP)" (106). These concepts are important in the analysis of colonial Cuba's cultural production, as well as in that of US thought regarding Cuba in the nineteenth century. The racialized narrative of salvation, military might, and development that justified the various systems of forced labor operating in Spanish colonization is couched in the racialized terms of civilization, development, and progress in both Cuban efforts to reform colonial institutions and in US ambitions towards the island and conceptions of its own practice of enslavement. In other words, similar discourses of modernity/coloniality, racial alterity, and empire building are at work throughout these texts regardless of their places of origin.

The concepts of abyssal thinking and the abyssal line introduced by Boaventura de Sousa Santos in *Epistemologies of the South: Justice Against Epistemicide* explain the enabling of coloniality in modern Western thought.[14] To illustrate these terms, Sousa Santos provides the example of the abyssal thinking through which the metropolis perceives the colony (118–19). An invisible abyssal line separates the metropolis from the colony; for those on the metropolitan side of the line, society is governed by "the regulation/emancipation dichotomy." On "this side of the line," one exists as a legal entity and is knowable, civilized, and part of the social contract. Those on the "other side of the line" are invisible, unknowable, extralegal, and nonexistent. As Sousa Santos explains, "nonexistent means not existing in any relevant or comprehensible way of being. Whatever is produced as nonexistent is radically excluded because it lies beyond the realm of what the accepted conception of inclusion considers to be its other" (118). On the colonial side of the line in this example, "the appropriation/violence dichotomy" applies: "Because the colonial territories were unthinkable as sites for the unfolding of the paradigm of regulation/emancipation, the fact that the latter did not apply to them did not compromise the paradigm's universality" (119). Finally, the structures on the metropolitan side are "grounded on the invisibility of the distinction between this side of the line and the other side of the line" (119). Following this logic, Western thought conceives of a universal, civilized humanity on one side of the line, with the absence of humanity on the other: "[M]odern humanity is not conceivable without modern subhumanity" (123). This mode of thought, employed by those who consider themselves civilized and progressive, not only enables such practices as enslavement but also justifies policies of military intervention into nations deemed incapable of governing themselves.

Nineteenth-century nonfiction texts about Cuban enslavement frequently express coloniality and abyssal thinking through ideologies of race. The writers from both Cuba and the US studied here reveal a shared association of modernity, nationhood, and citizenship with European-derived whiteness. They do not, however, agree as to who may be considered white, modern, and civilized. While similarities in the white-centric racial ideologies expressed in texts from Cuba and the US arise from their shared participation in the

European discourse of empire building, the differences arise from a shift in the locus of enunciation rather than from a change in the logic of coloniality. In his article "*Islamophobia / Hispanophobia*: The (Re)Configuration of the Racial Imperial/Colonial Matrix," Mignolo defines the discourse of empire building and identifies its original formulation in Spain as the starting point for the contemporary discourses of fear and difference known as Islamophobia and Hispanophobia. As the theorists of decoloniality argue, modernity/coloniality begins with Spain's encounter with the American Hemisphere beginning in 1492. This same year also saw the conclusion of the centuries-long Christian Reconquest of Spain from Muslim rule and the expulsion of the followers of the two other "religions of the book" that threatened Christianity and the rule of the Catholic monarchs: the Muslims and the Jews (15). The Western theological discourse of classification and differentiation separating Iberian Christians from Muslims and Jews became the discourse of empire building as newly unified Spain expanded into the American Hemisphere, incorporating the Indigenous population and Afro-descendants into the same narrative of salvation and progress that ideologically supported the Reconquest (17). Within this discourse, Renaissance Spaniards, self-styled inheritors of the Visigoth kingdom of Hispania, are established as the model of universal humanity on the metropolitan side of the abyssal line, with potential threats and exploitable populations on the other (see José Manuel Nieto Soria for more on Hispania).

As Spain's imperial power began to decline both within and beyond Europe, the differentiating discourse of empire building that the Iberian country had articulated was then adopted by the rising powers of northern Europe in what is often called the "Black Legend" (Mignolo, "*Islamophobia/Hispanophobia*" 17). Rather than reinscribe the colorism implied by this twentieth-century term, I will use the terms "Hispanophobic discourse of coloniality" or "Hispanophobia" to discuss the "Black Legend" in its historical and contemporary forms as an iteration of the original discourse of coloniality that was turned against Spain and Spanish-speaking territories. As Mignolo points out, the Others rejected by Spain's rhetoric in its rise as an empire represent Spain in the Hispanophobic discourse of coloniality. Even while committing similar acts, Protestant English propagandists accused "Spaniards of being barbarians (for the atrocities they committed in the New World), and nam[ed] them Moors, Blacks, and Sarracens" (22). The Hispanophobic discourse of coloniality ascribes to Spaniards the same suspect religious and ethnic categories that Spaniards had attributed to Jews, Muslims, Indigenous peoples, and sub-Saharan Africans and, additionally, condemns an intolerant and superstitious Spain as the worst perpetrator of colonial atrocities. Over the centuries, the rhetoric of Hispanophobia incorporated the terminology of racial difference while nonetheless continuing to rely on the colonializing logic of the Reconquest and the Spanish Empire (16). In the American Hemisphere, white *criollo* intellectuals in nineteenth-century Cuba perceived Spanish identity as white and European, yet US writers of the same era reiterate Hispanophobic rhetoric in their nation's own discourse of empire building and limit whiteness largely to perceived Anglo-Saxon identity. Again following the logic of coloniality, writers from each place associate the Afro-descendant populations exploited by capitalist production with abyssal subhumanity. As part of this Hispanophobic conception, US writers largely view Cuba's Afro-descendant and Asian populations as being even further from white civilization and modernity than those of the US.

The decolonial framework developed by Quijano and Mignolo has been further expanded by women of color theorists and by critics who note an *andino-centrismo* in decolonial thought. For example, María Lugones argues that Quijano's original theorization does not interrogate the coloniality of gender, including patriarchy and heterosexuality intersected with racial prejudice. Rather, she proposes that the theorist "accepts the global, Euro-centered, capitalist understanding of what gender is about. These features of [Quijano's] framework serve to veil the ways in which nonwhite colonized women have been subjected and disempowered" (190). Turning to the work of Kimberlé Crenshaw and other women of color feminists, Lugones argues that understanding intersectionality makes women of color visible and allows for further exposure of the operations of coloniality: "It is only when we perceive gender and race as intermeshed or fused that we actually see women of color" (193). As Eurocentered capitalism was instituted globally, a racialized gender system was imposed on subjugated populations in places where it did not necessarily exist previously, and thus created new hierarchies within these populations that further served coloniality. For example, Oyèrónkẹ́ Oyěwùmí demonstrates that gender was not a principle that organized Yoruba society prior to the imposition of Western coloniality (196). Initiated by colonization and maintained by the coloniality of power, women of color have been subjected to a process of gendering and racializing that puts them in a position of gender inferiority that also denies them the status that is accorded to bourgeois white women, who are the focus of much feminist theory (203). Building upon Lugones's work, Yuderkys Espinosa Miñoso describes the ongoing process of decolonization of feminism being carried out by Latin American women of color theorists as one that is moving beyond the concept of a universal female oppression to interrogate "la matriz moderno-colonial racista de género" (the racist modern-colonial matrix of gender; 154). The present manuscript is written with the goal of contributing to the decolonization of feminism and feminist literary theory, which has already been greatly powered by women of color theorists from Latin America and the US but which is nonetheless ongoing.

Additionally, there is a continued need to expand further the geographic and cultural considerations that are embedded in much Latin American decolonial thought, which tends to theorize coloniality and decoloniality from an Andean perspective. As Nelson Maldonado-Torres proposes in "El Caribe, la colonialidad, y el giro decolonial," "El Caribe y el pensamiento caribeño aparecen de manera fundamental pero típicamente no registrados en los estudios sobre la colonialidad, la decolonialidad, y el giro decolonial" (The Caribbean and Caribbean thought appear in a fundamental way but typically are not acknowledged in studies of coloniality, decoloniality, and the decolonial turn; 561). Theorists from the Caribbean, particularly Frantz Fanon and Aimé Césaire, are notably cited in decolonial thought, but the history and peoples of the Caribbean are less so.[15] Maldonado-Torres reminds us that the Caribbean was the first place in which so-called "New World" colonialism took place and which also saw the implementation of the various types of European colonialism and neocolonialism over the centuries (561). In addition to genocide and the assimilation of Indigenous populations, the Caribbean experienced the massive, violent relocation of people from Africa for centuries. Maldonado-Torres refers to the colonization of the Caribbean as "una verdadera catástrofe demográfica, ambiental, y metafísica . . . [y] un *big bang* sociocultural y politico . . . sin el cual es imposible entender al mundo moderno" (a true demographic, environmental, and metaphysical catastrophe . . . [and] a sociocultural and political big bang without which it is impossible to understand the modern world; 561). The Caribbean is also the site of powerful resistance to coloniality. Maldonado-Torres points to the importance of the Haitian Revolution as the first successful war of independence for a Latin American nation, and proposes that its challenge to coloniality has more in common with the wars of independence of the twentieth century than with those of mainland Latin America in the nineteenth (565). As the present study will indicate, the specific case of nineteenth-century writing about Cuba further contributes to expanding the perspectives of decolonial thought, particularly because of the longevity of original Spanish colonialism in Cuba, which coexisted with later colonial forms of accumulation of capital and racialized devaluation of labor, and because of the island's diverse sociocultural make-up.

DECOLONIAL LANGUAGE USE

The words that we use matter, so I have chosen to address terminology in the colonial languages of English and Spanish here with these brief remarks. While we continue to seek designators that are more widely satisfactory, I employ terms here that reflect current Spanish-language usage and perspectives while also trying to be clear for academic readers from a variety of disciplines. I use *US* rather than *American* or *America* whenever possible and, like John C. Havard, *US American* to refer to the northern country's inhabitants (2). *Latin America* refers to the areas south of the US that were colonized by Spanish, Portuguese, and French-speaking peoples; *Spanish America* means the Spanish-speaking areas of Latin America and the Caribbean. I refer to the larger region as *the American Hemisphere* and try to avoid the English-language plural *the Americas*. To speak of Cuba's population of color, I use the terms *African* to indicate African-born, *Afro-Cuban* and *criollo* to indicate Cuban-born, and *Afro-descendant* as a way of referring collectively to the population of African heritage in Cuba in the nineteenth century. The Spanish term *criollo* is used here in the Cuban sense, meaning "born in Cuba" rather than in Europe or in Africa; it is not an indicator of race but of birthplace. I do not use the English *creole* because it implies racial difference or impurity, and for that reason it is not an appropriate translation for either the general Spanish-language meaning, which in other circumstances is an indicator of whiteness, or the Cuban one.

MODERNITY/COLONIALITY AND RESISTANCE IN NARRATIVES OF CUBAN ENSLAVEMENT

CUBAN CONTEXTS

To contextualize the enslavement of Afro-descendant people in Cuba and elsewhere in the American Hemisphere, we turn again to 1492. Upon arrival in the Caribbean, Colón followed the Iberian peninsula's long-standing practice of enslavement justified by religious difference by immediately enslaving the purportedly godless Taínos. When the Indigenous population of the Caribbean precipitously declined following the arrival of the Europeans, the transportation of a "justly" enslaved non-Christian workforce from Western Africa to the American Hemisphere provided a new source of labor for colonization in the drive to accumulate capital. Over the centuries, the abyssal thinking that justified trafficking and enslavement generally shifted from positing the right of the victor and religious difference to the assumption of racial alterity. By the early nineteenth century, a variety of discourses, from the theological and philosophical to the pseudoscientific, supported concepts of racial difference in which whiteness was associated with Europe, civilization, progress, and reason, while Blackness was abyssally identified with Africa, underdevelopment, degeneration, and inferior mental capacity. Although the terminology changed, the premise established by Spain's original discourse of empire building, in which "a discourse of devaluation of human beings" is linked to the accumulation of capital, continued to justify enslavement and other forms of forced labor (Mignolo, "*Islamophobia / Hispanophobia*" 18).

The scale of enslavement of Afro-descendant people started to increase in colonial Cuba near the conclusion of the eighteenth century, when the island began to undertake massive importations of unfree laborers, which resulted in important demographic and cultural developments on the island. This change was fueled by the confluence of multiple factors: the demise of forced labor and sugar production in Haiti following the Haitian Revolution (1791–1804), the rise of abolitionism in Britain, the continued global demand for inexpensive sugar, and the termination of the Spanish royal monopoly on the human trade from Africa to Cuba (Ferrer, "Cuban Slavery and Atlantic Slavery" 270–71). Captive workers from Africa quickly became more readily available in Cuba after 1789, and the island soon became the most productive of the world's sugar colonies. At least 300,721 enslaved laborers were taken from Africa to Cuba between 1790 and 1821, which was more than all importation of captives prior to 1790 (Murray 134). The Cuban model of enslavement differed from that of the English-speaking Caribbean and the US in that the supply of mostly male laborers was constantly replenished by the transatlantic traffic rather than largely through reproduction. Despite the fact that Spain signed several treaties with Britain to end the trade over the course of the century, shiploads of unfree African-born workers continued to arrive in Cuba until 1867.

The decade of the 1830s witnessed the greatest numbers of forced laborers brought to the island while also marking the beginnings of a Cuban nationalist discourse that was critical of Spanish colonialism, which some members of the wealthy class of *criollos blancos* had come to consider retrograde. The literary members of Cuba's elite class theorized a nascent Cuban national identity that was understood to be racially and culturally white. However, the influential thinkers of this era were faced with a population in which *criollos blancos* had become the minority. In addition to holding the abyssal view that Afro-descendant people were unprepared for citizenship and self-regulation, Saco, Del Monte, and their contemporaries also demonstrated considerable fear of a widespread, violent uprising like that in Haiti. For example, as part of his critique of enslavement, Del Monte illustrates fears of a race war that would devastate the white population: "[H]ay aquí muchos negros esclavos y estamos rodeados por todas partes de ellos, y levantarán contra los blancos y los matarán y se arruinará la isla, . . . [y] el único remedio que nos queda es el prohibir de veras el tráfico" (There are many black slaves here and we are surrounded by them on all sides, and they will rise up against the whites and kill them and the island will be ruined, . . . [and] the only solution left to us is to prohibit the slave traffic definitively; *Escritos* 154–55). The fear of Blackness expressed by these *criollos blancos* is another iteration of the logic of coloniality that shaped Spain's first incursions into the American Hemisphere (Mignolo "*Islamophobia/Hispanophobia*," 17n1).

As a means of diminishing the threat of a massive rebellion like Haiti's, as well as moving Cuba towards modern, light-skinned nationhood, Saco and Del Monte argued for the need to gradually eliminate the outdated institution of enslavement and to promote *blanqueamiento*, or a whitening of the population through the erasure of Blackness. As Gema R. Guevara summarizes from his letters, "Saco suggested that if Cuba was to have a place in the world of nations it had no alternative 'but to whiten and whiten.'. . . Saco argued for a racial process that would result in eventual citizenship for the descendants of Cuban slaves, provided that they first became ethnically a lighter-skinned people and shed their African cultural practices " ("Inexacting Whiteness" 106). In other words, "modernizing" *blanqueamiento* is a colonialized and abyssal concept: Following the logic of colonial settlerism, whitening is only achieved by the erasure of physical and cultural African and Afro-Cuban identity. Although both whitening and the elimination of enslavement were understood to mark progress for Cuba, the exploitative and racialized nature of labor conditions on the island are exposed by the failed efforts to replace or supplement enslaved African and Afro-Cuban workers with lighter-skinned, ostensibly paid laborers throughout the century.

The repeated interracial triangulations that demonstrate the ideology of whitening in many of the fictional works of the Del Monte *tertulia* of writers are not generally featured in the nonfiction Cuban texts studied here. Nonetheless, the colonialized thought shaping the allegories of whitened nationhood is also apparent in these works. In Manzano's *Autobiografía de un esclavo* (1835), for example, the claim to *mulatez* and rejection of Blackness are key elements in the author's justification for having escaped from enslavement. While this is understandably one of the more controversial aspects of the *Autobiografía* for contemporary readers, it is part of Manzano's successful appropriation of white discourse in a narrative written at great risk to the author for a white readership that also demonstrates the coloniality of racial ideologies. In the texts by white authors studied here, a range of perspectives on racial identity and enslavement are apparent, although the pernicious association among whiteness, modernity, and civilization nonetheless persists even for those most opposed to enslavement. The most sympathetic of the white authors is Anselmo Suárez y Romero, particularly as he portrays himself in "El cementerio del ingenio;" in this artículo, he laments over and memorializes the violent deaths suffered by numerous enslaved Afro-descendants on his family's sugar plantation. Additionally, the author documents African and Afro-Cuban cultural elements in his essays in ways that suggest that he does not adhere to the view that all Afro-descendant cultural practices are primitive, demonic, and foreign. At the same time, however, Suárez y Romero's *artículos* reflect a narrative perspective that denies equality with those whom he observes. Francisco Baralt's *artículo de costumbres* presents a much more extreme case of abyssal thinking through its characterization of Afro-Cuban dance as a savage and indecent spectacle (155–158). A counterpart to the plantation fiction produced in the US after the Civil War, José E. Triay's "El calesero" memorializes waning enslavement and warns of the dangers presented by free people of color. The only work by a female Cuban author studied here, the Condesa de Merlin's *La Havane* appropriates the language of political liberalism represented in France by the works of Alexis de Tocqueville and Gustave de Beaumont while entirely rejecting the principles of equality and liberty in her defense of Cuban enslavement.

Even while reinscribing coloniality, these texts also present examples of individual rebellion and group solidarity. Manzano's autobiography presents a multifaceted justification for his self-liberation from enslavement, and the author's physical and rhetorical bids for freedom were ultimately successful. Suárez y Romero's *artículos* similarly describe examples of individual and collective resistance through escape, suicide, adherence to African identity, and solidarity among people of color. As Salvador Bueno writes of Cuban *costumbrismo*, enslavement and racial identity are ever-present topics of nineteenth-century Cuban literature even when they do not superficially appear to be (Prólogo xii). Whereas the fictions of *blanqueamiento* attempt to erase them, Cuba's people of color cannot be written out of these nonfiction texts. The incessant fear of Black violence provided justification for harsh measures of control, but it also reveals the fact that uprisings and individual acts of resistance were frequent. While they vary in their presentations, each of the writers studied here reiterates the centrality of Africans and Afro-Cubans to all facets of life on the island.

When the writers of the 1830s and 1840s began to critique enslavement and colonial practices in Cuba, the practice of enslavement was well-entrenched throughout the Spanish, Dutch, and French Caribbean colonies; in Brazil; and in the US. Nonetheless, Britain ended the practice of colonial enslavement of Afro-descendant people in 1833; the French and Dutch followed suit in in 1848 and 1863, respectively. The US abolished enslavement with the ratification of the Thirteenth Amendment in 1865. In Cuba, however, the Spanish colonial administration strictly protected enslavement as long as it appeared to guarantee the loyalty of *criollos blancos* and generated wealth. The slow end to the institution in Cuba finally began with the halt of the Spanish transatlantic traffic and the abolitionism promoted during La Guerra de los Diez Años (Ten Years' War, 1868–1878). The colonial administration definitively terminated enslavement in Cuba in 1886 and lost the colony just over a decade later.

US CONTEXTS

With independence, the US began to express the North Atlantic iteration of the discourse of coloniality, which was phrased as divinely ordained territorial expansion, which would be called Manifest Destiny by the mid-nineteenth century, and which would not acknowledge its own ideological descent from the rhetoric of Spanish conquest and colonialism. John Quincy Adams, the creator of the Monroe Doctrine, named Cuba as an essential acquisition for the US in 1823. He wrote, "It is scarcely possible to resist the conviction that to annex Cuba to our federal republic will be indispensable for the continuance and integrity of the Union itself" (cited in Rodríguez and Targ 18). Formal efforts to purchase the island were made by the Polk administration in 1848 and by the Pierce administration in 1854. The Compromise of 1850 brought new intensity to the national debates over domestic enslavement and made Cuba an even more attractive potential acquisition in the eyes of pro-enslavement factions. Filibustering expeditions such as those launched by Narciso López in 1850 and 1851 had wide national support despite their illegality.[16] Mid-century designs on the island came to a height with the production of the failed Ostend Manifesto (1854), which declared that the US had the right to overtake Cuba should attempts at purchase fail. Interest in the slaveholding colony waned only briefly during the US Civil War and rose again during the conflicts that led to the strategically located island's independence.[17] In a reflection of the wide interest in Cuba among US readers, more than two hundred travel narratives about the island were published between 1820 and 1900, with most being produced at mid-century and in the final decade (Guevara, "Geographies of Travel and the Rhetoric of the Countryside" 14).[18] Whether they favor such action or not, US writers typically operate under the assumption that annexation would be in Spanish Cuba's best interest and that some form of intervention would inevitably occur. In contrast, Cuban writers could only openly advocate for annexation to the US when living in exile, and the moderate support for annexation shown earlier in the century was largely gone by the time José Martí famously warned Latin America about "the monster" to the north.[19]

Areas that had been colonized or otherwise occupied by Spain make up considerable portions of what is now the US. By 1850, the North American country had gained control over the following regions formerly held by Spain: the Louisiana Territory (1803), Florida (1821), Texas (1845), and the US Southwest (1848).[20] Taking over these territories by various means was justified through the same logic of empire building that was employed first in Spanish and later in English colonization in the American Hemisphere. As articulated in the US, the discourse of coloniality proposed that the Anglo-Saxon people of the US were chosen by God to spread civilization, progress, and modernity across and beyond North America. As expressed by an early congressman from Massachusetts, the generations moving westward were "destined by Providence to carry westward, to the utmost bounds, the blessings of civilization and liberty" (Richardson, cited in Horsman 89). After mid-century, the discourse of expansionism relied increasingly on the terminology of race: "By 1850 the emphasis was on the American Anglo-Saxons as a separate, innately superior people who were destined to bring good government, commercial prosperity, and Christianity to the American continents and to the world. This was a superior race, and inferior races were doomed to subordinate status or extinction" (Horsman 1–2). Although not all in the US supported the rapid expansion of territory, particularly if it meant the spread of enslavement and/or the incorporation of populations of color, the special character attributed to Anglo-Saxons suggested that the continued expansion of US power and influence was both inevitable and beneficial.

The US discourse of coloniality follows that of the nations of northern Europe, particularly England, in its reliance upon a Hispanophobic presentation of the Catholic Spaniard against whom to define a white, Anglo-Saxon, Protestant national identity. For example, Eric Griffin argues that the antithesis of the Hispanophobic image of Spain was central to the development of a sense of nationality in early modern England: "[I]t was 'not-Spanishness' . . . that for several centuries gave the English their surest sense of national identity" (71). The reliance on this presentation of Spain and Spanish-speaking countries in the establishment of white, Anglo-Saxon identity in US discourse is a topic of growing interest among scholars of US literature, such as María DeGuzmán and John C. Havard.[21] As these critics note, the immoral literary Spaniard is increasingly described in racialized terms over the course of the nineteenth century. As María DeGuzmán illustrates, the Spaniard may be light in complexion but is morally suspect in comparison with the Anglo-Saxon, darkening his or her racial category to "not-right-white or . . . *off-white*" in US discourse (original emphasis, 4). Spain in this formulation is often portrayed as having a simultaneously appealing and repelling alterity that in either case provides a foil to white "Anglo-American imperial identity" (DeGuzmán xiii). Just as it is not unusual in the twenty-first century for English-speakers in the US to refer to Spanish-speakers as "Spanish" regardless of their national origin, Hispanophobic rhetoric and its racialized logic was often also widely applied to the Spanish-speaking populations in the American Hemisphere in US cultural production, and does not always distinguish between Spaniards and colonial descendants. Summarizing their racialized treatment in US literature of the era, Havard writes, "Hispanophone people exhibit peculiarly Hispanic deficiencies rooted in the Spanish character as was illustrated by the Black Legend, and those deficiencies are products in varying ways of racial inferiority" (Havard 9). Further, the racial mixing that was common and often promoted as *blanqueamiento* in Latin America is treated in US thought at the time as a process of racial degradation that brings out the worst tendencies of each race in unfortunate mixed offspring (Havard 8).

Employing North Atlantic frameworks, DeGuzmán and Havard analyze what I refer to as Hispanophobia and the Hispanophobic discourse of coloniality in US literature, but unlike the theorists of decoloniality, they identify not Spanish but rather Northern European colonization as its point of origin. While containing important arguments and bringing the role of Hispanophobia to greater attention in US literary criticism, these studies nonetheless reflect the failure of North Atlantic postcolonial theory to capture the full extent of the history of modern European colonization. DeGuzmán employs the familiar term "the Black Legend" throughout *Spain's Long Shadow*, and identifies Northern Europe rather than Spain itself as its source. Havard refers to the negative characterization of Spanish-speaking peoples as *Hispanicism* (Havard 10).[22] A primary strength of Havard's word choice is that it corresponds to criticism of the word *Hispanic* as it is often used in the US, particularly on official documentation, as a racialized catch-all term for Spanish speakers.[23]

Nonetheless, *Hispanicism* may not be the best term available for this concept for theoretical and linguistic reasons. Where DeGuzmán points to the continuity of the Black Legend in US cultural production, Havard argues that Hispanicism "owes a debt to the Black Legend of Spanish depravity," but is different enough to merit a distinct name (4). He proposes that the increased racialization of nineteenth-century discourse, Spain's decline in imperial power, and characterization of Latin Americans as torpid rather than bloodthirsty distinguishes Hispanicism from the Black Legend (4–10). However, following Mignolo and decolonial thought, we see that what Havard describes as Hispanicism is a continuation of the discourse of coloniality and hierarchical taxonomy that began with imperial Spain but was then redeployed by North Atlantic powers. Havard's further characterization of Hispanicism illustrates this point. He writes, "In the antebellum period, . . . Anglo-American observers became more concerned with Spain's large Celtic and Jewish populations, its history of Muslim rule, and its frequent commerce with Africa" (5). This closely reflects Mignolo's characterization of the Black Legend as first propagated by England: "[T]he discourse of race in England, during the European Renaissance, does not contradict the Spaniards' classification—on the contrary, they made the Spaniards the target, for Spaniards were the Moors, Jews, Indians, and Blacks" (*"Islamophobia / Hispanophobia"* 20). The shift over several centuries from a primarily religious taxonomy to a racialized one is a change in terminology but not in the essential logic of coloniality. Mignolo writes, "Christian theological classification overruled, with time, all the others and served as the basic structure for the secular classification of races in the late 18th and 19th centuries" (*"Islamophobia / Hispanophobia"* 16). Thus, I argue that Hispanophobia as it appears in nineteenth-century US literature is a continuation of rather than a departure from the previous iterations of the discourse of coloniality, first by Iberian and then by Northern European imperial powers.

Havard recognizes that his choice of term could cause confusion in that *Hispanicism* is already a term for words borrowed from Spanish that also looks a lot like *Hispanism* (10). For academics who research the Spanish-speaking world, these English words are already familiar and used regularly. Either of these translates to only one word in Spanish, *hispanismo*. Like its English cognate, *hispanismo* can refer variously to a word originating from Spanish, to the study of the language and cultures of the Spanish-speaking world, or to the promotion of a Spanish or Spanish-derived identity.[24] *Hispanicismo* would be a neologism in Spanish, which would not be bad in and of itself, but it would most likely be confused with *hispanismo* or any number of other words in Spanish that begin with *hispan-*, such as *hispanidad* or *hispanización*. These terms are used in Spanish in a wide variety of contexts with at times quite different implications, ranging from expressions of identity to critiques of cultural and racial assimilation in Latin America to designators for fields of academic research. Without contextualization, *hispanicismo*, as well as *Hispanicism*, could easily be taken for something quite different from the concept that Havard is trying to convey, in addition to suggesting that it is a significantly different form of discourse.[25]

A further dimension that distinguishes my approach from those of both Havard and DeGuzmán additionally stems from the decolonial recognition that Orientalism is a key feature of Spain's original discourse of coloniality, and therefore is also fundamental to Hispanophobia. While Islamophobia appears in discourses and contexts not directed at Spanish-speaking populations, it nonetheless should also be understood as integral to Hispanophobic characterizations because they both arose from the same system of theological classification that later relied on racialized language. However, critics trained within North Atlantic frameworks tend to address Orientalism as distinct from rather than central to the Hispanophobic discourse of coloniality. For example, while recognizing the considerable reliance on Orientalism in the US characterization of Cuba, DeGuzmán views it as a distinct discourse: These are "Orientalist representations of Spain and Spaniards *tied together* with strands of the Black Legend" (emphasis added; DeGuzmán xxix, 139–85). Following Mignolo's argument that the Hispanophobic discourse of coloniality embodies the non-Christian Others who are rejected in the discourse of empire building, the "-isms" identified with British and French colonialism and characterized as distinct ideologies in North Atlantic theory originated with the Spanish discourse of empire building. Put another way, Hispanophobia contains within itself not only Orientalism, anti-Black racism, and anti-Semitism but also the colonializing logic of all such discourse. I argue that this understanding of Hispanophobic rhetoric helps to clarify the continuity of the discourse of empire building in nineteenth-century US literature and also accounts for its application to quite diverse populations in the Spanish-speaking areas of the American Hemisphere. The nineteenth-century Hispanophobic representation of Cuba in the US considerably emphasizes the island's perceived Islamic, Semitic, and African characteristics, and attributes unique despotism and violence to imperial Spain.

Like those of Spain, US literary presentations of Cuba alternate between Hispanophilia, which is an Orientalizing focus on the exotic, Moorish elements of the island, and Hispanophobia, which is a negative characterization of the violence and despotism of the Inquisition and the Conquest as unique to imperial Spain. When treated as distinct from their Spanish forebears, non-African Cubans are generally portrayed as indolent inhabitants of a tropical paradise who have been spoiled by dependence on enslaved labor and the warm climate. Havard makes a similar point when he states that in the prevailing view, "reliance on slave labor enervated the creoles, making them even more lazy and passionate than might be expected of peninsular Spaniards" (8). In either case, Cuba's premodern, uncivilized, and non-white inhabitants are characterized as inhabiting the far side of the abyssal line. Within this framework of darkened Spanish despotism and Cuban ineptitude, US-authored texts typically represent Africans and Afro-Cubans as occupying a lower rung on the ladder of civilization than Black US Americans, whether enslaved or free.

When writing about enslavement in Cuba, even writers considered progressive in the US tend to espouse positions that accept Cuban enslavement as a benevolent and civilizing institution. Maturin Murray Ballou frames Cuba's Afro-descendant population as dangerous, as he warns of a coming race war that will devastate white populations. Julia Ward Howe argues that Afro-descendant slaves in the Caribbean must "go to school to the white race," i.e., in the US, before they could be considered capable of living in freedom (*A Trip to Cuba* 12). Howe evaluates the Afro-descendants whom she encounters using the terms of blackface performance, finding them less acceptable than their Northern counterparts. For the pro-enslavement Eliza McHatton Ripley, Afro-descendant enslaved people in Cuba are incompetent and incomprehensible workers who could only be admired for their physical strength. The Black US Americans who Ripley illegally transported to Cuba as part of her household serve as intermediary figures between the enslaved and indentured island workforce and the "enlightened" North Americans running the plantation. For Cuban intellectuals such as Del Monte, the corruptions of enslavement and colonial institutions merited reform and, later, independence, provided that sufficient *blanqueamiento* could be achieved. For North American writers, the discourse of empire is recast with Spaniards, Cubans, and Africans in positions of undesirable alterity, suggesting that US intervention into the fate of the strategically located island is necessary, justified, and inevitable. In these texts, abyssal thinking attributes whiteness, enlightenment, modernity, and civilization to the US, and darkness, backwardness, superstition, despotism, and violence to Spain's Cuba and its various populations.

US writers visiting Cuba during the tumultuous decades leading up to and following the Civil War not only expose the ongoing discourse of empire building through their characterizations of Cuba: They also are observers of important developments on the island. For example, while they have been generally excluded from literary and academic considerations of Cuban identity and culture until recently, the indentured Chinese brought to Cuba after 1847 are frequently described by US visitors of the era. Further, censorship and closely guarded battle zones made it difficult for Cubans to write about the events of the first major war for independence in Cuba, La Guerra de los Diez Años (1868–1878), while it was ongoing. US accounts of this war offer important insights into the first rebellion that united Cuba's residents, at least rhetorically, across racial identifications, nationalities, and social classes, and that was supported at a discursive level by an idealized vision of Cuban national identity as raceless. At the same time, this war was also viewed by US writers as a reflection of the issues surrounding their own Civil War. As with the Cuban-authored texts, evidence of resistance to coloniality appears even in Ripley's *From Flag to Flag*, which is the most overtly pro-enslavement English-language text included here.

THE STRUCTURE OF *CUBAN SLAVERY FROM THE INSIDE OUT*

Each of the texts approached in this book has unique characteristics necessitating some differences in methodology, but together they contribute to our understanding of the operations of modernity/coloniality and the discourse of empire building in colonial Cuba and, in its Hispanophobic iteration, in nineteenth-century US representations of Cuba. In turn, this reading sheds light on our contemporary situation. My analysis begins with Cuban texts from the late 1830s and early 1840s in the three chapters that make up Part I, "Writing from Inside Cuba." Part II, "Writing from Outside Cuba," also consisting of three chapters, focuses on narratives by authors from the US who visited or lived in Cuba during the latter half of the century in periods of heightened interest in Cuba from the North. The view of Cuban enslavement in Part I is internal, and analyzes representations of enslavement during the massive increase in sugar production and the establishment of Cuban national literature in the first half of the century. In Part II, the view is external, looking into Cuba in the latter half of the century during upheavals in the US over enslavement and forced labor, growth in US imperial designs, and the first major challenges to Spanish colonial power on the island. The perspectives on enslavement vary somewhat in the texts studied here, but all reveal the racialized, abyssal thinking of coloniality that justifies the practice of enslavement, as well as the maintenance of the colonial matrix of power. At the same time, these texts also provide episodes of resistance and of lateral relationships of solidarity that either had the potential to or in fact did challenge coloniality. In the Cuban texts, even while addressing the entrée of Enlightenment ideals into the colony, the abyssal line continues to demarcate degrees of racial difference and the perceived ability to live as a free legal entity. In the US texts, the abyssal line divides by concepts of racial and national difference, attributing white civilization to the US and premodern, darkened barbarity to Spanish Cuba. Read together, these texts reveal that the abyssal line is not a fixed point, and they expose the European discourse of empire building that continues to operate in the American Hemisphere today.

Chapter 1 is dedicated to the most widely known of the Cuban texts studied here, Juan Francisco Manzano's *Autobiografía de un esclavo* (*Autobiography of a Slave*), which is nonetheless understudied, given its importance for the study of slave narratives in the American Hemisphere. Manzano's is the only first-hand testimony that was written in Spanish by an enslaved person of African descent while enslavement was still in practice.[26] Previous critics have proposed that Manzano adheres to a Delmontine model of the submissive enslaved character. In contrast, I argue that Manzano's self-portrait departs considerably from the fictional Cuban models of his era. The author builds a justification for his rebellious escape from enslavement by simultaneously reinscribing and subverting the various oral and written forms of discourse ranging from the literary to the legal to the religious that maintained the operations of coloniality in Cuba in the 1830s. To borrow the terms expressed by Lorde, Gordon, and Gordon, Manzano uses the tools of the master to build his own house and to free himself from enslavement.

Chapter 2 analyzes several previously unstudied texts of *costumbrismo criollo* (Cuban local color sketches) by Anselmo Suárez y Romero, Francisco Baralt, and José E. Triay. Like its peninsular counterpart, Cuban *costumbrismo* engages with liberal Enlightenment ideals while at the same time idealizing past traditions in a changing world. As observers of the consolidation of modern nation-states in the wider world, white Cuban authors looked to define a Cuban identity to promote, along with their push to reform colonial practices and an island culture perceived as decadent. Colonial censorship and total economic dependence on the institution of enslavement severely limited direct discussion of enslavement. The rare examples provided by the *artículos* studied here reinscribe coloniality in their abyssal presentation of Afro-descendants in Cuba and of the authors as white arbiters of human status. At the same time, however, these narratives also provide significant examples of the transculturation that occurred in both Spain and Cuba as a result of coloniality, the ways in which African-derived cultural practices facilitated solidarity and resistance, and the development of the Afro-Cuban culture claimed as the hallmark of Cuban identity today.

The final installment of Part I, chapter 3 analyzes two little-studied sections of *La Havane* (1844), by María de las Mercedes Santa Cruz y Montalvo, primarily known in Spanish as the Condesa de Merlin. The three-volume *La*

Havane recounts a voyage from the author's adopted home of France to her native Cuba via the US. The present manuscript is the first to outline Merlin's extensive reliance on and recasting of the writings of her aristocratic French contemporaries, Alexis de Tocqueville and Gustave de Beaumont, in the account of the author's visit to the US and in "Lettre XX," also published as a separate tome with the title *Los esclavos en las colonias españolas* (*Slaves in the Spanish Colonies*, 1841). Merlin's deployment of liberal terminology associated with the two French political theorists would suggest that the author is a proponent of Enlightenment values, yet her assessment of the US concludes with a rejection of democratic governance as oppressive to the individual. In her treatise on enslavement, the author carries this rejection of the twin tyrannies of liberty and equality to its logical conclusion with her promotion of Cuban enslavement as a benevolent and patriarchal institution. Recalling the horrors and mob rule of earlier revolutions influenced by Enlightenment concepts, Merlin shares abyssal fears of Black violence not only with her Cuban contemporaries but also with the famous French theorists of democracy.

Part II of this manuscript addresses texts written by US writers who travelled to or lived in Cuba in the nineteenth century. Chapter 4 is a study of Maturin Murray Ballou's *History of Cuba; or, Notes of a Traveller in the Tropics: Being a Political, Historical, and Statistical Account of the Island, from Its First Discovery to the Present Time* (1854). An author better known for his outlandish fictional tales of adventure, Ballou sensationalizes his "history" of Cuba by relying on the Hispanophobic characterization of Spain and Cuba and the familiar concept of the island's majority Afro-descendant population as a dangerous threat. Not only relying on previous travel narratives and works by proponents of Manifest Destiny, Ballou's text is also influenced by such Cubans as Merlin and Francisco de Arango y Parreño. Like many of his Cuban counterparts, Ballou proposes that whitening is the solution to Cuba's problems; however, his definition of whiteness as pertaining to Anglo-Saxon Protestants is at odds with that of the *criollo* intellectuals. Asserting racial, political, and economic superiority for the US over Spain and Cuba, Ballou further illustrates the Hispanophobic approach to Cuba's Afro-descendant population by claiming that there is a developmental difference between recent arrivals and those born in Cuba; the implication is that under the care of off-white Spaniards and Cubans, this population has not yet arrived at civilization. Demonstrating "the hubris of zero degrees," Ballou rationalizes US intervention in Cuba as necessary, justifiable, and worth the investment (Castro-Gómez 278–80; Guevara "Geographies of Travel" 12–13).

Julia Ward Howe's little-studied *A Trip to Cuba* (1860) is the topic of chapter 5. In contrast to the popularly held view of Howe as both a committed feminist and abolitionist, Howe clearly reinscribes the Hispanophobic discourse of coloniality in *A Trip to Cuba*. While she bristles at the restrictions placed on herself as a female traveler, Howe's egalitarianism evaporates when touring slaveholding colonies in the Caribbean. Reinscribing the coloniality of race and gender, the author does not find common cause between herself and any of the women of Cuba. Narrating her visits to multiple sugar and coffee plantations in Cuba, Howe presents blackface-inspired scenes of merriment or of insensibility to cruel treatment by Orientalized slaveholders rather than expressing opposition to enslavement. The author of "Battle Hymn of the Republic" instead argues that the institution of enslavement provides a necessary civilizing process for the Caribbean's Afro-descendant population, which has not yet been "improved" by contact with true whiteness, that of the Anglo-Saxon. Viewing the situations in the US South and in Cuba as comparable, the author concludes her narrative with the proposal that divinely sanctioned Northern intervention is the only solution for each.

Chapter 6 is a study of Confederate Eliza McHatton Ripley's *From Flag to Flag: A Woman's Adventures and Experiences in the South During the War, in Mexico, and in Cuba* (1889). Ripley's understudied tale recounts her family's Civil War–era flight from their Louisiana plantation to a Cuban one via Texas and Mexico. As a postbellum plantation narrative, Ripley's memoir reflects efforts by white supremacists who strove to maintain racial inequality in a US that was becoming increasingly multiracial after the Civil War. At the same time, Ripley's account differs from other such narratives because of its Cuban setting. The author reinscribes the Hispanophobic discourse of coloniality as she relates her efforts to manage a multiracial and multinational unfree workforce in an Orientalized Cuba. Providing an unusual portrait of the coexistence of enslavement and Chinese indenture, Ripley nonetheless reinscribes Hispanophobic coloniality by establishing a hierarchy of reliability that ranks illegally enslaved Black US Americans most highly, followed by indentured Chinese, and ends with Cuba's enslaved Afro-descendants. Reflecting the wide US interest in and divided perspectives on the Cuban wars of independence, the author additionally rewrites La Guerra de los Diez Años as a minor conflagration divorced from abolitionism and wide participation by people of color and suggests a false parallel to the US Civil War. Within a decade of the publication of Ripley's memoir, the US replaced Spain as the ruling power in Cuba for a period of several years.

Cuban Slavery from the Inside Out ends with brief concluding remarks and an epilogue that outlines some of the ways in which nineteenth-century expressions of coloniality continue to influence cultural production in and about Cuba today. The myth of Cuban racial equality and the proposal of a post-racial society formulated by nineteenth-century freedom fighters continue to be embraced in twenty-first century Cuba. Following the revolutionary government's 1961 claims to have abolished racism, the continuity of racialized thought on the island remains a topic that is not publicly addressed. Viewed from the perspective of many Black US writers and activists, the rhetoric and appearance of racial harmony on the island has appeared to present an alternative to US segregation and racial violence, although the asylum that it offered did not always work out as anticipated. Travelling to Cuba again in large numbers in the twenty-first century, US visitors reinscribe coloniality by promoting images of the island as exotic, premodern, and suspended in time.

PART I
WRITING FROM INSIDE CUBA

CHAPTER ONE

THE MANY DISCOURSES OF JUAN FRANCISCO MANZANO

Disruptions to Coloniality in *Autobiografía del esclavo poeta*

Juan Francisco Manzano's *Autobiografía del esclavo poeta* (*Autobiography of a Slave Poet*, 1839) is the only known first-hand account of slavery in a Spanish colony written by an enslaved Afro-Hispanic person prior to the institution's abolition.[1] The only other first-hand account, Esteban Montejo's *Biografía de un cimarrón* (*Biography of a Runaway Slave*, 1966), was dictated to ethnographer Miguel Barnet almost a century after the official abolition of slavery.[2] Despite its importance, Manzano's autobiography is still understudied in scholarship on Cuban and Latin American literature and is little known outside of Hispanic studies. The original handwritten manuscript of the *Autobiografía* held in the Biblioteca Nacional José Martí presents a challenge because of its nonstandard language use and format. Today's reader might have difficulty deciphering the handwritten text or even typed transcriptions. However, Manzano's message is nonetheless clear: He speaks for himself in his own narrative and demonstrates full control over his rhetoric. Over the course of his autobiography, Manzano operates multiple modes of discourse that otherwise support the colonial matrix of power to create an autobiographical self who is ready to claim his position on the free side of the abyssal line. While there are illustrative adherences to the discourse of coloniality as articulated through literature, religion, law, and racial ideologies, Manzano's narrative differs in significant ways from the fictions of his white contemporaries and employs the discourse of power to empower and liberate himself. While the simple fact of his identity as an enslaved writer challenges coloniality, Manzano uses the discursive tools of the master to construct an Afro-Cuban identity ideally designed to set him free.

Juan Francisco Manzano was born into enslavement in 1797 in the household of the Marquesa Justiz de Santa Ana, who he remembers as a doting mother figure.[3] In 1809, Manzano became subject to the control of the domineering Marquesa de Prado Ameno, and the arbitrary cruelty that characterized his life thenceforward began. The existing portion of the *Autobiografía* concludes with the author's self-liberation from the countryside to the city of Havana, which occurred at some point during the years 1814–1817. Despite prohibitions against it, Manzano taught himself to read and write during his youth; his published poetry brought him to the attention of Domingo del Monte. At some point after Manzano's escape, Del Monte requested that he write the story of his life and raised a collection to purchase the poet's freedom in 1836. Manzano lived a life that was full of difficult challenges, and he faced at least one additional life-threatening crisis as a free man of color. When the poet Gabriel de la Concepción Valdés (Plácido) was arrested and tortured by colonial authorities, he falsely accused Manzano and Del Monte of being participants in the Conspiración de la Escalera (the Ladder Conspiracy, 1844). As a result, Manzano was imprisoned and tortured. In contrast, the white and wealthy Del Monte had already left Cuba and eventually settled in Spain. There is no evidence that Manzano wrote again after his imprisonment. The author died in Havana in 1853, leaving behind a body of literary work that included poetry, a play (*Záfira: Tragedia en cinco actos*, 1842), and his life narrative.

The discourses at work in Manzano's autobiography in many ways appear to adhere to the ideologies of power operating in colonial Cuba. Contemporary scholarship on Manzano's text, which often seeks to identify the author's resistance to oppression, contends with this by investigating the extent to which the text itself is a true reflection of what the author wanted to say. For example, Ivan Schulman asks whether Del Monte instructed the poet to write about specific events (Introduction 16). Although they were promoters of reform, a number of the white Del Monte writers were also members of the elite *sacarocracia* and slaveholders themselves. Wholesale denunciation of that class and their ideologies would have led not only to the alienation of his patron but also would have threatened Manzano's life. Even formerly enslaved narrators in the US were often obliged to write "*for* and *to* a white audience" (original emphasis, Nayar 198). English-language slave narratives were frequently informed by abolitionists' desires to have case histories to use in support of their arguments and to reflect their own antislavery and religious agendas (199). Del Monte may have had something similar in mind when requesting that Manzano write down his own case history and was himself authoring reports on colonial conditions in Cuba for potential allies abroad. We can only speculate as to the extent to which Del Monte specifically and the intended audience generally influenced Manzano's text. Moreover, colonial censorship led even elite white writers to self-censor; for an author in Manzano's position, openly criticizing colonial institutions and colonializing ideology would have been very dangerous (Branche 77).

Further complicating the question of whether or not Manzano's text truly communicates what the author wanted to say is the fact that the original text does not conform to reader expectations for published material, and it has been subjected to a number of textual interventions and interpretations. The handwritten manuscript does not follow standard spelling, syntax, punctuation, or formatting, and to complicate matters, an unknown person, probably Anselmo Suárez y Romero, marked up and wrote upon Manzano's handwritten manuscript (Luis, Introducción, *Autobiografía* 31). Unlike the white writers of the *tertulia*, who performed their own revisions, Manzano was obliged to surrender his manuscript to Del Monte for redacting. To make the text more accessible for the nineteenth-century readers that he wanted to reach, Del Monte initiated an editing process that turned out to be highly destructive. Manzano wrote his *Autobiografía* in two halves and passed them on to Del Monte, who then gave each part to a different editor. The first section was entrusted to Suárez y Romero, and the second to Ramón de Palma. The former redacted his portion of the text, making the corrections and alterations that he deemed necessary, and it was included in the portfolio of antislavery literature that was given to Richard Robert Madden before his departure from Havana (Luis, Introducción 50–58).[4] There is only conjecture as to what fate befell the second part of Manzano's autobiography (Schulman, Introduction 28). Madden then took a text already altered by Suárez y Romero and made further changes for his abridged English translation (Luis, Introducción 19, 35; Molloy 44–46).[5] The text was not published in full in Spanish until José Luciano Franco's 1937 transcription, which Luis characterizes as careless and erroneous: "Esta versión presenta frecuentes descuidos y errores de interpretación que distorsionan el texto original" (This version presents frequent inattention and errors of interpretation that distort the original text; Luis, Agradecimientos 11). More recent, modernized editions and translations of the text have also been published, again with the goal of making the narrative more accessible for readers.[6] This brief history supports Sylvia Molloy's argument that Manzano's text has been "inordinately manipulated" (38). While Madden's translated and abridged edition is the most altered, William Luis argues that most of the available edited and transcribed versions diverge enough from Manzano's original that they are in fact different texts from the handwritten autobiography (Introducción 19–20). Because of the many interventions into the narrative in most existing published editions, I rely here on Luis's transcription of the original handwritten manuscript as published in *Autobiografía del esclavo poeta y otros escritos* (2007).[7]

Scholarship additionally points to the effects of internalization of racist and other colonializing thought by marginalized people as a means of accounting for the ways in which Manzano's autobiography appears to reinscribe ideologies that support the colonial matrix of power. For example, the text's elevation of whiteness and devaluation of African and Black identity suggests the effects of colonization on oppressed populations. Stuart Hall articulates that during "'the colonial experience' . . . [t]he ways in which black people, black experiences, were positioned and subjected in the dominant regimes of representation were the effects of a critical exercise of cultural power and normalization. . . . They had the power to makes us see and experience *ourselves* as 'Other'" (225). In analyzing the construction of the self in the *Autobiografía*, Schulman characterizes Manzano as ambivalent and isolated: The narrator is "an individual disconnected from his African kin and shut off from the world of the Creole or Spanish whites" (24). Molloy describes Manzano's having to incorporate his text into white literary tradition as "fostering the *twoness* so many Black writers have described" (39). To what extent is colonization of the mind reflected in the *Autobiografía*? There are convincing arguments to be made that Manzano self-censored, anticipated his readers' expectations, and internalized the predominant ideologies of his day. However, it is difficult to say with certainty to what extent or which of these concepts offers the key to understanding the narrative and to identifying resistance within the text itself.

DISRUPTIONS TO ORAL AND WRITTEN DISCOURSES OF POWER

Because we can only speculate as to how much the text truly reflects what the author desired to communicate, I propose to analyze the deployment of the various modes of the discourse of coloniality within Manzano's text in order to identify the author's departures from them. These discursive alterations range from subtle to overt, but they all challenge the colonial matrix of power. For a number of scholars, the written enunciation of the discourses of power by an enslaved person is in and of itself an act of defiance.

Manzano was legally forbidden to write, yet he persisted in doing so. Molloy, for example, considers Manzano's poetry to be transgressive even if reductive because of his legal status: "Manzano's poetry, I argue, is original precisely *because* it is so imitative, because it is such a deliberate and total act of appropriation of the reading and writing that had been denied him" (52). Addressing a wider Latin American context, Jerome Branche states that "[t]he appropriation of written discourse demonstrates the awareness among free and enslaved Africans and Afrocreoles of the relationship between writing and the politico-legal superstructure, as well as their determination to use whatever means were available to achieve their liberation" (68). To use the terminology presented by Audre Lorde, Lewis Gordon, and Jane Anna Gordon, Manzano employs the master's tools to build his own house (cited in Mignolo and Walsh 7).

Nonetheless, the resistance discernible in Manzano's text is not due only to his identity and status in the colony but also to the ways in which he adapts multiple modes of discourse to support a multifaceted case for his freedom. The first of the rhetorical modes engaged by the *Autobiografía* that I will address are those of literary and autobiographical discourse. Molloy proposes that Manzano did not have a literary model, or discourse, to follow when writing the story of his life and discusses the alignment between the autobiographer's created self-image and Del Monte's generally abyssal view of people of color that nonetheless allows for a few exceptional individuals (40–41, 53). Representing the figure of the "exceptional slave," Manzano could write an autobiography useful for Del Monte's purposes in that it would reflect "the opinion of an enlightened middle class" while outlining the horrors of slavery (40). Schulman contends that Manzano did in fact have literary models: the prose works of the Del Monte *tertulia* (Schulman, Introduction 36–37n66). Ultimately, however, Molloy and Schulman appear to be making the same point, which is that Manzano's autobiographical self closely aligns with the ideologies projected in the written texts of the white members of the Del Monte *tertulia*.[8] Schulman further states that "Manzano in this narration emerges as the incarnation of the slave figure that the novelists of the Del Monte group created, that is, a generous and noble exception to a degraded race, a fundamentally obedient and faithful servant" (Introduction 27). However, I argue that Manzano does not cast himself as the doomed figure of Delmontine antislavery fiction: There are important distinctions between the writer's narrative self and the enslaved characters produced by the *tertulia*. Fashioning his own life story, Manzano presents an urban, cultured, Cuban, and *mulato* identity that is the most likely to win his bid for freedom from the powerful systems stacked against him.

The linear, chronological construction of his life story and his literary references suggest that Manzano was in fact familiar with models beyond those of the *tertulia*, including autobiographical and other narrative forms. The writer makes literary allusions throughout the text, including a reference to one of Europe's most famous autobiographers, Jean-Jacques Rousseau (318). There is also the possibility that the well-connected members of the *tertulia* knew of slave narratives that predate Manzano's, such as Olaudah Equiano's best-selling *The Interesting Narrative of the Life of Olaudah Equiano* (1789) and Ottobah Cugoano's *Narrative of the Enslavement of Ottobah Cugoano, a Native of Africa* (1787). Del Monte, for example, had traveled widely and maintained an extensive international correspondence in multiple languages prior to asking Manzano to write his life story. Historian José M. Aguilera Manzano writes that "the Havana faction was nurtured through the ideas and works received from the Peninsula, from different areas of the United States, Paris and, in smaller measure, London" (71). Finally, the canonical prose works by Manzano's Cuban contemporaries are not first-person autobiographies, fictional or otherwise, and generally do not represent the first-person perspective of the enslaved. The enslaved characters tend to be spoken about in nineteenth-century Cuban antislavery fiction much more than they speak for themselves.[9]

As an autobiographer who was not supposed to write, Manzano reflects upon his acquisition of written discourse similarly to other authors of slave narratives, such as Equiano, Cugoano, and Frederick Douglass (1845), and in distinction from Delmontine fictions. Each of these writers recounts his development of literacy and recognizes written communication as a discourse of power.[10] Addressing Equiano's work, Carl Plasa states that "by affirming himself as a writing subject, Equiano suggests that he too possesses those qualities of 'reason' and 'humanity' which the Enlightenment would like to preserve as purely white" (16). Theorists of decoloniality would point out that this process begins not with the Enlightenment but during the sixteenth century, but the colonialist association of reason and humanity with whiteness nonetheless continues to operate. In his autobiography, Douglass explains that the denial of literacy functions as a tool of enslavement. Having heard the master request an end to his tutoring, Douglass writes, "I now understood what had been to me a most perplexing difficulty—to wit, the white man's power to enslave the black man. From that moment, I understood the pathway from slavery to freedom" (cited in Nayar 219). Cuban antislavery fictions rarely feature the acquisition of literacy by enslaved persons.

Manzano's life narrative clearly articulates the association among power, intellectual capacity, and both oral and written forms of communication, as well as his drive to make use of the most effective means of discourse available. Before he learns to write, young Manzano demonstrates great skill at memorization, composition of poetry by memory, painting, and other talents that require intelligence, creativity, and artistic sensibility, all of which are otherwise abyssally associated with whiteness. While he at times is praised for his capacities, the narrator also makes clear that his early displays of intellect present a threat to the status quo. For example, after the Marquesa de Prado Ameno overhears Manzano telling an original story to a mixed audience, she mandates a humiliating punishment. The day after he was overheard, he relates that "me pusieron una grande mordaza y parado en un taburete en medio de la sala con unos motes de tras y delante de los cuales no me acuerdo" (they put a large gag on me and stood me on a stool in the middle of the living room with signs hanging from my front and back which I forget what they said; 308).[11] The marquesa's power is asserted through the written discourse of the signs placed on his body, and the gag is meant to silence the dangers of his voice and his creativity.

Manzano's command of different registers of spoken Spanish that are considered elevated, such as literary and ecclesiastical modes, also participate in the author's depiction of himself as an educated *mulato criollo* within a highly stratified slaveholding society. While the presentation of his racial identity will be further examined below, the narrator's portrayal of his abilities in spoken Spanish help to define his status as an intelligent *mulato* born in Cuba and in differentiation from the enslaved *negro bozal*, who holds the lowest possible position in colonial Cuban society. The word *bozal* was employed for forced laborers recently taken from Africa, which was the case for many enslaved in Cuba for much of the nineteenth century. Owners of Cuba's *ingenios* (sugar plantations) believed that frequently replacing the majority male workers was more economical than providing the care needed for longer life expectancy under the harsh conditons of sugar production. Not speaking the language of the colonizer, Spanish, or having limited familiarity with it was an indicator of denigrated *bozal* status. The *Diccionario de la Real Academia* presents a range of meanings for *bozal*, many of which are related to controlling or taming animals by placing something on or near their mouths, as in "muzzle" but also in "lead," as for directing a horse (*Diccionario*, under "bozal"; see also Branche 84n63). The *Diccionario* further states that in reference to enslaved people of color, *bozal* means "recently taken from his/her country" and, in older Cuban Spanish, "[p]ersona que pronuncia mal la lengua española, a semejanza del antiguo negro bozal" (person who speaks the Spanish language poorly, similarly to the antiquated foreign Black; *Diccionario*, under "bozal"). In combination, these definitions indicate that coloniality assigns the *negro bozal* a subhuman, uncivilized, incomprehensible, and alien status; clear speech is not expected from the *bozal*, but would be dangerous should it emerge. As a *criollo* born in Havana, Manzano is a native speaker of Spanish. Moreover, he controls literary and other modes of spoken Spanish, which are otherwise associated with those in power, in ways that distinguish him from the low status *bozales* but that also threaten the slaveholding authority.

As he matures, the author recognizes that learning to write will be of much greater service to him than recitation, and his determination to become literate results in rebellion. After memorizing one of Don Nicolás's rhetoric lessons, Manzano states that "[yo] conosia el poco fruto q^e. sacaba de aquello pues nunca abia occasion de aser uso de ello, entonses determiné darme otro mas util q^e. fue el de aprender a escrivir" (I knew that I was getting little benefit from that because I would never have the occasion to make use of it, so I determined to give myself another more useful skill that of learning to write; 326). Literacy was prohibited for the enslaved in Cuba, and Manzano is admonished on multiple occasions for his steadfast pursuit of it. Once he begins to practice handwriting, he is repeatedly ordered to stop because it is an activity above his station: "yo pasaba todo el tiempo embrollando con mis papeles no pocas veces [Sr. Márquez] me sorprendió en la punta de una mesa q^e. abía en un rincon imponiendome dejase aquel entretenimiento como nada correspondiente a mi clase" (I spent all my time entangled with my papers not a few times [Sr. Márquez] surprised me at the end of a table that was in a corner imploring me to stop that amusement because it was not suitable for my position; "[Sr. Márquez]" added for clarity, 326).[12] Manzano defiantly resorts to practicing secretly at night, copying poetry by Juan Bautista Arriaza: "[T]odos se abian de acostar y entonces ensendia mi cabito de bela y me desquitaba a mi gusto copiando las mas bonitas letrillas de Arriaza" (Everyone would go to bed and then I would light my little bit of candle and I would get revenge to my liking by copying the loveliest poems by Arriaza; 326). In Manzano's *Autobiografía*, the relationship between power and written discourse is made explicit, and the author demonstrates a defiant drive to access it and to develop his intellect using the prohibited tools of the master.

In conformity with Western autobiographical conventions, Manzano's life story begins with the circumstances of his birth. Unlike many of the enslaved characters of Delmontine fiction, however, Manzano is not the product of a violent or illicit union. As Sara Rosell points out, the *tertulia* writers typically portray extramarital, abusive, and even incestuous affairs between free white men and enslaved Black women, making the literary protagonists and their families illegitimate and improper: "[L]a temática siempre se desarrolla alrededor de los abusos hacia la mujer negra por parte del hombre blanco o la imposibilidad en la raza negra de constituir una familia legítima" (The theme is always developed around white man's abuses of the Black woman or the impossibility for the Black race to constitute a legitimate family; 15). The titular character of Cirilo Villaverde's canonical novel, *Cecilia Valdés*, for example, is placed in an orphanage at birth in order to disguise the identity of her married white father (17). Even for more "exceptional" enslaved characters, the circumstances of birth are either undiscussed, as is the case for Suárez y Romero's Francisco, or clouded by mystery and bastardy, as is the case for Gómez de Avellaneda's Sab (109).

Manzano's origin story is one of respectability and legitimacy that upholds the class/race discourse of colonial Cuba, yet also signals important disruptions.[13] The very first words of the *Autobiografía* are the full name and aristocratic title of his first *ama*: "La Sra. Da. María Beatriz de Justiz Marqueza de Sta. Ana, esposa del Sor. Dn Juan Manzano" (The Señora Doña Beatriz de Justiz, Marquesa of Santa Ana, wife of Señor Don Juan Manzano; 301). Class/race privilege is reinscribed by the respectful inclusion of the marquesa's title, name, and marriage before any discussion of Manzano's own parents. At the same time, both the class/race hierarchy and the purported familial relations of enslavement are inverted as Manzano claims his position in the family as part of his bid for freedom. The author next describes his parents' high rank within the household: they are referred to as *criados* (house servants) rather than as *esclavos* (slaves) and work in urban domestic service. He explains that the Marquesa de Santa Ana had the custom of selecting the loveliest of her enslaved *criollas* to serve her as *criadas de razón* until they were married; Manzano's mother, María del Pilar, was chosen for this position and became the marquesa's highest ranking female servant (299).[14] Similarly, Manzano's father, Toribio de Castro, was "el primer criado de la casa" (the top servant in the house; 300). The narrative indicates that the two were married around the time that Don Nicolás was born to the white family (300). Thus, Manzano himself is established as the legitimate child of married, Cuban-born parents who are highly placed in the household of a titled and wealthy family. Unlike the beginnings described in many antislavery fictions, there is no scandal, mystery, or violence attached to Manzano's parents' relationship or to his birth. However, marriage was a right upheld by Cuba's enslavement laws and was viewed by colonial authorities as a means of pacification of the enslaved (De la Fuente 359).

Following a Rousseauian vein, Manzano characterizes his earliest years as a golden age of innocence in which he is treated by his first mistress like a member of her socially prominent family. Although of the same generation as white offspring who were later known by aristocratic titles, the author was the only child born in the house at that time, either black or white, and as a result he had a special relationship with the marquesa. She called him, "el niño de su bejez" (the child of her dotage), and he refers to her as "mama mia" (mother mine; 300). He was so beloved by the marquesa that even his parents were not allowed to discipline him without her permission. Anticipating his reader's potential doubts about his favored position, Manzano reinforces his claim to veracity when he states that there are still living witnesses who can attest that he spent every waking moment with his mistress (300).

Manzano continues to enjoy a happy life with strong connections to the white family while living with his white, upper-class godmother, Trinidad de Zayas, and describes his participation in events important for the white Manzano family. He mentions that he was a witness to "el bautismo famoso del señor Dn Pedro orreylli" (the famous baptism of Señor Don Pedro Orreylli; 303) in a way that suggests he is writing for a reader familiar with this event and that establishes the narrator as part of the select group of those present. Likewise, he regularly names prominent white *criollos* with whom he comes into contact, underscoring the notion that he has a social network comprised of upper-class supporters and also attesting to the accuracy of his account. In his godmother's house, Manzano is allowed so much freedom that he is innocent of the knowledge of his enslaved status: "[T]odo esto sin saber si tenia amo o nó ... entraba y salía de la casa [como de unos amos] sin q^e. nadie me pusiese ostaculo" (All of this without my knowing whether I had a master or not ... I came and went from the house [like a master] without anyone trying to stop me; 303). As José Triay points out in "El calesero," childhood was a luxury reserved for Cuba's free-born, wealthy children; enslaved people were forced to work from a young age (421). Manzano's description of his earliest years suggests that his experience was that of a free white child rather than that of an enslaved Afro-Cuban. The utopian nature of Manzano's earliest youth serves both to provide a stark contrast with the cruel treatment he later receives from the Marquesa de Prado Ameno and also to establish his position in a class/race-conscious social order that prioritizes perceived legitimacy, lighter skin tones, and Cuban over African birth.

Branche proposes that Manzano's autobiography relies upon "a simple binary structure" that divides his life into two contrasting parts, the first being his happy early childhood and the second pure torment under the control of a domineering tyrant (78). Molloy, however, points out that that Manzano's fate in the Prado Ameno household is determined by the marquesa's extreme and haphazard changes of disposition, and that Manzano expresses some ambivalent feelings about her (46–47). On the one hand, his residence there is defined by terrible and arbitrary cruelty. On the other, he also expresses pride in the family's displays of wealth and culture and his own elevated position in the hierarchy of the enslaved. The first aspect of life with the Marquesa de Prado Ameno on which Manzano elaborates is his wardrobe, which defines his urban household status. Further establishing his position of privilege, Manzano receives special treatment from Doña Joaquina, a member of the new marquesa's household. She treats him "como a un niño" (like a young master), suggesting that she treats him like a white child and a family member. He is separated from the other Black children and given the same food as the white *amos*, which is a signifier of privilege: Doña Joaquina "me bestia peinaba y cuidaba de q^e. no me rosase con los otros negritos de la misma mesa como en tiempos de señora la Marqueza de Justis se me daba mi plato q^e. comia a los pies de mi señora la Marqueza de [p] Pr. A." ([Doña Joaquina] dressed me combed my hair and took care that I didn't mix with the other Black children at the same table like in the day of the Señora Marquesa de Justiz I was given my plate to eat at the feet of my lady the Marquesa de Prado Ameno; 304). Passages such as these suggest adherence to the class/race hierarchy at work in colonial Cuban society and in Delmontine discourse. Many of the "exceptional" characters in Cuban antislavery fiction are portrayed in domestic rather than agricultural work, suggesting that they are more refined because of their proximity to white European culture and because they do not perform hard agricultural labor.

The discourse of white-authored Cuban antislavery literature relies on images of violence and cruelty as one means of creating sympathy in the reader for the suffering enslaved character and of indicting the corrupting influence of enslavement (Schulman, Introduction 16–17). Violence and abuse also figure prominently in Manzano's narrative and attest to the extent to which he suffers. The author's literary treatment of this topic partially overlaps with those of his white cohort, yet also reflects the difficulty of being the narrator of his own traumatic experience. In alignment with the long-suffering, tragic, enslaved characters of antislavery fiction, Manzano's narrative voice expresses great sorrow at his treatment and rarely demonstrates emotions that would alienate a white *criollo* readership, such as anger or desire for revenge.[15] In contrast to literary characters, however, Manzano's torment is not exacerbated by impossible love or immoral lust as in many of the Delmontine fictions, but rather because of the caprice of one slaveholding woman. Manzano describes undergoing psychological and physical mistreatment that is frequent, violent, unwarranted, and disproportionately harsh for the alleged infractions. Among the most haunting of the punishments for young Manzano is his solitary confinement in a dark coal cellar inhabited by deformed rats that crawl over him (304–5). The violence and frequency with which he is whipped and locked in the cellar weakens his body and stunts his physical development: "[E]sta penitencia era tan frecuente q^e no pasaba semana en q^e no sufriese de este genero de castigo do o tres veses, . . . yo he atribuido mi pequeñez de estatura y la debilidad de mi naturaleza a la amargosa vida q^e. desde trese a catorse años he traida" (This penitence was so frequent that I didn't go a week without suffering this type of punishment two or three times, . . . I have attributed my slight stature and physical frailty to the bitter life that I have led since I was thirteen or fourteen years old; 305). Manzano is beaten for inconsequential boyhood lapses and for misunderstandings on the part of the Marquesa de Prado Ameno that make clear her terrible cruelty.

When describing the worst of the physical abuse that he receives, Manzano's text reflects the difficult position in which he is placed as the narrator of his own dehumanizing torment. One consideration is the potential to offend his intended white readership, many of whom were slaveholders. While white *tertulia* authors portray the violence of enslavement in their own literary works, the presentation of the same cruelty by an enslaved writer could become an accusation. Branche proposes that Manzano's depictions of receiving physical punishments from brutal Black males deflects the blame for the violence away from white readers: The diversion is "a rhetorical tactic of scapegoating of the whip-wielding negros, as the victim seeks a place to locate blame, while highlighting the wretchedness of his own condition" (78–79). This point is well taken, although I would add to this that the move to the household of the vindictive Marquesa de Prado Ameno is signaled as the primary cause of Manzano's suffering. Her gender and her total opposition to the ideal mother figure of the Marquesa de Santa Ana make her vulnerable to criticism from the enslaved narrator.[16]

To maintain his intended reader's empathy, Manzano must resist a portrayal of himself that would suggest he is dehumanized by the brutal conditions of enslavement (Schulman, Introduction 27). In some of the most painful scenes that he recounts, the narrator refrains from outlining the full extent of the violence. For example, in relating a painful episode in which both he and his mother are beaten, Manzano declines to relate the entirety of the event: "[P]asemos en silencio el resto de esta exena dolorosa" (Let's pass over the rest of this painful scene in silence; 312). Later, Manzano begins to describe a severe beating that he suffered for having plucked a petal from a geranium, but then conceals the remaining details, writing "corramos un belo p`r`. el resto de esta exena mi sangre se ha derramado yo perdí el sentido" (let's draw a veil over the rest of this scene my blood was spilled I lost consciousness; 321).[17] Not only are these very traumatic events, but they could also damage the implicit argument built into the narrative for Manzano's ability to live as a free legal entity on the "civilized" side of the abyssal line. Manzano's use of ellipses draws attention to the torture that is part of enslavement and a significant point of criticism within Cuban antislavery discourse, while also providing him with a way to avoid irrevocably consigning himself to an abyssally subhuman status. Finally, Molloy argues that silence and withholding information are signs of resistance in Manzano's writing (43).[18] The decision whether or not to tell all is one that the *tertulia*'s fictional characters cannot make.

AFRO-CUBAN DISRUPTIONS TO COLONIALIZING CHRISTIAN DISCOURSE

Christian spiritual autobiography has long been recognized as an important model for slave narratives written in English, and ideologies of evangelical Protestantism are central to critiques of enslavement in the nineteenth-century Anglophone world.[19] Writing for a different audience, however, Manzano does not relate a religious awakening or conversion. Rather, the author makes regular references to Catholicism and related social structures throughout the narrative in ways that support the construction of his Cuban identity and also make clear his integration into Havana society. With the exception of Matthew Pettway's *Cuban Literature in the Age of Black Insurrection: Manzano, Plácido, and Afro-Latino Religion*, there is little published scholarship on the role of religious discourse in Manzano's text. In a line of thought that accords with Mignolo's articulation of coloniality, Pettway characterizes colonial Christianity as participating in "Spanish Catholic acculturation designed to extinguish African cultural histories and supplant African ethnic identities with pejorative racial categories" (51–52). In other words, Christianity in colonializing discourse is a marker of "civilization," whiteness, and enlightenment that places "primitive" African religions and cultures on the far side of the abyssal line in the Spanish colonial context in Cuba.

The narrator's adherence to European Catholic practices weaves him into the social fabric of Havana in ways that at times reinscribe his enslaved condition but that also create networks of support with the potential to challenge the status quo. The ritual of baptism is mentioned several times in the *Autobiografía*. This rite is central to the Spanish discourse of coloniality because it represents the first step towards salvation for conquered populations. Pettway characterizes Manzano's description of his baptism, for which he wears his mistress's own baptismal gown, as "a performance of belonging . . . even though it reiterated his slave status" (53); this event reinscribes the pseudofamilial relationship between the slaveholder and the enslaved. Manzano additionally invokes his baptism to establish his position in the enslaved hierarchy, his Cuban birth, and his belonging to the cultured city. He is deeply offended when the Marquesa de Prado Ameno claims that he is the worst of the enslaved born on the rural plantation: "[E]sto era otro genero de mortificasion . . . yo sabia muy bien q^e. estaba bautisado en la Habana" (This was another kind of humiliation . . . I knew very well that I was baptized in Havana; 335).

The narrative begins to disrupt the role of European Christianity in pacifying enslaved populations more openly through the presentation of author's relationship with his white godparents. *Padrinazgo* (godparenting) is an important religio-cultural institution in Latin America, in which the godparent provides protection and assistance to the godchild in a relationship often conceived as familial. As practiced in colonial Cuba, white godparenting of enslaved children is not conflated with ownership but rather with protection and guidance. In urban environments, this traditional practice became a way for enslaved people to establish networks of support. Alejandro de la Fuente describes the custom in which enslaved parents of color selected white godparents for their children as both common and strategic: "These sponsors could be valuable, particularly when slaves came in contact with colonial institutions to press for rights under Spanish law" (357). Manzano clearly establishes his status as godchild to the upper-class Trinidad de Zayas in the narration of his idyllic early years, and thereby demonstrates his network of support within the wealthy white community. The Catholic institution of *padrinazgo* becomes another means by which Manzano asserts his humanity, incorporation into society, and capacity to live as a free legal entity.

Manzano's narrative further challenges the colonializing discourse of Christianity by twice claiming that he had divine protection on the night of his self-liberation. In arguing that the saints that he venerates safeguarded him during his flight, Manzano disrupts the idea of Christian obedience for the enslaved. Anticipating his later escape for the reader, Manzano writes midway through his narrative that the saints guided and protected him that night: "[T]odavía creo q^e. ellos me depararon la ocasión y me custodiaron [el dia] la noche de mi fuga de matanzas p^a. la Habana como beremos" (I still believe that they provided me with the opportunity and protected me [the day] the night of my flight from Matanzas to Havana as we will see; 319). Later in the text, he reiterates this by describing his prayers to the saints before freeing himself from the plantation: After saddling the horse, "me puse de rodillas me encomendé a los santos de mi debosion me puse el sombrero y monté" (I got on my knees I entrusted myself to the saints of my devotion I put on my hat and mounted; 340). The author's presentation of his self-liberation as divinely sanctioned is of itself a challenge to the conventional, colonializing Christian discourse of resignation and acceptance imparted to the enslaved.

In addition to challenging the role of Christianity in pacification of the enslaved, the author's references to the saints reflect a mixed Afro-Cuban identity and not a wholesale adoption of European Catholicism. Pettway convincingly argues that Manzano's appeal to the saints and other allusions to spirituality and the supernatural are expressions of transculturated Afro-Cuban religious beliefs and practices.[20] Addressing the author's devotion to certain saints, Pettway explains that "[t]hroughout Latin America and the Caribbean, persons of African descent encoded African-inspired religious beliefs in the symbolic practices of Catholicism and, [sic] the Catholic saints provided a remarkably fertile terrain for this type of transculturation. Manzano spoke about, revered, and otherwise engaged the saints in ways very consistent with an African Atlantic pattern of ritual, reverence, and reciprocity" (134).

Although his word choices correspond to conventional Catholic terminology, Manzano's inclusion of African-influenced beliefs in the narrative challenges the association between European whiteness and Christian salvation otherwise operating in the discourse of coloniality. This is a notable departure from the works of Manzano's white contemporaries: Afro-Cuban religion "is nowhere to be found in Delmontine reformist fiction" (Pettway 150). The intellectual promoters of *blanqueamiento* proposed erasing all signs of African culture from the Cuban populace, yet the African influence on Manzano's belief system is discernable for past and present readers alike. Pettway proposes that there is "evidence that some contemporary observers understood that when African descendants spoke of the saints, they did so investing the word with shifting and unstable meanings that signified different things to diverse readerships" (140). Francisco Calcagno, for example, characterizes Manzano's religious devotion as being mixed with "ignorant fanaticism" (cited in Pettway 138–39). Notably, Suárez y Romero's edition of Manzano's text does not alter this particular aspect of the narrative, and of course Manzano himself makes the decision to relate his transculturated beliefs. I argue that the author's presentation of mixed religious belief participates in the overall narrative construction of an Afro-Cuban *mulato* self that is neither fully white nor in total conformance with the state religion. Additionally, I propose that this aspect of Manzano's religious discourse is one of very few suggestions of solidarity with Afro-Cubans and Africans in the text; these traditions are shared orally within Afro-descendant families and communities and were not part of institutionalized religious instruction.[21]

THE DOUBLE-EDGED SWORD OF LEGAL DISCOURSE

Manzano also regularly invokes legal discourse in the narrative, yet this is another aspect of the text that has received very little scholarly attention.[22] Luis affirms the author's familiarity with the law: "Manzano era conciente de las leyes de la época y manejó en su manuscrito el discurso legal con la perspicacia suficiente para protegerse de posibles denuncias" (Manzano was aware of the laws of the era and handled legal discourse in his manuscript with sufficient wisdom to protect himself from possible accusations; *Autobiografía* 25). Throughout the narrative, Manzano constructs a legal case against his continued enslavement based on the rights of the enslaved under colonial Cuban law. Illustrating the adaptation of the ideologies of the Reconquista to colonization in the American Hemisphere, colonial Cuba's enslavement laws date back to the thirteenth-century Siete Partidas of Alfonso X the Wise, which were themselves influenced by Roman codes (De la Fuente 356). Although the law granted masters control over the enslaved, it also protected rights for the enslaved and followed a principle that laws should in general favor freedom as humanity's natural status (356). Appealing to one's rights under the colonial enslavement codes was something of a double-edged sword: Juridical and legal discourse are clearly found among the master's tools. Official recognition of the rights of the enslaved served as a form of pacification: Enforcing individual rights "encouraged reliance on colonial institutions while discouraging other forms of resistance, contributing to social stability and peace" (De la Fuente 349). At the same time, taking one's case to court "represented avenues for advancement and goals for other slaves struggling for freedom . . . [and] demonstrated that it was possible to challenge the master's authority in court," and some enslaved individuals were able to improve their conditions through legal appeals (360). De la Fuente asserts that the expansion of the free population of color, largely located in Havana, "cannot be attributed to natural growth alone. . . . [T]he right to self-purchase continued to be exercised in nineteenth-century Cuba " (365). Working within a legal system that pitted slave-owning interests against the rights of the enslaved, Manzano appeals repeatedly to his rights under Cuba's enslavement laws (360). By engaging in a written legal argument, Manzano transforms himself from one who is accused to one who accuses, aiming his accusations at the slaveholder who denies him his rights (Ramos 10–11).

Manzano begins to build his legal case when narrating the events that led to his unexplained transfer to the household of the Marquesa de Prado Ameno. He states that his first *ama* (mistress) left him in the care of his white godmother after her death: "S^{ra}. D^a. Joaquina me condujo a la casa de mi madrina donde luego supe q^e allí me abia dejado mi señora" (Señora Doña Joaquina led me from my godmother's house where I later found out that my lady had left me; 303). He proposes that he leaves his happy home because he was sought out by "algunas antiguas criadas de la casa" (some former household servants; 303). The narrative voice relates that he is sent to the home of the Marquesa de Prado Ameno for a visit and then is never returned to his godmother's home. Manzano communicates confusion about these events: "no se desir lo q^e. aqui paso lo sierto es qe. al dia siguiente . . . cuando me queria ir a la casa de {**mi**} amada madrina no se me llebó; ella fue a buscarme y yo no fui que sé yo" (I don't know how to say what happened here the truth is that the following day . . . when I wanted to go to {**my**} beloved godmother's house no one took me; she came to look for me and I didn't go what do I know; 303).[23] Surely this was bewildering to Manzano as a child, and it would make sense that the *amos* would not think it necessary to explain to an enslaved child why he was sent from one house to another. The adult Manzano narrating this extremely important change in his circumstances reports that he is not able to clarify what happened. The transfer to the Marquesa de Prado Ameno's household is characterized in the narrative as both an accident and counter to the expressed wishes of the late, idealized Marquesa de Santa Ana. With this, the author begins to cast doubt on the legality of the Marquesa de Prado Ameno's claim to him and to build the case for his freedom.

Over the course of the *Autobiografía*, Manzano claims to have legally free status several times and enumerates the multiple ways in which the Marquesa de Prado Ameno has denied him his legal rights. The excessive and extreme violence that he suffers at the will of the Marquesa de Prado Ameno is one of several important arguments that contribute to his legal case. Cuban enslavement laws regulated the severity of physical punishments that could be administered, and the enslaved in Spanish colonies had "the right to recourse against cruel masters" that stipulated several options for relief in such cases (De la Fuente 350). Although the language is cautiously chosen, the narrative voice makes it very clear that the Marquesa de Prado Ameno breaks the law by denying Manzano his freedom and his rights. In addition to explaining that his first mistress left him in the care of his godparents, Manzano insinuates that she also intended to free him upon his reaching the age of majority (318). Finally, the narrator also claims to be *coartado*. A practice also found in the Siete Partidas, *coartación* in colonial Cuba meant that the enslaved and the slaveholder would agree upon a set price of freedom to be granted upon payment, an arrangement that was legally binding for both parties (De la Fuente 358).[24] Not long after his first intimation that he should have been freed upon reaching his majority, the narrator describes his mother suddenly informing him that she has the money for his freedom: "Juan aqui llebo el dinero de tu libertad . . . ya no te bolberan a castigar mas" (Juan I have here the money for your freedom . . . from now on they won't keep punishing you; 322). María del Pilar goes to present the sum to the mistress but returns empty-handed and without her son being freed (322). Finally, the marquesa does not respect the property rights of the enslaved family following María del Pilar's death. She refuses to honor certificates of debt owed and to make payments from María del Pilar's belongings to the woman raising Manzano's free sister (331–33).

I argue that the denial of his rights forces an awakening for Manzano that is the inverse of a spiritual one: He loses faith in the humanity of his mistress.[25] The author realizes that his right to freedom will not be recognized, and he turns permanently against the Marquesa de Prado Ameno: "[D]esde el momento en q^e. perdi la alhagueña ilusión de mi esperanza ya no era un esclavo fiel" (From that moment in which I lost the promising dream of my hope I was no longer a faithful slave; 333). Even after this anti-awakening, Manzano continues to seek a legal resolution for his difficulties by asking to be hired out rather than be sent again to the sugar plantation: "[M]e determine pedir papel p^a. buscar amo, asombrose mi señora de esto y me dijo q^e. si yo no conosia bien q^e si ella me llebaba era p^r q^e lo debia de aser . . . [y] me bolvió la espalda" (I determined to ask for papers allowing me to be hired out, my lady was shocked by this and told me that didn't I well know that if she sent me it was because that was what had to be done . . . [and] she turned her back on me; 328). Despite this being a common urban practice and a legal option for recourse in the case of cruel masters, the marquesa rudely refuses to recognize Manzano's right to contract himself out for pay (De la Fuente 354).

Once these legal options have been exhausted, an unnamed servant points out not only that Manzano is being mistreated but also that there is one more legal avenue that he can pursue. This is another of the few instances in the narrative that suggests some degree of solidarity for Manzano. Near the conclusion of the *Autobiografía*, a free servant remarks that a light-skinned and talented *criollo* like Manzano deserves better: "[H]ombre q[e.] tu no tienes berguenza p[a]. estar pasando tanto trabajos cualquiera negro bozal está mejor tratado q[e]. tú, un mulatico fino con tantas abilidades como tú al momento hallará quien lo compre" (Man are you not ashamed of being put through so much torment any African fresh off the boat is treated better than you, a light mulatto with so many abilities like you will find someone to buy you in an instant; 338).[26] In another of the few moments that suggests solidarity with others for Manzano, the same interlocutor urges him to appeal to the island's highest authority, the captain general: "[M]e abló mucho rato conclullendo con desirme q[e]. llegando al tribunal de el capitan general asiendo un punctual reláto de todo lo q[e]. me pasaba podia salir libre" (He talked to me for a long time concluding by telling me that upon arrival at the captain general's tribunal making a timely report of all that had happened to me I could be freed; 338). The author thus builds a legal case throughout the autobiography for his escape and freedom based on the same laws that also govern and uphold enslavement.

Manzano is sometimes characterized in scholarship as fearful and passive, yet he is the active agent of his freedom in the *Autobiografía*.[27] His appeal to the law relies upon colonial legal discourse yet also directly challenges the authority of a white slaveholder and exposes the contradictions between the idealist elements of Spanish colonial law and the actual practice of enslavement. He openly approaches the marquesa about his legal options; when most of these are overruled by the cruel mistress, he escapes to Havana in order to seek out the captain general. Manzano does not present himself as physically dangerous, but he disrupts the marquesa's authority by documenting her denial of his rights and by continuing to press for recognition of them. He does not escape from "civilization" by heading for the maroon communities of the mountains, but rather flees towards the center of power and home to much of the free population of color, Havana. The long-suffering enslaved characters typically presented in fiction by Manzano's white contemporaries do not generally make either physical bids or legal arguments for freedom, but instead fatalistically accept their destinies on Cuba's sugar plantations. For example, Suárez y Romero's Francisco surrenders to despair after learning of Dorotea's dishonor (177). Gómez de Avellaneda's Sab does not run away with Teresa when she invites him to, but instead dies of a broken heart (220; 246). Most of the female characters of color created by members of the *tertulia* also become resigned to their tragic fates. Manzano, in contrast, outlines a legal pathway to freedom successfully pursued by other enslaved persons before and after him.

RACIAL DISCOURSE: BLACK, WHITE, AND IN-BETWEEN

The presentation of racial identity in the *Autobiografía* reinscribes the stratified view held in colonial Cuba that placed an abyssal line between whiteness and Blackness while also recognizing a range of mixed identities. This hierarchical conception is particularly well illustrated by one of the most often cited statements in the narrative, which is found near the conclusion of the text. Afraid of being remanded to the plantation, Manzano explains that he would be "en una palabra mulato y entre negros; mi padre era algo altivo y nunca permitio no solo corrillos en su casa pero nii qe sus hijos jugasen con lo negritos de la asienda . . . y en aquel momento determine mi fuga" (in a word mulatto and among Blacks; my father was kind of arrogant and never allowed gatherings in his house or his children to play with the Black children of the plantation . . . and in that moment I decided on my escape; 339). Fear of punishment and of being the lone *mulato* among Blacks provokes his escape from the *ingenio*. For some scholars, this constitutes a rejection of Black and African identity. For example, Richard L. Jackson is critical of the author's lack of solidarity when he writes, "Juan Francisco Manzano (1797–1854) and other slave poets in Cuba were ignoring their African heritage" (94). Luis considers the author's difficult position when he proposes that "to abandon his own frame of reference, of Africa and slavery" is a strategic move to gain his freedom (*Literary Bondage* 65; Branche 81–82). In Branche's analysis, however, Manzano is not rejecting an African identity, but instead is constructing a *mulato* one: "He could not abandon an [African] ethnic identity that he had never assumed" (81–82). Manzano is clear throughout the text that he is neither Black nor African—he is a Cuban-born man of mixed racial heritage.

Constructing a *mulato* identity is not only a question of Manzano's desire to alter his legal status and a likely reflection of the internalized racism of colonialism but also one of life or death. Life expectancy for agricultural workers on the *ingenios* could be as low as five years because of the dangerous working conditions and lack of care that slaveholders provided (Paquette 55). Speaking little to no Spanish and representing different dialects and language groups added to the risk: This was the case for many *bozales* and, later, for indentured Chinese. In his study of US investment in Cuban sugar plantations, Stephen Chambers refers to the sugar fields and factories as the "agro-industrial graveyard" because of the dangers that they held for workers (62). Manzano's narrative reiterates the negative view of Blackness that is a key component in the commodification of human bodies under the system of enslavement in Cuba and elsewhere in the American Hemisphere, yet it is also true that he wrote from a position of considerable vulnerability in a highly stratified slaveholding colony. The author's frequent references to himself as solitary and distant from the larger enslaved population would also allay the fears of organized rebellion so amply expressed in Del Monte's essays and letters.

In Delmontine discourse, the erasure of cultural and physical Blackness is presented as the path to modernity and nationhood. As Sara Rosell and Gema R. Guevara argue, the ideology of *blanqueamiento* fails in the literary projects of the white *tertulia* writers; the gendering of whitening means that Blackness cannot ever be fully erased.[28] Many of the antislavery fictions by Manzano's contemporaries describe their tragic, central characters as being of mixed race, yet there are also a few notable exceptions to this, such as Suárez y Romero's Francisco and Tanco's Petrona. Whether of mixed race or not, however, the literary enslaved characters created by Manzano's white contemporaries may demonstrate exceptional personality traits, but they never cross the abyssal line to freedom through *blanqueamiento*. The racialized discourse in Manzano's text in many ways corresponds to that employed by his white contemporaries and Cuban colonial society in its devaluation of Blackness, associated with ignorance and enslavement, and elevation of whiteness, linked to enlightenment and freedom, yet his status as a *mulato* is an integral part of the narrator's case for freedom. Manzano claims an in-between, mixed racial identity that permitted "upward socio-racial mobility" in a colonial society that at times allowed for racial fluidity and change of status (Branche 79–81). Further, his insistence on a *criollo*—i.e., Cuban—identity challenges the premise of Antonio Saco and Del Monte's *blanqueamiento* that to be Cuban and to participate in the modern nation requires the erasure of all degrees of Blackness. Rather, Manzano constructs an identity that is white enough to cross the abyssal line to the freedom that eludes the characters of Delmontine antislavery fiction, but is nonetheless a mixed racial identity.

CONCLUSION: CHALLENGES TO AND REINSCRIPTIONS OF THE DISCOURSE OF COLONIALITY

The modes of discourse that appear in the *Autobiografía* often participate in the maintenance of the colonial matrix of power in nineteenth-century Cuban written works and in the wider American Hemisphere. In Manzano's text, the author reinscribes certain elements of the discourses that uphold power, yet also adapts them to his purposes, all in the service of his overall argument in support of his freedom. His narrative illustrates the operation of coloniality in nineteenth-century Cuba while also revealing the ways in which it can be challenged. Manzano's use of oral and written discourses that were considered above his station threatened those in power. His employment of religious discourse indicates the ways in which colonial Christianity bound the enslaved to the slaveholder and reinforced obedience, while at the same time revealing the interracial network of support that *padrinazgo* created for the enslaved. The appearance of Afro-Cuban religious beliefs and practices in the text demonstrate that the author's literary self is not passing, but instead presents an identity that is mixed not only racially but also culturally.[29] Through reliance on the same laws that authorized enslavement, Manzano challenges the authority of the slaveholder and employs the tools successfully used by others in his position. The author's construction of a mixed racial identity reiterates colonialized denigration of Blackness but also points to the fluidity of racial identities recognized in Cuba and the possibility for social mobility.

Even with the adherences in his text to the discourse of power, Manzano was ahead of his time in his presentation of himself as an Afro-Cuban writer and intellectual. He presents an identity that is culturally and racially mixed well before white intellectuals began to promote Cuba's blend of Spanish and African influences as the defining feature of Cuban national identity in the first half of the twentieth century. Manzano's demonstration of intellectual and artistic accomplishments challenges the limitation in colonializing discourse of such capacities to the domain of whiteness alone. Despite the author's characterization of himself as solitary and isolated, Manzano's text nonetheless points to a greater level of incorporation into Afro-Cuban culture and community. As De la Fuente's research indicates, Manzano was clearly not the only enslaved person insisting on his legal rights and pursuing freedom. Further, the fact that a servant points out to Manzano that he can appeal to the captain general illustrates the dissemination of legal information running counter to slaveholding interests among the oppressed. Discernible African influence on Manzano's religious beliefs and practices also indicates both greater solidarity and a more culturally mixed identity than his narrative might otherwise suggest. As an enslaved person in colonial Cuba at a time when systemic change seemed very difficult to achieve, Manzano had only difficult options. By working within the system and at the same time making alterations to the discourse of power, however, the author documents a path to freedom that could be followed by others. The chapters that follow will outline the reinscription of the discourse of coloniality in texts by white authors as well as disruptions to that discourse, even when counter to apparent authorial intentions.

CHAPTER TWO

COSTUMBRISMO CRIOLLO

Enlightenment Ideals and the Discourse of Coloniality

Literary *costumbrismo* (reformist local color writing) as it developed in Spain and Cuba is intertwined with Enlightenment ideologies, Spain's loss of much of its empire, and the expansion of sugar production on the island.[1] This mode of writing typically promotes a liberal identity in the face of a rapidly changing country and offers moral correctives to perceived societal wrongs. To put this into the terms of decolonial thought, *costumbrismo* writes the transfer of political and economic power from the crown and the aristocracy to a new group that is empowered by capitalism and technology and that views itself as promoting liberal values such as tolerance and equality. Finally, aligning with the North Atlantic thought of the nineteenth century's rising colonial powers, the framework for *costumbrismo* dates modernity from the Enlightenment and associates it with moral, economic, and technological advancement. As with Romantic expression in general, literary *costumbrismo* rephrases the colonializing narrative of progress and salvation in Enlightenment terms of modernity, progress, equality, and freedom.

As adopted by white *criollo* writers, such as those of the Delmontine *tertulia* in Cuba, *costumbrismo* offers a literary mode through which aspects of Spanish colonialism can be satirized and Cuban claims to nationhood legitimated. A literary influence on the island for much of the century, reformist local color writing appears in novels as well as *artículos de costumbrismo* (local color sketches or essays), which may blend fact and fiction. Although their wealth and status typically place them economically in the upper class, politically disempowered *criollo* writers often promote a reformist position associated with Enlightenment values as well as their understanding of

Cuban national identity in their quest to gain greater political and economic agency from the Spanish colonial administration. Although *costumbrista* works typically seek to depict that which is especially representative of a society while providing moralizing correctives meant to improve the human condition, Afro-descendants and the institution of enslavement infrequently appear as primary subjects of Cuban *artículos de costumbrismo*. However, understudied *artículos* by Francisco Baralt, Anselmo Suárez y Romero, and José E. Triay provide exceptions to this general rule. While each of these authors presents Afro-descendant characters from an abyssal perspective, there are some differences of degree between them. Studied in conjunction, these *artículos* reflect the anxieties of white writers at key moments in the island's history regarding African influence, enslavement, and institutional changes. Further, even if counter to apparent authorial intent, these authors also document Afro-Cuban culture and practices in ways that allow for solidarity, preservation of identity, and challenges to colonializing power by people who were enslaved and marginalized during the colonial era.

COSTUMBRISMO AND ENLIGHTENMENT IDEALS

Peninsular *costumbrismo* is characterized by its nationalistic and moralizing features. Strongly influenced by the French *littérature de moeurs*, critiquing moral faults and promoting social and individual progress is at the heart of this genre of literature: "Por *moeurs* los franceses han entendido siempre todos los resortes morales del hombre y de la sociedad" (The French have always understood *moeurs* to mean all the moral resources of man and society; Montesinos 48). This reformist tendency combines with a search for defining national character rooted in conceptions of past traditions. Alarmed by political and social transformations in the early decades of the century, Spain's local color writers also sought the comfort of a unifying, traditional, and historic identity: "De aquí la tendencia a buscar lo castizo y a satirizar lo moderno y extranjerizado, a evocar el recuerdo calmante de la pachorrenta vida de antaño, y la inquietud maravillada ante la vertiginosa vida moderna" (Hence the tendency to seek the authentic and to satirize modernity and foreign influences, to evoke the soothing memory of the slow life of yesteryear, and the astonished anxiety produced by the speed of modern life; Montesinos 44). At the same time, the most prominent *costumbrista* writers strove to affirm the shift in political power to the rising middle class and a concept of modernity rooted in the Enlightenment: "In the 1830s Spanish writers had set parameters for the Costumbrista movement. Their examination of national types and of their impact on local customs proposed to reflect the rise to power of the middle class and the complex changes occurring in the Spanish political arena" (Ocasio 4).

The effects of the political and economic changes in Spain on literary *costumbrismo* are the focus of Susan Kirkpatrick's analysis of the work of the best-known peninsular *costumbristas*, Ramón de Mesonero Romanos and Mariano José de Larra. Coinciding with the rise of the popular press in Spain in the 1830s, the era's local color writing builds upon a preexisting indigenous strain of local color writing and also borrows from the journalistic traditions of France and Britain, two nations that had already witnessed the rise of capitalism and of the middle class and, adding to Kirkpatrick's list, I also include the two countries' considerable growth in imperial power (Kirkpatrick 29–30). In contrast, Spain had lost most of its colonies and the monarchy was in severe crisis in the 1830s. During this transitional time, the nascent Spanish bourgeoisie found expression for its interests in the *artículos de costumbres* authored by urban writers who reflected and represented those class interests (31). The primarily urban reading public, aware of living in a time of political and social change, was interested in consuming a new image of itself as pivotal to the modernizing nation while nonetheless legitimized by connections to past cultural traditions (31).

Enlightenment ideals and North Atlantic frameworks of modernity inform literary *costumbrismo*. José Francisco Martín offers a succinct list of the Enlightenment ideals important to liberal *costumbristas* such as Larra: "La confianza en el *progreso* material y moral del género humano . . . , la fe en la *razón* como instrumento capaz de explorar y comprender la realidad, junto a la *tolerancia* y la *libertad* defendidas por Larra ponen de manifiesto el marco ilustrado en el que se desenvuelve el problema de España en su obra" (Confidence in the material and moral *progress* of humankind . . . , faith in *reason* as an instrument capable of exploring and comprehending reality, together with the *tolerance* and *liberty* defended by Larra highlight the Illustration framework in which the problem of Spain is developed in his work; original emphasis, 228). In addition to espousing Enlightenment values, Martín proposes that Larra's concern for national development makes him a precursor to the Generación del '98, the group of writers who explore the country's existential crisis provoked by the loss of Spain's last colonies in the American Hemisphere and in the Pacific (223). Although they promote national ideologies and defend their country's international reputation against Hispanophobic imagery, Spanish *costumbristas* nonetheless appear to accept the premise that the more industrialized northern nations of Europe taking control of the colonial matrix of power were now at the forefront of modernity and that Spain had been left behind. Just as it did not prevent the continuation of enslavement in the newly formed US, the rise of liberal Enlightenment philosophy did not put an end to Europe's colonial era but rather provided new terminology for it as England and France extended their empires under the guise of modernizing and enlightening vulnerable populations in areas possessing great natural resources.

In Cuba, the liberal discourse of *costumbrismo* was adapted by upper-class writers seeking to legitimize their claim to increased political power and also to reform colonial practices. Salvador Bueno characterizes Cuban *costumbrismo* as primarily seeking improvement in severe colonial conditions: "Su proyección era predominantemente de crítica social y de carácter reformador" (Its trajectory was primarily one of social critique and of a reformist nature; Prólogo x). The confluence of multiple social, political, and economic factors led to the development of local color writing in Cuba—namely, the rise of the sugar aristocracy, the modest but notable increase in newspaper publication, and the spread of Enlightenment ideology fueling literary Romanticism, to which I also add the huge increase in human traffic from Africa to the island (Bueno, Prólogo x–xi). Whereas Cuba's nineteenth-century *costumbrista* novels have received considerable scholarly attention, many *artículos de costumbrismo* remain understudied. Bueno defines these local color sketches as "breves trabajos, en prosa casi siempre, que en forma concisa y con intención satírica, o meramente recreativa, describían usos, hábitos, costumbres, tipos característicos y representativos de una sociedad determinada" (short works, almost always in prose, that in a concise form and with satiric, or simply entertaining, intention, describe uses, habits, customs, characteristic and representative types of a specific society; Prólogo x).

Artículos de costumbrismo began to appear in Cuban newspapers as early as 1790, beginning with the *Papel Periódico de la Havana*. Late eighteenth-century Cuban *costumbrismo* describes local customs from the perspective of white *criollos* employing the Enlightenment framework of correcting vices to improve quality of life at individual and societal levels, even at the risk of angering colonial officials. An anonymous declaration published in the *Papel Periódico* describes the goal of local color writing and of the newspaper itself as providing a moral corrective: "Atacar los usos y costumbres que son perjudiciales en común y en particular corregir los vicios pintándolos con sus propios colores, para que mirados con horror se detesten, y retratar en contraposición el apreciable atractivo de las virtudes" (Attack widespread, harmful habits and customs and especially correct vices by painting them in their true colors, so that when seen with horror, they will be despised, and portray in contrast the appreciable beauty of virtues; cited in Bueno, Prólogo xi–xii). The preferred topics of Cuban *costumbristas* provide a liberal critique of the decadence and corruption of colonial life: Common themes include "la educación y el amor, censuras a los bailes, el juego y las modas extravagantes, satíricos ataques contra el afeminamiento y la equivocada instrucción de los niños. Y también, la temática, cada vez más candente, de la esclavitud" (education and love, censure of balls, gambling, and extravagant fashions, satirical attacks against effeminacy and misguided education of boys. And also, the increasingly burning topic of slavery; Bueno, Prólogo xii). Even in works of Cuban *costumbrismo* that seem on the surface to be benign, Bueno argues that discontent is a fundamental element: "[P]or debajo de esta mera descripción de hábitos populares, de figuras pintorescas, como trasfondo de este panorama colorido de la época palpita y hierve una protesta" (Underneath the simple description of popular traditions, of picturesque figures, like an undercurrent to the era's colorful panorama, a protest beats and boils; xiv).

In *Afro-Cuban Costumbrismo: From Plantations to the Slums*, Ocasio underscores the context of significant social transition for Cuban *costumbrismo* (4). Like the metropolis, Cuba was undergoing tremendous changes due to rapid demographic shifts, heightened control by the metropolitan government, the wars of independence in mainland Latin America, and technological advancement, particularly in sugar production. Although subject to strict official censorship, Cuban writers "adapted [Spanish] Costumbrista aesthetic trends to their own needs in their comprehensive analyses of national sociopolitical conditions.... One important trend was their often severe views of the state of Cuban customs" (5). Again like Spain, Cuba hosted numerous foreign visitors who wrote about Cuban culture through a North Atlantic lens, including Alexander von Humboldt, Abiel Abott, Richard Henry Dana, Fredrika Bremer, Maturin Murray Ballou, and Julia Ward Howe, to name only a few. Foreign critiques of local practices did not always sit well with Cuban readers beginning to take pride in their own national identity. In his introduction to Víctor Patricio de Landaluze's collection of *costumbrista* engravings and essays, *Los cubanos pintados por si mismos: Colección de tipos Cubanos* (*Cubans Portrayed by Themselves: Collection of Cuban Types*; 1852), Blas San Millán explains that nations may feel free to analyze themselves but smart at the criticisms of others: "Las naciones son como los individuos; el menor sarcasmo estrangero hiere agudamente *nuestra nacionalidad*, y no perdonamos á los que no nacieron en nuestro suelo" (Nations are like individuals; the slightest sarcastic remark from a foreigner wounds our *national pride* deeply, and we don't forgive those who were not born on our soil; original emphasis, San Millán, Introducción 1).

Whereas Peninsular *costumbrismo* is characterized as a discourse proposing national unification, the colonialized discourse of racial difference often makes the Cuban projection of identity exclusionary. As Ocasio argues, Cuban *costumbrismo* largely equates *cubanía*, or Cubanness, with whiteness (3). Similarly, Maida Watson is critical of the presentation of people of color in this predominant mode of writing: "El cuadro de costumbres cubano decimonónico y las escenas costumbristas—que aparecen en las novelas cubanas de la misma época—presentan un marcado racismo" (The nineteenth-century Cuban local color sketch and local color scenes—which appear in Cuban novels of the same time period—present a marked racism; 160–61). On the rare occasion that a published *artículo de costumbrismo* does highlight enslaved Afro-descendants, their portrayals generally rely on contented, passive, and otherwise nonthreatening stereotypes: "[T]hey described certain slave types, such as the faithful, hardworking field worker, or the old, 'retired' field worker" (Ocasio 5). However, as Watson argues, these literary works also present the opposing extreme, in which Afro-descendant people are characterized as wild and animalistic (161). The liberal, humanistic framework of *costumbrismo* is thus put to work not only to criticize the corrosive nature of enslavement but also to counter the perceived negative influence of uncivilized and underdeveloped Afro-descendants. This seeming paradox is explained by recognizing the abyssal view that many of these authors had of enslaved Afro-descendants and also by their interest in protecting their share of the colonial matrix of power.

Under strict censorship that made overt criticism impossible, the employment of this literary mode implies a liberal, reasoned critique of colonial institutions and endemic corruption. For much of the century, as Ocasio argues, explorations of Cuban identity centered around white "types" and European-derived culture, with few exceptions. However, as the century progressed and Cuban freedom from Spain started to hinge upon the involvement of Afro-descendants in the fight for independence, literary *costumbrismo* began to recognize the presence of Afro-descendants in Cuba and to contemplate a society without enslavement. Even when reinforcing coloniality and abyssal thought, *artículos* portraying Cuba's enslaved nonetheless highlight the centrality of African influences to the island's culture and the development of Afro-Cuban cultural practices that challenge the structures of power.

FRANCISCO BARALT: ABYSSAL VIEWS COUNTERED BY *LA TUMBA FRANCESA*

Costumbrista writers find fertile ground in the topic of dances as gatherings that illustrate the status and morality of the attendees. Villaverde's *Cecilia Valdés*, for example, portrays two types of balls that are defined by the racial identities of those present and by the corresponding levels of morality attributed to them. *El baile de cuna* (Afro-descendants' ball), primarily attended by people of color but also by white men seeking sexual partners, is associated with loose morality and chaotic racial mixing (Watson 172).[2] In contrast, the upper-class, whites-only ball is portrayed as a respectable gathering considered appropriate for unmarried, upper-class white women to attend (174). Put another way, *el baile de cuna* is a threat to colonial social order and hierarchy, but the whites-only ball serves to uphold it. Whereas balls in salons and urban spaces are regular subjects of Cuban *costumbrismo*, dances that take place on plantations among the enslaved are much less frequent topics. Francisco Baralt and Anselmo Suárez y Romero provide exceptions to this. Although the two overlapped chronologically, these authors offer quite different assessments of Afro-Cuban music and dance as developed on the island's plantations. Of the *artículos* studied here, Baralt's "Escenas campestres: Baile de los negros" ("Country Scenes: The Blacks' Dance," 1846) most clearly upholds the colonial matrix of power in its linking of a white Europe with civilization and modernity, as well as the inverse association of a dark Africa with the uncivilized and the primitive. The characterization of Afro-descendants in this *artículo* as savage and indecent suggests that like the attendees of Villaverde's *baile de cuna*, they, too, could be dangerous to colonial order and morality. While clearly relying upon an abyssal assessment of Afro-descendants, the *artículo*'s account of a plantation dance, Oriente's *tumba francesa* (French drum), nonetheless points to the importance of music and dance as loci for solidarity and communication among the enslaved and the potential for transculturated art forms to challenge the status quo.

Baralt's essay begins with a lengthy discussion of dance as the most elevated human art form: "De todos los ejercicios del cuerpo que el hombre ha elevado a artes, se puede decir, sin gran temor a equivocarse, que ninguno se halla más generalizado, más extendido, en grado más eminente de perfección que el de la danza" (Of all the exercises of the body that man has elevated into art, one can say, without great fear of being wrong, that none is more widespread, more far-reaching, in the most eminent degree of perfection than that of dance; 151). In line with the Enlightenment framework of human progress, the author traces the development of Western dance from the ancient Egyptians to classical Greece and Rome and then to Europe. As a culmination of this historical progress, the highest form of this affective art occurs in civilized Europe: "[E]l idioma que los hombres usan no alcanza para expresar lo que se ve, lo que se siente y lo que se piensa en uno de esos espectáculos de hadas que la civilizada Europa alcanza sólo a montar como corresponde" (The language used by men is inadequate to express what one sees, what one feels, and what one thinks during one of those fairy spectacles that civilized Europe alone is able to stage as it should be done; 153–54).

At this point, however, Baralt clarifies that the point of this essay will not be to discuss dance as manifested among civilized peoples, but rather to portray a "throwback":

> Yo voy a presentar el baile en este artículo, no como se encuentra en casi todos los pueblos civilizados, más o menos adelantado por el estudio y la observación, gobernado por el gusto y regido por la decencia, sino que, dando *un salto atrás*, voy a tomarlo en su estado *natural, rústico y grotesco*; voy a presenter el baile del *salvaje*; . . . ese baile traído del África.
>
> I will present dance in this piece, not as it is found among almost all civilized people, more or less advanced by study and observation, governed by taste and ruled by decency, rather, taking *a leap backwards*, I will present it in its *natural, crude, and grotesque* state; I will present the dance of the *savage*; . . . that dance brought from Africa. (emphasis added, 154)

The juxtaposition between civilized Europe and so-called "savage" traditions in Cuba reflects a deep ambivalence about the African-influenced culture on the island's plantations. The *artículo*'s lengthy discussion of the historical development of Western dance appears at first glance to suggest a legitimating connection between European and Afro-Cuban dance from the author's perspective: The creation of art forms is a uniquely human activity and an indicator of cultural accomplishment. However, as Watson points out, for many Cuban *costumbristas*, balls and popular dances in Cuba reflect "la influencia nociva que la cultura africana ejercía sobre la cultura de los blancos" (the noxious influence that African culture exercised over the whites' culture; 169). Despite the initial link that Baralt appears to establish with European cultural traditions, he reiterates the opinion that the music and dance of Cuba's enslaved Afro-descendant people is primitive, obscene, and grotesque.

Baralt criticizes the music that accompanies the plantation dance for perceived simplicity: The beat of the drums produces "una armonía monótona y fastidiosa sin variedad ni cadencia" (a monotonous and tiresome harmony lacking variety and cadence; 155). Similarly, *el canto*, the song, is "monótono, sin glosas ni adornos, como lo son siempre las de los hombres incultos y cercanos aún al estado primitivo" (monotonous, without refrains or flourishes, since they are always the songs of ignorant men still close to the primitive state; 156). Again hinting at a legitimating connection to European art forms, Baralt uses Italian music terminology to describe the dance: "[E]l tango redobla sus golpes, su compás es vivo y arrebatado, y toca ya al último grado del *allegro* cuando va disminuyendo para volver a caer en el *andante* más pausado" (The dance doubles its beat, its rhythm is lively and rushed, and then just as it reaches the highest grade of *allegro*, it slows to again fall into the slowest *andante*; original emphasis, 157). Following his account of the first two dancers to perform, Baralt claims that he has described these dances in a limited way because they are too obscene for full representation: "Yo me avergonzaría de pintarlas con sus colores naturales; la descripción que de ellas hago llega hasta donde la decencia lo permite y se queda muy lejos de la realidad" (I would be ashamed to paint them in their natural colors; the description of them that I make goes only to where decency permits and stops far short of the reality; 157). Once all the participants have joined the performance, Baralt compares the dance to gatherings of witches and demons, thereby reinscribing the discourse of coloniality that characterizes vulnerable populations as needing Christian salvation and oversight: He claims that an outsider "que sin anterior preparación se hallara transportado al sitio donde pasa la escena, que asistía a un sábado de las brujas, a un agitado pandemónium" (an unprepared [outsider] finding himself where this scene occurs, would think he was attending a witches' sabbath, an agitated pandemonium; 158).

Baralt's condemnation of African-influenced music and dance reflects the colonializing premise that Europe is the seat of civilization, human progress, and Christian salvation. However, his response could also be informed by the extent to which these artistic expressions represent a threat to the slaveholder's power. Given his focus on eastern Cuba and the fact that he refers to it as "esa *tumba* o *tango*" (that *drum* or *dance*), Baralt appears to be describing Afro-Haitian-Cuban *tumba francesa* (French drum), in which French ballroom and African dances are performed to West African drum rhythms and accompanied by vocals (154).[3] *Tumba francesa* originated in the French colony of St. Domingue and was introduced into Cuba through Oriente with the arrival of French colonial coffee planters, who brought enslaved people with them when escaping the Haitian Revolution. Inviting an understanding of transculturation that considers both the African authenticity and also the originality of this new creation, Adriana Méndez Rodenas considers *tumba francesa* to be of "singular importancia . . . para ilustrar los procesos de transculturación" (singular importance . . . in illustrating the processes of transculturation; "Poéticas de la transculturación" 150). *La tumba francesa* is a transculturated art form that continues to be a powerful expression of Afro-Cuban identity today.

Prior to the abolition of enslavement in Cuba, performance of the *tumba francesa* on coffee plantations gave the opportunity for Afro-descendants to gather in groups and dance to drum rhythms brought from Dahomey. *Tumba francesa* is an example of what Fernando Ortiz refers to as *contrapunteo* (counterpoint), or a response to a forced transfer from one culture to another (Méndez Rodenas, "Poéticas" 151).[4] This form of song and dance is not an imitation but a talking back; French ballroom dance is put into dialogue with West African drumming and alternates with West African dances (153). The lyrics that accompany the dance, often sung in either French or Spanish patois, permitted the utterance and dissemination of information and ideas that were otherwise dangerous to speak. Ortiz characterizes the *cantos* (songs) of the *tumba francesa* as spoken newspapers reporting on current events (cited in Coca-Izaguirre et al. 343). Manuel Coca-Izaguirre et al. add to this characterization by explaining that the songs also provide commentary on the news shared in addition to narrating historical events (343). Further, humor and mockery appear frequently in the *cantos*, indicating that they provide an opportunity to caricature the powerful (343; 345–46).

Baralt presents the description of the music and dance as well as that of a New Year's Day feast prepared for the enslaved as novel and scandalous entertainments for a reader assumed to share the same colonializing and abyssal values. His own trip to the plantation was motivated by a desire to witness the special feast: "Yo había ido expresamente a la hacienda para ver ese banquete" (I had gone deliberately to the plantation in order to see that banquet; 159). Unlike *artículos* that appear more calibrated to criticize the cruelty of slavery, this sketch reinscribes the dehumanizing discourse of coloniality. At the same time, the author presents ambivalence when confirming the African influence on popular Cuban dances such as *la chica, el fandango,* and *el bolero* (154). Further, despite the author's reductivist characterization of it, this *artículo* documents a performance of *tumba francesa*, a transculturated art form that expresses Afro-Cuban diasporic identity, serves as a means of communication and solidarity for the enslaved, and constitutes a new cultural form arising from the dialogue among African, European, and Caribbean elements. Finally, the radical expression of *la tumba francesa* is made clear by the ways that it has been revisited in twentieth-century interpretations of periods of unrest and revolution in Cuba (Coca-Izaguirre et al. 342; Méndez Rodenas, "Poéticas" 157–58).

ANSELMO SUÁREZ Y ROMERO: SOLACE BUT NOT SOLIDARITY

Anselmo Suárez y Romero (1818–1878) was an influential participant in the Delmontine *tertulia* and is best known for *Francisco, o las delicias del campo* (written 1838; published 1880), which literary criticism has traditionally characterized as antislavery.[5] Although the novel was strongly critiqued later in the century, colonial censorship considered *Francisco*'s presentation of enslavement and white brutality too dangerous for circulation. The novel was not published until decades after it was composed and, like *Cecilia Valdés*, first appeared in print in the US rather than in Cuba. As were many of the white members of the Domingo del Monte *tertulia*, Suárez y Romero was also a slaveholder belonging to the elite class. This author spent a considerable amount of time on site managing the family's sugar plantation, Ingenio Surinam (Silverstein 62). In letters, he reports feeling isolated and seeing nothing but sad scenes at Surinam: "[Estoy a]islado en el injenio, sin ver de dia y de noche mas que enormes fábricas, monótonas y sin gusto, el batey, los cañaverales, y luego para acabar de entristecer el cuadro, sin ver otro espectáculo que el de hombres infelices trabajando incesantemente para otros" (I am isolated at the sugar mill, seeing nothing day and night but the huge factories, all the same and unpleasant, the refinery, the cane fields, and then as a final, sad touch to the picture, without seeing any other sight than unhappy men working ceaselessly for others; cited in Cabrera Saqui 23). Encouraged to write about plantation life by Del Monte, Suárez y Romero composed *Francisco*, as well as a number of *artículos de costumbrismo*, while in residence at Surinam and as a daily witness to the most brutal iteration of enslavement in Cuba, that of the sugar plantation (Ocasio 26–28). Suárez y Romero died in Havana in 1878, just before his novel *Francisco* was finally published for the first time.

Compared to *Francisco*, Suárez y Romero's *artículos de costumbres* are significantly understudied, despite providing ostensibly nonfiction accounts of plantation culture. Ocasio and Stephen Silverstein are among the few critics to offer recent analyses of the author's shorter works.[6] Ocasio characterizes

Suárez y Romero's local color sketches as humanizing the enslaved in a way rarely seen in the works of his contemporaries, particularly since they so infrequently appear in Cuban *costumbrismo* at all, especially prior to 1881 (22–59). Silverstein, in contrast, argues that the author in fact intended to promote the continuation of enslavement by encouraging a program of *buen tratamiento* (good treatment) in his local color sketches (60). However, Silverstein does not consider racialized thought in his argument, which is a significant component of the argument against enslavement in essays by Saco and Del Monte, and also appears to discount the *tertulia* writers' statements in favor of gradually ending enslavement (62). Following Schulman's characterization of the *tertulia* writers as reformists, I consider that Suárez y Romero's use of inherently moralizing *costumbrismo*, his consistently melancholy tone, and his unusual decision to write about enslavement implies criticism of the harsh conditions of sugar production (Introduction 17). However, the *costumbrista* altruism in the *artículos* is limited to the author's own anguish over enslavement, and his heavy reliance on the stereotype of the contented slave results in an abyssal rather than a humanizing presentation of Afro-descendants. Notable similarities between the novel *Francisco* and the sketches further distance the latter from an objective presentation of enslaved people of color. Where Suárez y Romero surpasses a contemporary such as Baralt, however, is in his acclaim of Afro-Cuban plantation culture and his recognition of the dangerous, inhumane conditions of work in sugar cultivation.

In a reversal of Juan Francisco Manzano's insistence on his distance from the rural enslaved collective, Suárez y Romero consistently depicts himself as drawn to the company and cultural practices of the enslaved Afro-descendant people on Surinam. Unlike Manzano, however, Suárez y Romero's racial and class status is never in doubt, nor is it forgotten by those around him; he seeks to relieve his solitude and melancholy among the Afro-descendants held on the plantation but does not look for solidarity with them. This is particularly well illustrated in "Ingenios," which is part of a series describing plantation life that was written in 1840 and published nearly two decades later in Cuba in *Colección de artículos* (1859; Ocasio 24). Although Ocasio credits the author with as much of a critique of enslavement that Cuban censorship would allow, he argues that Suárez y Romero provides "no indication of cultural pride in slave culture" (25; 59). However, in the first paragraph of "Ingenios," the narrator announces that his long stay at Surinam will allow him plenty of time to study "*nuestras* costumbres" (*our* customs; emphasis added, 309), incorporating what he describes of plantation life into a shared

Cuban culture. Moreover, Suárez y Romero's emotional description of Afro-Cuban music and dance in this *artículo*, particularly when contrasted with Baralt's assessment, suggests that the author positively values the African-influenced culture of the plantation (311–13).

The narrative begins with a celebration of Cuba's natural beauty and an expression of national pride: The speaker states that he will dedicate himself to "la contemplación de tantas maravillas y magnificencias con que Dios quiso embellecer estas tierras de los trópicos, y en especial a nuestra adorada patria la preciosa isla de Cuba" (the contemplation of so many marvels and the grandeur with which God wanted to beautify these tropical lands, and especially our beloved fatherland the lovely island of Cuba; 309). However, Suárez y Romero's portrait of the sugar plantation quickly turns to the ecological devastation caused by clearing the tropical forest in order to plant a single crop. Additionally, the narrator sees the huts for enslaved people, which he describes as the shantytown of the plantation microcosm: "Los bohíos se hallan a corta distancia detrás de las fábricas, y pueden por su miseria y desnudez considerarse como los suburbios o arrabales del pequeño pueblo a que un ingenio se parece" (The huts are found a short distance behind the factories, and can, because of their squalor and bareness, be considered the suburbs or slums of the small town that the sugar plantation resembles; 309). Revealing his perspective as a white master, Suárez y Romero remarks that picking coffee on a *cafetal* is a mild, even entertaining, occupation: "Siquiera en los cafetales recolectar el café es una operación muy sencilla, antes distrae que molesta a los negros, es cosa que se hace jugando hasta por los criollitos" (Even harvesting coffee on the coffee plantation is a simple operation, it sooner distracts than bothers the Blacks, it's something done while playing even by the smallest children; 310). At the same time, he acknowledges the extreme physical demands to which the enslaved are subjected on sugar plantations. The alternating seasons on the sugar mill, "la zafra y el tiempo muerto" (the sugar harvest and the dead season; 310), are both terrible. When sugar is not being harvested, captive workers must plant cane in the rain and mud. During the harvest, the labor required is unbearable:

> Cortar caña, si es tiempo de molienda, al resistero del sol durante el día, meterla en el trapiche, andar con los tachos y las pailas, atizar las fornallas, juntar caña, acarrearla hasta el burro, cargar el bagazo; y por la noche hacer estos trabajos en los cuartos de prima y de madrugada al frío y al sereno, muriéndose de sueño, porque para diecinueve horas de fatiga sólo hay cinco de descanso.

> Cutting cane, if it is milling season, during the day when the sun is at its hottest, putting it into the sugar mill, walking with the bins and the pans, stoking the oven fires, gathering cane, hauling it to the donkey, carrying the bagasse; and during the night, laboring at the hours of Prime and dawn in the cold and under the night sky, dying of exhaustion, because for nineteen hours of hard work there are only five of rest. (310)[7]

Suárez y Romero's lachrymose narrator loses heart before the devastating features of the *ingenio*, which he relates directly to an intended reader that he perceives as being like himself: "Yo no sé, amigo mío, por qué se me abatieron entonces las alas del corazón" (I don't know, my friend, why the wings of my heart began to fold; 310). In Romantic fashion, the humane and sensitive narrator's feelings of loneliness and sorrow are projected onto the landscape and buildings of the plantation, but the overt criticism of slavery is limited here to a commentary on the hard work of sugar cultivation specifically.

Because it is a Saturday on the *ingenio*, the enslaved workers, conforming to the stereotype of the contented slave, ask for permission to "bailar el tambor" (dance the drum; 311). The narrative suggests that this request is for recreational dancing, but the drum had many important uses in the *contrapunteo* of nineteenth-century Afro-Cuban religion and culture. This scene provides Suárez y Romero the opportunity to explore the topic of African-derived music and dance on the plantation. In contrast to Baralt, Suárez y Romero stands out as an early admirer of the African influence in Cuban music and dance, which are claimed among the hallmarks of Cuban identity today. As Claudette M. Williams points out in her analysis of *Francisco*, Suárez y Romero's treatment of plantation music and dance is a notable precursor to twentieth-century *negrista* representations of African-derived cultural practices (64). Eager to observe the festivities, the narrator follows the enslaved people to an open space near their huts where they will dance together. Revealing the great imbalance of power between himself and those who are enslaved, the narrator explains that he has to hide in order to satisfy his own desire to watch: "[M]e escondí detrás de un árbol, porque en habiendo algún blanco delante, los negros se avergüenzan y ni cantan ni bailan; y desde allí pude observarlos a mi sabor" (I hid behind a tree, because when there is a white person before them, the Blacks become ashamed and neither sing nor dance; and from here I could watch them to my taste; 311). As Ocasio also notes, the author does not appear to have any compunction about watching, even knowing that it would make the performers uncomfortable (52). Suárez y Romero characterizes Afro-descendants as ashamed to be seen dancing, yet their unwillingness to be observed could reflect the desire to protect religious and other cultural practices or to find relief from the invasive gaze of their oppressors. As Molloy argues of Manzano, holding something of themselves back is a form of resistance for Afro-descendants (43). Similarly, Williams points to postcolonial literary analyses of silence as containing subterfuge in her discussion of Francisco's unspoken resistance to power (53).

Suárez y Romero's narrative persona forgets his sorrows while enthusiastically describing the sounds and movements as the drums begin to beat: "¡Qué bulla, qué gritería, qué desorden, amigo mío!" (What an uproar, what shouting, what chaos, my friend!; 312). He then rhapsodizes about Afro-Cuban songs featured on the *ingenio*. Each plantation has its own set of songs, but there are tunes common to all because they have been brought from Africa by the *negros de nación*, which is a more neutral term for African-born Blacks than *bozales*, and the songs are also learned by the *criollo* enslaved. Whereas Baralt highlights the primitive and indecent nature of Afro-Cuban dance, Suárez y Romero celebrates the music that is a constant presence, ranging from work songs to those of Christian holidays and rituals. The author connects the songs with order on the plantation, associating them with productivity and Christianity. However, the African and African-influenced songs are another of the means by which the enslaved promote solidarity amongst themselves and talk back to the institutions intended to pacify and exploit them. Relying on an ethnic stereotype also associated with the discourse of enslavement in Cuba, Suárez y Romero points out that the *minas* of West Africa are like the Italians in Europe: They produce the best music (313).[8] Unlike Baralt, who complains of monotony, Suárez y Romero finds this music deeply affective: "La música de estos negros llega al alma, habla al corazón" (The music of these Blacks touches the soul, speaks to the heart; 313). As Ocasio points out, enslaved characters very rarely speak in Suárez y Romero's *artículos* (56). Here, however, they are singing, dancing, and drumming, communicating among themselves, and the author finds it profoundly moving. Again contrasting with Baralt's more threatening stereotype, Suárez y Romero does not suggest indecency or wickedness in the dance that forms part of *nuestras costumbres*. Just as occurs in *Francisco*, the solidarity of the music and dance is abruptly ended by the appearance of the overseer: "El tambor desmayó al instante" (The drum fell quiet in an instant; "Ingenios" 313; *Francisco* 102). A community gathering is broken up by a figure of plantation authority into a group of solitary individuals returning to their shelters: "[C]ada cual se fue a su bohío" (Each one went off to his hut; 313). Not only is the dance abruptly broken off, but the essay also quickly concludes.

Suárez y Romero's "El cementerio del ingenio," published in Cuba in 1864, is a powerful recognition of the death toll produced by sugar cultivation, presenting a grim picture of the institution even while projecting an abyssal gap between the author and his literary subjects.[9] Written more than two decades later than "Ingenios" and just three years prior to the termination of human trafficking from Africa, significant changes in Cuba could account for the greater recognition here of the physical and emotional dangers of enslavement compared to the 1840 *artículos*. Suárez y Romero begins by explaining that even though the main house is full of visiting friends, he decides to take a sunset walk alone through the *ingenio*. The scene he paints is again one of Romantic melancholy, and he soon finds himself at the sugar mill's cemetery. Addressing the vast number of deaths on the plantation over the last one hundred years, the author expresses feelings of guilt and responsibility: "Más de quinientos esclavos de todos sexos y edades estaban reunidos en aquel breve pedazo de los terrenos tantas veces regados con el sudor de sus frentes, y yo, que había sido uno de sus dueños, debía afligirme a su memoria" (More than five hundred slaves of all sexes and ages were reunited in that small portion of the land watered so many times by the sweat of their brows, and I, who had been one of their owners, must suffer sadness to honor them; 338). Arriving at the cemetery produces a flood of emotion and memories for the writer, and he sobs as the feelings overtake him.

While more often describing them as part of a nameless collective in his earlier *artículos*, in "El cementerio del ingenio," the author proceeds to memorialize enslaved individuals who were interred in the cemetery while nonetheless relying on stereotyped characterizations. Only three of the deaths that the narrator recounts in the *artículo* resulted from advanced age. He begins with Pedro, "un negro anciano de nación macuá" (a very old African man of the *macuá* nation [i.e., from Mozambique]; 338). Despite his old age and gruff demeanor, the author and his brothers spent many hours in his company. Carlos, who was the family's *calesero* (carriage driver), lost his eyesight and was sent to the *ingenio* to be cared for by his own family, where he died soon after. Fernando was a *negro bozal* who lived many years but always had a cloud of sadness surrounding him. He never learned to speak Spanish: "[S]us cantares fueron siempre, únicamente, los cantares africanos, nunca bailó sino al compás del tambor, y con sus *carabelas*, jamás habló otra lengua que la de su tribu" (His songs were always, and only, African songs, he never danced but to the beat of the drum, and with his *compatriots*, he never spoke any language other than that of his tribe; original emphasis, 341).[10] Ocasio describes Fernando's refusal to assimilate to the culture of the colonizer as a "self-marginalization" (48).

The remaining and larger number of deaths described in "El cementerio del ingenio" result from various forms of violence and cruelty, outlining the horrors of enslavement. Those of Teodoro and Rogerio present the most overt signs of active resistance to power through escape and suicide.[11] Teodoro was a frequent runaway who was often kept in shackles (338). Once the chains were removed, he would escape again. During one of his flights, Teodoro hanged himself before he could be attacked by the search dogs: "Un día Teodoro, al percibir desde un jobo entre cuyas ramas se había escondido, los ladridos de los perros, se echó al cuello un lazo con un arique; y cuando aquéllos le clavaron los dientes en los pies ya estaba ahorcado" (One day Teodoro was hidden among the branches of the cedar tree; upon hearing the dogs barking, he threw a rope of palm fiber around his neck; and when they sank their teeth into his feet he was already hanged; 338). Rogerio, a *mina* like the fictional Francisco, is described with admiration for his physical strength, hard work, and industry in keeping a small farm for himself (339–40; *Francisco* 64). Rogerio secretly left the plantation to visit his girlfriend and was set upon by a group of enslaved men from a different plantation when returning. He escaped after killing two of his attackers and then hanged himself from a mamey tree. Offering a Romantic motivation for his suicide that also recalls *Francisco*, Suárez y Romero supposes that Rogerio hanged himself out of fear that he would be prohibited from visiting his girlfriend again, rather than acknowledge that suicide could be a choice made in order to evade physical torture as punishment (340; *Francisco* 175–77).

Three of the enslaved laborers in "El cementerio del ingenio" who the narrator remembers are horrifically killed because of the sugar plantation's dangerous working conditions. For the reformist purposes of *costumbrismo*, recounting of these accidents supports the argument that the *ingenios* needed to modernize and provide more humane working conditions. Twenty-year-old Gertrudis is described as having been beautiful and always happy: "Con la risa perennemente en los labios y sin cesar cantando, Gertrudis caminaba por el sendero de su existencia como si estuviese sembrado de flores" (With a smile always on her lips and singing without ever stopping, Gertrudis walked along the path of her life as if in a bed of roses; 340). One day when she fell asleep while at work in the *trapiche*, Gertrudis's arm was caught in the crushing machine; she was killed and her body mutilated (340). Another of the plantation's slaves, José, fell into a boiling vat of sugarcane juice and was scalded alive (341). The author's childhood companion and playmate, Wenceslao, took a fatal fall from a palm tree when the stirrups of his climbing irons broke (341). Each of these people died a violent and early death as a direct result of the dangerous work they were forced to undertake on a sugar plantation. Finally, Dorotea, who recalls the fictional Dorotea of *Francisco*, also died prematurely, and her narrative treatment reflects the association between whiteness, beauty, and respectability of colonialized racial discourse as well as the author's Romantic sentimentality. Dorotea was "una mulata [que no] tenía pasas, sino lacios cabellos, su tez era casi blanca y todas sus maneras y palabras demostraban que había sido criada de mano de alguna familia decente" (a mulatta [that did not] have kinky but rather straight hair, her skin was almost white and all her habits and words indicated that she had been a handmaid of a respectable family; 339). She and her baby had been sent to the plantation as punishment for an unmentioned crime committed in the city. She died from unnamed causes four months after arriving at the *ingenio* (339). Her similarity to the fictional Dorotea suggests that she, too, died from sorrow (*Francisco* 177).

The slaveowner in the *artículo* has outlived most of the enslaved people that he knew as a child: "Y en verdad, de toda la dotación que yo había conocido en los primeros años de mi vida, pocos eran los esclavos que aún existían" (And truthfully, of the whole team that I had known in the first years of my life, there were few slaves that were still alive; 342). Were the *artículo* to end here, it would perhaps be read as a powerful critique of enslavement. However, the sketch concludes with a reaffirmation of the abyssal line separating the author from those whom he otherwise claims to recognize. Suárez y Romero states at the beginning of the essay that he is guilty and must suffer, which he does by remembering and weeping over those who are buried in the cemetery. Having done this is cathartic for Suárez y Romero, and he proposes that his emotional self-flagellation has earned him divine forgiveness: "[A]l levantarme para volver al batey, sentí que una dicha, nunca hasta entonces experimentada, inundaba en celestial arrobamiento lo más íntimo de mi corazón" (Upon rising to return to the main part of the plantation, I felt that a happiness, never felt before that moment, flooded in heavenly ecstasy the very center of my heart; 342). The narrator returns to the main house and spends the rest of the day with his guests, still feeling unadulterated happiness sent from heaven (342). Ocasio is also critical of this conclusion, arguing that the happy ending precludes the *artículo* from being abolitionist (48). Although he refers to earlier *artículos*, Silverstein argues that the author's "cathartic tears" not only absolve the slaveowner of his sins but also serve the purpose of promoting reform not to end but to sustain enslavement (60). Williams also refers to the composition of *Francisco* as cathartic for Suárez y Romero, but offers a more sympathetic reading of the novel as an antislavery work than do these two critics of Suárez y Romero's *artículos de costumbrismo* (43). Although the horrific conditions of enslavement on a sugar plantation are clearly outlined in "El cementerio del ingenio," the text nonetheless stops short of recognizing the full humanity of those forced to live in such conditions and highlights the distance that the author perceived between himself and his literary subjects.

Suárez y Romero's critique of enslavement and his stereotyping of enslaved characters was strongly criticized by the next generation of writers in a Cuba that was approaching abolition and independence, particularly Antonio Zambrana and Enrique Piñeyro (Luis, *Literary Bondage* 46–50; Silverstein 59). However, the contrast between Suárez y Romero's acclaim of Afro-Cuban plantation culture and the disdain expressed for it by his contemporary, Baralt, is worth noting. Unlike the promoters of total *blanqueamiento*, Suárez y Romero counts the African-influenced culture of the plantation among *nuestras costumbres* and testifies to the affective power of Afro-Cuban art forms and to the extreme conditions and dangers of the sugar plantation, and reveals resistance and solidarity among Afro-descendants on the plantation.

JOSÉ E. TRIAY: MEMORIALIZING SLAVERY AND MARGINALIZING BLACKNESS

Originally from Andalucía, José E. Triay (1844–1907) became a noted journalist and author in Cuba, although today his work is significantly understudied.[12] Triay belongs to a later generation of *costumbristas* than Baralt and Suárez y Romero, and this is reflected in his work. By 1881, the publication date for Triay's "El calesero" ("The Carriage Driver"), Cuba had experienced the first war for independence, La Guerra de los Diez Años (1868–1878), during which both wealthy *criollos* and Spanish colonial officials alike realized that they would need the support of Afro-descendants to win. Additionally, the human traffic from Africa to Cuba had finally been stopped (1867), the intermediary *patronato* system of labor established (1880–1886), and the end of enslavement made inevitable (1886).[13] Racial discourse was transitioning from the *blanqueamiento* of the Delmontine era to what would be the promotion of a raceless Cuban identity in the final decade of the century by pro-independence writers such as José Martí.[14] Relying on stereotyped presentations of people of color, "El calesero" reflects the anxieties of a white *criollo* population witnessing the end of the institution that had powered the island's economy for centuries and the incorporation of freed people of color into a stratified colonial society. In contrast to the consolidation of national identity projected in earlier Spanish *costumbrismo* by writers navigating social transformations, Triay's *artículo* reinscribes abyssal hierarchy by positing that freed Afro-descendants will contribute to criminality and disorder rather than belong to civilized and productive society. Triay thus presents a Cuban counterpart to US authors such as Eliza McHatton Ripley and Joel Chandler Harris, who idealized plantation life to reinscribe white supremacy after the Civil War.

Triay's literary generation included more Afro-descendant characters and images in their published literary representations of Cuban culture than earlier authors did. For example, the mid-century illustrated collection *Los cubanos pintados por si mismos* (*Cubans Portrayed by Themselves*, 1852) addressed only white character types, but Antonio Bachiller y Morales's later *Tipos y costumbres de la isla de Cuba* (*Types and Customs of the Island of Cuba*, 1881), which includes Triay's "El calesero," presents several written sketches and illustrations featuring Afro-descendant "types." While the 1881 collection acknowledges the existence of people of color in Cuba in a way that many prior published *artículos* did not, it nonetheless projects an abyssal view of them. Raquel Gutiérrez Sebastián proposes that the written and illustrated representations of Afro-Cubans and Africans in *Tipos y costumbres* are similar to those performed in Cuba's *teatro bufo*, popular vaudeville-type productions that relied on blackface and other highly stereotyped representations that started to appear the same year that La Guerra de los Diez Años began (42).[15]

Triay's subject, the *calesero*, is a common "type" recurring in both Spanish and Cuban *costumbrismo*. Suárez y Romero's Francisco, for example, is a faithful carriage driver before being sent to the sugar plantation. In *costumbrismo*, the *calesero* is typically described as a handsome and handsomely dressed Black man, and often is characterized as a seducer of racially mixed women (Ocasio 127, 133). Among the few critics to study Triay's *artículo*, William Luis concludes that the author's stereotyped *calesero* is "a Francisco type," portrayed as passive and contented (*Literary Bondage* 44). However, I argue that Triay's *calesero* is a conglomeration of several abyssal stereotypes associated with both enslaved and free Afro-descendants that permits both a nostalgic presentation of enslavement and an association between free Black men and criminality. When enslaved, the Afro-Cuban coachman is a contented, musical, and happy-go-lucky servant. Once free, he will drift towards a life of criminality on the margins of the city.

Reminiscent of earlier Spanish *costumbristas*, Triay begins by characterizing the modernization of the city as alarming: "La Habana de hoy no es La Habana de ayer. Ha crecido, y se ha transformado. El progreso lo ha invadido todo; todo lo ha trastornado, subvertido, modificado, siguiendo esa ley ineludible que lleva los ríos al mar y no los vuelve nunca a su cauce" (The Havana of today is not the Havana of yesterday. It has grown, and it has been transformed. Progress has invaded everything; it has upturned, subverted, changed everything, following that unavoidable law that carries rivers to the sea and never returns them to their beds; 417). The narrative voice then looks back to a soothing vision of an earlier Havana which, prior to 1861, was divided by the original colonial walls into two populations (417).[16] Inside the walls, one finds the wealthy and cultured old city, which is home to most of the city's white population. Society's lowest classes, consisting predominantly of people of color, reside outside of the walls. Triay characterizes life within the walls as civilized: Here is "la ciudad del comercio, de la vida, del movimiento, de la riqueza" (the city of commerce, of life, of movement, of wealth; 417). Outside the walls, one finds the barbaric outlying neighborhoods of El Manglar, Jesús María, and El Horcón. These districts were popularly associated with Blackness and criminality as the haunts of *los curros negros*, an Afro-descendant group that lived in Sevilla for generations before being sent to Cuba (Ocasio 148).[17] In the few *artículos* in which they appear, such as José Victoriano Betancourt's "Los curros del Manglar," *los curros* are curiosities for their flamboyant clothing and speech patterns, which serve as evidence of their transculturation in Spain and again in Cuba, but they also are dangerous threats because of their reputations as killers and criminals. Triay's coachman is not a *curro*, but he will end up in the same marginalized neighborhoods that this group dominated earlier in the century.

Further reflecting upon modernity, the narrator considers the reduced use of the formerly ubiquitous carriage variously called the *quitrín*, *volante*, or *calesa* (calash), which makes the *calesero* a character of the past who should be memorialized (419).[18] Throughout his depiction of the carriage driver, the narrator employs a light yet mocking tone that is complicit with colonialized disregard for the humanity of enslaved people. The presentation of the coachman is immediately stereotyped: "El *calesero* es, casi siempre, negro, y se llama José. Generalmente, nació en la casa de sus amos, y su origen es tan oscuro como el color de su rostro" (The carriage driver is almost always Black and named José. Generally, he was born in his masters' house, and his origins are as dark as the color of his face; 420). In addition to attributing illegitimacy to him, the narrator portrays the generic "José" as unable to learn without being subject to violence: "No adquirió la ciencia de guiar el carruaje sin trabajo ni pena, . . . y el *cuero*, aplicado con severa energía sobre sus espaldas, fue su mejor maestro" (He did not learn the science of driving the carriage without work or torment, . . . and the *whip*, applied with severe energy across his back, was his best teacher; original emphasis, 420). The narrator's convivial tone when describing brutality does not suggest a critique of the cruelty of enslavement but instead reinscribes racialized thought. Seen as a written counterpart to *teatro bufo*, this presentation of repeated lashings of an enslaved Afro-descendant who is either lazy or slow to learn appears intended as farcical humor.

As Triay describes it, the job of the enslaved *calesero* brings with it many privileges and advantages, from fine clothing to plenty of free time. The coachman plays as a child and is allowed to "retire" at the end of his career with "free time" to reflect on his "días de glorias" (421). Following the example of other *costumbrista* models, the young *calesero* here is also stereotyped as an easygoing Don Juan Tenorio: "José fue el Tenorio de la casa, la envidia de los mozos de la cuadra y el héroe entre los hombres del barrio" (José was the Don Juan of the house, the envy of the stable boys, and the hero of the neighborhood men; 421); he enjoys the hunt much more than an easy conquest. If "José" becomes the confidant of the slave owner's daughter, *la niña*, he can avoid being sent in punishment to the sugar plantation. Finally, resorting to additional stereotypes, Triay describes the illiterate *calesero* as a natural entertainer: "[S]abía tocar el punto en la guitarra.... También contaba unas décimas muy sabrosas, ... y en la cocina y en el zaguán, contaba sus cuentos, que tenían el privilegio, con gracia o sin ella, de hacer reír" (He knew how to play the *punto* on the guitar.... He would also recite savory poems, ... and in the kitchen and in the hallway, he would tell tales that were worthy, whether agreeable or not, of making you laugh; 422). Manzano's account of his own experience, in which he is prevented from sharing stories and poems and beaten for no reason, provides a notable point of contrast here.

Unlike most of Delmontine writers earlier in the century, Triay is not prevented by either official or self-censorship from referencing *coartación*, or setting the conditions for self-purchase, and from ambivalently celebrating the concept of freedom near the *artículo*'s conclusion. For Manzano, self-emancipation is a legal path to freedom that would provide the opportunity to work a trade and to join the social fabric of the city. Contrasting with Manzano's plan to become a productive citizen, however, in "El calesero," *coartación* does not lead to incorporation into respectable Havana society, but rather to poverty and criminality in the marginalized neighborhoods beyond the city walls. Once he is no longer under white supervision, the former *calesero* associates with people of dubious backgrounds and joins them in their enterprises: after his *coartación*, "[c]onocía a toda la gente de antecedentes dudosos, conocía los últimos barrios, tenía otras amistades y otros trabajos.... De Marte pasaba a Mercurio" (he knew all the people of dubious backgrounds, he knew the lowest neighborhoods, he had other friendships and other work.... He went from Mars to Mercury; 422). No longer a faithful servant, the freedman now inevitably serves the god of trickery and thieves. At the same time, however, the narrative upholds the abstract concept of liberty that forms part of the Enlightenment framework of *costumbrismo* and also supports Cuban independence from Spain. The narrator argues that one who has not been enslaved cannot appreciate the freedom that the impoverished "José" now has: "Esta libertad no la puede valorar el que no la ha perdido" (This liberty cannot be appreciated by one who has not lost it; 422). The liberal value of freedom is celebrated, but the extension of human equality to the freedman is not.

To conclude the essay, Triay again returns to the theme of modernization in Havana, relegating the Black *calesero* to the past and to the margins. The aristocratic class has now exchanged the useful but simple *quitrín* for fancier carriages: "[S]ustiyó con el cupé, el landó, la berlina, el cabriolé, su cómodo quitrín" (They've "substituted the coupé, the landau, the Berlin carriage, the cabriolet, for their comfortable calash; 423). Similarly, the driver of today is also different from the enslaved *calesero* of the past: "[E]l cochero es de otra familia, de otra clase, de otro color que el calesero" (The chauffeur is from another family, another class, another color than the carriage driver; 423). The enslaved Black coachman has been replaced by the higher-status, lighter-skinned, and free chauffeur. The final words of the *artículo* offer an ironic exaltation of the *calesero*: "También pasaron los tiempos de la andante caballería; pero por eso ¿habrá borrado la historia de sus páginas las proezas del caballero, como Bayardo, sin mancha ni tacha? El calesero ha muerto. ¡Viva el calesero!" (The days of the errant knights have also passed; but because of that, will history have erased from its pages the deeds of the knight, such as Bayardo, without stain or blemish? The carriage driver is dead. Long live the carriage driver!; 423). Triay proposes that the picturesque character type of the enslaved *calesero* should be memorialized, yet the freed Afro-descendant is abyssally relegated to the realm of disorder and criminality at the fringes of cultured society.

CONCLUSION: ABYSSAL VIEWS CHALLENGED BY AFRO-CUBAN CULTURE

In the contemporary reevaluation of nineteenth-century white-authored literary works traditionally labelled as antislavery, a decolonial approach to the liberal, Enlightenment framework deployed in *costumbrismo* reveals the ways in which such writers sought to reform Cuban society, yet stopped short of dismantling colonializing thought. The institution of enslavement is subjected to some critique even within the confines of colonial censorship, but the abyssal views of white supremacy and of Black inferiority that justified enslavement is consistent throughout the sketches studied here.

Baralt's *artículo* most clearly expresses a view of enslaved Afro-descendants as primitive, uncivilized, and threatening that provides literary support for an ideology of erasure such as *blanqueamiento*. Suárez y Romero's *artículos* illustrate the remorse of the slaveholder yet also rely on the stereotype of the passive enslaved person, which is the other side of the coin, so to speak, of the dangerous character illustrated in Baralt's sketch. Suárez y Romero outlines the extreme, deadly conditions of sugar production, but ultimately forgives himself for his complicity with the institution. The abyssal view of Afro-descendants continues even as enslavement is being phased out in Triay's "El calesero." The formerly enslaved Black coachman who was once a charming entertainer disappears as he is relegated to the criminal outskirts of society and replaced with more desirable free and white laborers. The Enlightenment concept of human equality is denied to the Afro-descendant in a literary form otherwise associated with liberal values.

Looking beyond the narrative perspective, however, these *artículos* also capture Afro-Cuban cultural practices that facilitate communication, solidarity, and preservation of identity among Afro-descendants. These sketches reference various aspects of the centuries-long African diaspora in Spain and in the Caribbean and highlight the transculturated and counterpoint traditions that developed as a result. Baralt's description of Afro-Haitian-Cuban *tumba francesa* and Suárez y Romero's of plantation music and dance document significant examples of the ways in which enslaved Afro-descendants on plantations circumvented the controls designed to prevent communication while building a culture that is characterized as fundamentally Cuban today. The latter author's recounting of escapes and suicides is another recognition of resistance to the slaveholder's power. Triay's reference to the neighborhoods particularly associated with *los curros negros*, descendants of people forcibly taken to Sevilla in the early years of the human traffic from Africa, serves as a reminder of the cultural variety among the Afro-descendant population in Cuba and also that the ways in which marginalized populations respond to economic deprivation are viewed as threats to those holding institutional power. Finally, the increased appearances of Afro-Cuban character types in later Cuban *costumbrismo* reflects wider acknowledgement of their participation in Cuban culture and of their importance in the fight to free Cuba from colonial status.

CHAPTER THREE

THE TYRANNIES OF LIBERTY AND EQUALITY

The Condesa de Merlin's Colonialist Travels

La Havane (1844), by María de las Mercedes Santa Cruz y Montalvo, la Condesa de Merlin, is an extensive collection of letters documenting the author's travel from her adopted homeland, France, to her native Cuba with a short stay in the US. Addressing a wide range of topics, the three-volume work has sparked controversy since the time of its publication. Shortly after its serialized publication in Cuba, Merlin was accused by members of Domingo del Monte's *tertulia* of plagiarism and of espousing a pro-colonial point of view.[1] Contemporary scholarship on *La Havane* continues to engage with the issues of the author's extensive and often unstated reliance on prior texts and of the extent to which she promotes or counters coloniality. Literary critics have identified a number of Cuban sources that shaped Merlin's letters, but the significant influence of works by Alexis de Tocqueville and Gustave de Beaumont on *La Havane* has been almost entirely overlooked. Evidence in *La Havane*'s little-studied US letters and "Lettre XX," published in Spanish as *Los esclavos en las colonias españolas* (1841), indicates that the two French authors' well-known texts are important unacknowledged sources. Merlin invokes aspects of Tocqueville and Beaumont's theories, terminology, and narrative strategies, which gives her work the appearance of conforming to an Enlightenment framework of values. However, unlike the two French theorists, I argue that Merlin rejects liberal political concepts entirely, particularly those of equality and liberty, and supports continued colonization and enslavement in Cuba in the early sections of *La Havane*.

The details of the author's tumultuous life, which produced material for numerous autobiographical narratives, help account for the colonialized views expressed in *La Havane*. Mercedes Santa Cruz y Montalvo (1789–1852) was born in Havana to a wealthy family that was a stronghold of the *sacarocracia* (Méndez Rodenas 19).[2] As Salvador Bueno outlines, the Jaruco family had been established in Cuba "desde los primeros tiempos de la conquista" (from the earliest times of the conquest) and benefitted greatly from the sugar boom in Cuba that followed the Haitian Revolution ("Un libro polémico" 107). Like Gertrudis Gómez de Avellaneda, Merlin spent her childhood in Cuba, but was taken in early adolescence to live in Spain. She later married a French aristocrat, Antoine Christophe Merlin, who was an aide-de-camp to Joseph Bonaparte. After Spain's defeat of Napoleon's army, Merlin accompanied her spouse to Paris and established a noted salon. Financial troubles that followed the count's demise in 1839 led the Condesa de Merlin to turn to writing as a means of supporting herself (Bueno "Un libro polémico" 108; Méndez Rodenas 24; Torres-Pou 67, 79).[3] Merlin's difficulties were further exacerbated by her opposition to the policies of Louis Philippe, "the Bourgeois King," whose July Monarchy denied her a widow's pension (Torres-Pou 79). Recalling Flora Tristán, Merlin decided to cross the Atlantic with a dual financial purpose: to claim an inheritance from her family and to write a marketable book about her travels.[4] The multivolume *La Havane* was the literary outcome of Merlin's journey and, along with others of the author's many works, has been analyzed in critical texts such as Adriana Méndez Rodenas's *Gender and Nationalism in Colonial Cuba: The Travels of Santa Cruz y Montalvo, Condesa de Merlin*, Susana Regazzoni's *La Condesa de Merlin: Una escritura entre dos mundos o de la retórica de la mediación*, and articles and book chapters by Salvador Bueno, Sylvia Molloy, Claire Emilie Martin, Joan Torres-Pou, Ariana Huberman, and Daylet Domínguez.

Written during and after her journey in the early 1840s, *La Havane* consists of a total of thirty-six letters. Many of the epistles are addressed to Merlin's daughter, Madame Gentien de Dissay, while others are dedicated to such figures as George Sand, Viscount Simeon, Baron de Rothschild, and Viscount Chateaubriand (Bueno, "Un libro polémico" 113). As Méndez Rodenas characterizes it, *La Havane* is a text that defies generic categorization: It is "an ambitious book that recorded the political, economic, and social organization of the island of Cuba. Its most salient sections have to do with the history of the colony, the status of women in Creole society, and the pressing question of slavery" (24). *La Havane* begins with the narration of the author's visit to the US, which has been little studied but provides important insights into her colonialized perspective. In these letters, I argue that Merlin follows Tocqueville and Beaumont in rejecting what they called the "tyranny of the majority" created by political equality and also by critiquing racism in the northern states of the US, yet differs from her two contemporaries by also repudiating the concept of liberty, which she labels a destructive force. The employment of these Enlightenment concepts as dangerous is reiterated in the treatise on enslavement that follows shortly after the US letters in the text. Where Tocqueville and Beaumont directly critique the cruelties of enslavement, Merlin argues in favor of what she characterizes as a benevolent institution in Cuba. Pointing to the example of the Haitian Revolution, all three writers subscribe to the abyssal view that the emancipation of enslaved Afro-descendants will inevitably end in a violent race war that will destroy the white population. Thus, Merlin establishes the discourse of coloniality early in the text in such a way that informs the discussion of Cuban institutions and the representation of Afro-descendants throughout *La Havane*'s three volumes.

The extent to which Merlin relies on Tocqueville and Beaumont's texts in the US letters and the enslavement treatise has not been explored elsewhere in the scholarship on her work, with the exception of a brief reference to Tocqueville by Torres-Pou that does not identify the differences between Merlin's and her compatriot's thought (78). However, an understanding of how Merlin employs her compatriots' terminology while departing from their theories is central to explicating her colonializing views. Not only were these three aristocratic writers contemporaries and active in Parisian intellectual circles but there is also considerable textual evidence in *La Havane* of familiarity with the two political theorists' well-known works. Merlin undertook her journey in 1840, only eight years after Tocqueville and Beaumont had spent nine months in the US studying the newly established penitentiary system. Upon their return to France in 1832, Tocqueville and Beaumont collaboratively produced several international bestsellers. Both men were also active in the relatively cautious *Société française pour l'abolition de l'esclavage* which was founded in 1834.[5] Although it was then and is now often visited by tourists, Merlin followed Tocqueville and Beaumont's footsteps when she visited Eastern State Penitentiary, also called Cherry Hill Prison, which the two theorists analyze in *On the Penitentiary System* (Merlin 107–23; Tocqueville and Beaumont 187–98; 232–66). Merlin's use of phrases, concepts, and rhetorical strategies associated with the two authors' works, particularly Toqueville's *Democracy in America* and Beaumont's *Marie, or Slavery in the United States: A Novel of Jacksonian America*, indicate that she followed their textual footsteps as well.

TOCQUEVILLE, BEAUMONT, AND THE COLONIAL MATRIX OF POWER

A large body of scholarship is dedicated to Tocqueville and, to a lesser extent, to Beaumont, placing a comprehensive overview of the two beyond the scope of this study. I focus here on the elements of their work most pertinent for analyzing Merlin's text. While Tocqueville has received the greater part of scholarly attention in US criticism, recent studies that focus on *Democracy*'s treatment of race, enslavement, and incarceration by such scholars as Sara M. Benson, Margaret Kohn, and Louis J. Kern point out that Tocqueville and Beaumont collaborated extensively on their published works (S. Benson 466–67; Kohn 169; Kern 150). Appointed by Louis Philippe's government to study and report on the US penal system, the two theorists visited prisons throughout the US in 1831–1832. Before Merlin began her journey in 1840, the two men had published several internationally prominent works, including the coauthored *On the Penitentiary System in the United States and Its Application in France* (1833), volume 1 of Tocqueville's *Democracy in America* (1835), and Beaumont's *Marie, or Slavery in the United States: A Novel of Jacksonian America* (1835), which is a combined novel and antislavery treatise.[6]

Sara Benson characterizes Tocqueville and Beaumont as descendants of the ancien régime who grew "up in the confines of aristocracy's civil death" (470). Although his parents were spared, many of Tocqueville's family members were guillotined during the French Revolution, producing in the author a fear of mob rule and a belief that democracy dominated by majority public opinion in the US "had gone 'too far'" (470–71). As aristocrats who had lost their inherited privileges, Tocqueville and Beaumont were excluded from power in France: Becoming experts on the US prison system presented a route back into "the circles of French governance" (471). The journey was pivotal for the development of the two writers' liberal political theories. Richard Avramenko and Robert Gingerich propose that the study of prisons provides an early configuration of the concern expressed shortly after in *Democracy* that dystopia that can occur in a democracy in which institutions enforce full equality and thus servitude in in citizens (58–59). In the penitentiaries, the writers observe prisoners "stripped of their basic religious freedoms, deprived of the bonds of association, and subjected to the tyranny of public opinion by the steady discipline of the warden" (61).

In volume 1 of *Democracy*, democratic governance in the US is characterized as a "tyranny of the majority," a term which, as is discussed below, appears throughout Merlin's US letters (Tocqueville 239–42). Tocqueville's conception of the aristocracy as a class persecuted by ignorant revolutionary mobs informs his interpretation of democratic institutions in the US and is especially pertinent to Merlin's use of the two theorists' terminology. Guy Aiken explains that Tocqueville and, by implication, Beaumont, turn the idea that "the majority is always right" in US democracy into "a sweeping generalization about the unchecked might of the majority in democracy everywhere" (185). For these theorists, the concept of equality among citizens creates the conditions in which the masses—the singular, unchecked power in the country—would become omnipotent and inevitably tyrannize or oppress the minority (189). Tocqueville clearly formulates the tyranny of the majority as a class struggle in which the impoverished masses oppress the wealthy few: "In the United States, where the poor man governs, the rich always have to fear lest he abuse his power against them" (*Democracy* 230). The pair conceived of the Enlightenment concept of individual liberty, a right enjoyed by the aristocracy in previous eras, as a counter to the tyranny of the majority (Pitts 191). As Gurminder K. Bhambra and John Holmwood further clarify, Tocqueville and Beaumont understood aristocracy, with its duties and privileges, to serve as a "moderating influence on the possible excesses of democracy" that they perceived in the US (57).

Tocqueville's and Beaumont's commentaries on enslavement and racial prejudice in the US also inform Merlin's work. Scholars are not in agreement as to whether coloniality is expressed in the two political theorists' discussions of these topics. Kohn, for example, writes that published works by both Tocqueville and Beaumont in conjunction identify the contradictions between liberal ideals, racism, and enslavement and predict that anti-Black racial prejudice would continue to threaten the country even after the abolition of enslavement (175). In the "Three Races" chapter that concludes the first volume of *Democracy*, Tocqueville overtly denounces the institution of enslavement: "[T]here is one evil that enters the world furtively . . . ; it is deposited as a cursed seed on some point of the soil; . . . this evil is slavery" (ellipses added, 326). As the seed metaphor indicates, enslavement is like a pernicious weed that is only eradicated with difficulty once it has been established. "Three Races" is also critical of the white population's racial intolerance, which deprives free people of color of their rights and forces them into a "precarious and miserable existence" (337). Contemporary criticism reads Beaumont as being the more sympathetic of the two writers to the problems of racial prejudice and the ways in which people of color are treated in both the free states and those where enslavement was then legal.[7] In *Marie*, Beaumont clearly states his objection to enslavement, stating that the institution "outrag[es] all the sacred laws of morality and humanity," and challenges the concept of racial inferiority, although not definitively (198; 202–4).

As Alvin B. Tillery outlines, antebellum Black US American reviewers were critical of Tocqueville's treatment of race in *Democracy*. These writers proposed that the text "reif[ied] arguments that had been deployed against them during their bondage" (4) and identified "a strain of scientific racism" in it (9). Despite this early critique, scholarship did not generally engage with the abyssal and colonializing content of *Democracy* until relatively recently, particularly in conjunction with Tocqueville's long-term support of colonization in Algeria. Two scholarly texts that address these issues are Gurminder K. Bhambra and John Holmwood's *Colonialism and Modern Social Theory* and Kevin Duong's "The Demands of Glory: Tocqueville and Terror in Algeria." Bhambra and Holmwood write that Tocqueville viewed the US as a white nation: The author subsumed "democracy in America under the narrative of one race—that of the English colonists" (68). Moreover, the text displays "deep racial prejudice" (68) in which people of color constitute a threat to the white settlers' system of possession and an inability to "contemplate their inclusion as free and equal human beings" (70). Duong's approach locates the origins of Tocqueville's support for colonialism in his liberal political formation and characterizes the settler colonialism that the theorist promoted as an abyssal program of extermination. As Peter Wolfe argues, settlerism, whether promoting integration or extermination, always follows a "'logic of elimination' that racializes indigenous populations" (cited in Duong 34). During the same time period in which he authored *Democracy in America*, Tocqueville argued for homogenizing racial mixture for the French colony in Algeria "to form a single people from two races" (cited in Duong 35). When the local population proved itself resistant to French rule, Toqueville advocated total war after 1841 to eliminate the Indigenous population altogether in the service of necessary glory for France, which would ensure that the European nation would function properly as a democracy (35). These decolonial approaches to Tocqueville's work thus identify the ways in which the author's liberal political expressions operate in the maintenance of the colonial matrix of power.

As antebellum readers observed, scientific racism is reinscribed in *Democracy* even while it is questioned as suspect. Among the clearest examples of this are the two authors' assertions that the Black population thrives only in the warm climate of the southern US and not in the cold north (Tocqueville 343; Beaumont 212). Further, these writers share an abyssal belief that enslaved people of color operate in an unenlightened state, unaware of their deprivation of liberty and thus are not a threat to national unity. In the "Three Races" chapter, this is made particularly clear: Tocqueville writes, "Negroes can long remain slaves without complaint; but having joined the number of free men, they will soon become indignant at being deprived of almost all the rights of citizens" (345). This is, of course, in direct contradiction to the historical fact of numerous uprisings in places where enslavement was practiced, including Nat Turner's rebellion, which happened not long after the two French writers' arrival in the US.

Although the Haitian Revolution is not overtly referenced in *Democracy*, Bhambra and Woodholm argue that Toqueville's perception of that event informs Tocqueville's—and by implication the like-minded Beaumont's—statements about enslavement and race in the US (75). Tocqueville understood Haiti's deadly racial violence to have resulted from the spread of the Declaration of the Rights of Man in the colony and from immediate rather than gradual emancipation. As a result, despite stating opposition to the institution of enslavement, both writers identify the emancipation of enslaved people of color as the real threat to the future of the US as a nation. Tocqueville's expression of the dangers posed by a large, enslaved nonwhite population in the "Three Races" chapter is the more apocalyptic: "The most dreadful of all the evils that threaten the future of the United States arises from the presence of blacks on its soil" (326). Moreover, he argues that racial hostility will inevitably result where the two races coexist: "Everywhere that whites have been most powerful, they have held Negroes in degradation or in slavery. Everywhere that Negroes have been strongest, they have destroyed whites" (328). Following this logic, Tocqueville argues that the only solution for the states where enslavement is already practiced is to maintain it for "the longest possible time" (346). More ambiguously, Beaumont proposes that "[i]n my opinion, slavery must be either abolished or maintained in all its severity" (*Marie* 199). If abolition does occur, Beaumont writes, "some means must be found to make [Black people] disappear from the society where they have been slaves" (*Marie* 208). Both theorists refer to colonization, or rather deportation, as an ideal yet impractical solution (Tocqueville, *Democracy* 345; Beaumont, *Marie* 209). Thus, the two theorists propose that racial mixing, which they understood as a means to erase Blackness, is the only viable alternative if the country is to remain united. In an argument that mirrors his proposal to create one governable race from two in Algeria, Tocqueville writes that in the US, the "Negroes and whites must intermingle entirely or separate" (*Democracy* 341). Tocqueville and Beaumont's prediction of extreme racial violence, on the one hand, and their proposal for homogenizing racial mixing to erase dangerous Blackness, on the other, sound very much like the often-criticized stands taken by Cuban theorists José Antonio Saco and Domingo del Monte. However, the argument that the most dangerous violence would most likely erupt after abolition rather than before it marks a departure from the fears of uprisings by the enslaved expressed by many white slaveholders in the US South and Cuba alike.

TYRANNIES OF LIBERTY AND EQUALITY IN MERLIN'S US LETTERS

Without explicitly referencing either Tocqueville or Beaumont, Merlin characterizes US democracy as a tyranny of the majority, but without the more positive assessments of representative government and Enlightenment values that scholars such as Donald J. Maletz attribute to *Democracy* as mitigating factors (751). Torres-Pou likewise characterizes Merlin's position in the US letters as *antidemocrática* (72n13). Merlin indeed goes farther than Tocqueville and Beaumont in her critique of US democracy by rejecting both equality and liberty as dangerous causes of disorder when wielded by the uncouth masses. This characterization begins with her arrival in New York. Upon disembarking, Merlin reports hearing loud criticism of English aristocrats from the US crowd while being warned by her fellow travelers to watch her pockets (56). These comments set the tone for the author's assessment of the North American country as a place tyrannically ruled by a proletarian and criminal majority. In "Lettre VII," public transportation without class distinctions leads to a reflection on the costs of equality and liberty for the individual and the incompatibility of the two concepts: "On achète bien cher la liberté collective, quand on la paye par l'esclavage individuel.... [L]a liberté est sacrifiée á l'égalité, l'égalité immolée à la liberté" (One pays dearly for collective liberty, when one pays for it with individual slavery.... [L]iberty is sacrificed to equality, equality immolated by liberty; 91). During her visit to Washington, DC, Merlin characterizes the minority Whig politicians as defenders of "la haute class, la bourgeoisie, opprimée par le despotisme populaire" (the upper class, the bourgeoisie, oppressed by popular despotism; 156–58). Echoing Tocqueville and Beaumont, Merlin characterizes life in the US as a reversed class struggle: "Ici, le riche est toujours opprimé par le pauvre et refoulé par la jalousie des masses" (Here, the rich man is always oppressed by the poor one and held back by the envy of the masses; 91). Without the safeguards of aristocratic distinction and its attendant benefits, including police protection, Merlin feels unsafe and reports being the victim of multiple unresolved thefts during her sojourn.

Françoise Mélonio writes that philanthropy "was the fashionable public commentator's indispensable calling card, and the penitentiary question was assuredly the topic with the highest status" in France under the July Monarchy (cited in Avramenko and Gingerich 61). In keeping with this vogue,

Merlin occupies herself with visits to schools for the deaf and the blind in New York and to Philadelphia's Eastern State Penitentiary, the same facility that was toured by Tocqueville, Beaumont, and other prominent Europeans, including Charles Dickens.[8] Although she is largely complimentary of the charitable schools, Merlin's assessment of the penitentiary is contradictory (Torres-Pou 74–75). The author begins with a brief discussion of the problems facing French prisons and initially offers a positive assessment of the new penitentiary's imposing building and of the new system of separate confinement as a means of reforming convicted criminals. Merlin also offers a rare view into the conditions of female imprisonment in Eastern State Penitentiary when marveling at the elaborate decorations in the cell of one such prisoner (113).[9] However, she abruptly turns from praise to censure when she directly copies several pages of a report documenting abuses committed by officials in Eastern State that was published by the Prison Discipline Society, without explaining that the penitentiary was under a system of regular review or giving the source for the information (Torres-Pou 74). In much the same way that Tocqueville and Beaumont's assessment of equal treatment forced upon prisoners offers a preview of their theory of the tyranny of the majority in US democracy, Merlin's recounting of problems in Eastern State Penitentiary relegate such issues to being yet more examples of corruption in US institutions (Torres-Pou 75).

Merlin's US letters also follow Tocqueville and Beaumont in censuring racism in the North American country while nonetheless simultaneously reinscribing abyssal thought. Explaining that none of her acquaintances will accompany her to a Black church, she criticizes the prejudice held against Black US Americans: "Le nègre est ici une sorte de pestiféré que l'orgueil des blancs tient toujours à distance" (The black here is a type of plague carrier that the pride of the whites keeps always at a distance; 137). However, in contrast to the whitening logic of settlerism promoted by Tocqueville, Beaumont, Saco, and Del Monte, Merlin presents miscegenation not as a solution for racial strife but rather associates it with scandalous behavior and utopian socialism. Describing a group of "fervent" abolitionists ejected from their quarters, she writes that "ils on voulu mettre en pratique la théorie sacrée de l'amalgamation, blancs, mulâtres et noirs des deux sexes se sont couchés pêle-mêle. . . . [Parmi eux,] les biens sont communs et le marriage interdit" (they wanted to put into practice the sacred theory of amalgamation, whites, mulattos, and blacks of the two sexes were lying about pell-mell. . . . [Among them,] goods are communal and marriage prohibited; 136). Additionally, Merlin characterizes the free people of color that she encounters in the Northern US as threatening (Torres-Pou 71). For example, she is afraid of the mixed-race valet at her lodging in New York, describes him as having a "figure sinistre" (ominous face; 57), and reports being haunted by his visage in her chamber at night (87–88).

Merlin directly invokes the specter of the Haitian Revolution in her US letters when she denounces violence against white slaveholders as an example of the tyranny of the majority created when the enslaved seek their freedom. Recounting her visit to Philadelphia, Merlin reflects upon the meaning of the word *liberty*, presenting it not as a human right but as a source of oppression, violence, and bullying. When Merlin was a child, her uncle used to tell her "terribles histoires où ce mot *liberté*, toujours mêlé à ceux d'emprisonnement, d'assassinat et massacre, me faisait pleurer á sanglots" (terrible stories in which the word *liberty*, always mixed with those of imprisonment, of assassination and of massacre, that would make me sob; 129). One such tale was that of a friend of her uncle who lost his family and his fortune during the Haitian Revolution. Similar to Tocqueville's characterization, the narrator explains that the desire for liberty, which was first expressed in France and then spread to the colonies, led the enslaved to commit atrocities against the "weaker" white masters: "Les esclaves l'apprirent et ce soulevèrent à leur tour pour devenir libres; et comme les blancs, leurs maîtres, étaient les plus faibles, ils les massacrèrent" (The slaves learned of it and rose up in turn to become free; and because the whites, their masters, were the weaker, they massacred them; 131). She then recounts frightening episodes of mob violence that she witnessed in both Spain and France, also carried out in the name of liberty (132–33). By this logic, the rebellion in Haiti becomes an example of the tyranny of the majority, in which the enslaved mass of people of color rises up to decimate the smaller, unprotected class of wealthy whites.

Merlin's reflections on liberty end in a denouncement of the corrupt US government and of the tyrannical, uncouth majority (133). Rhetorically asking what she has discovered in the country with the most representative government in the world, she responds that she finds only corruption, crime, intolerance, and the sacrifice of individual tastes and habits to the demands of the masses (133). She argues that one who has observed the country up close would not desire American democracy for France: Men who love their country "ne souhaiteraient jamais à la France un avenir américain, s'ils avaient visité les États-Unis" (would never wish for France an American future, if they had visited the US; 118). Setting the tone for the remainder of *La Havane*, Merlin's US letters entirely reject the liberal political principles of human equality and liberty as well as promote an abyssal view of Black US Americans, thereby reinscribing the discourse of coloniality early in the text.

UNVEILING THE DISCOURSE OF COLONIALITY IN
LOS ESCLAVOS EN LAS COLONIAS ESPAÑOLAS

Before reappearing as "Lettre XX" in the complete *La Havane*, *Los esclavos en las colonias españolas* was published as a political pamphlet in Spanish in 1841 and figures among the least-studied of the author's nineteenth-century Spanish-language publications.[10] The existing scholarship that engages with the central argument of *Los esclavos* identifies Cuban, Spanish, and British sources that contribute to Merlin's text but does not reference Tocqueville and Beaumont. However, in this treatise on enslavement, Merlin continues to rely on the liberal terminology and narrative strategies employed by her French contemporaries, refers to US race riots discussed by both authors, and plagiarizes information from Beaumont's *Marie*. In a continuation from the US letters, Merlin invokes yet rejects the concepts of liberty and equality that are upheld as central to democratic government in liberal discourse. By openly discounting these Enlightenment concepts, Merlin clearly demonstrates a commitment to colonization in Cuba that parallels Tocqueville's support of colonization in Algeria, but without the program of whitening that the latter supports. Finally, in presenting Cuban enslavement as a patriarchal and Christian institution that civilizes savage people, Merlin temporarily sets aside Enlightenment terminology to engage openly with the original phrasing of the discourse of coloniality. The duality, ambiguity, or slippage that some contemporary criticism attributes to Merlin's positions on race and enslavement is due to her concurrent use of an Enlightenment linguistic framework alongside that of the sixteenth-century discourse of coloniality, which are conventionally understood to be contradictory. Regardless of her terminology, however, Merlin's commentary on enslavement and abyssal views of Afro-descendants promotes the maintenance of the colonial matrix of power through colonial institutions in Cuba.

The limited scholarship available on Merlin's treatise is not in agreement as to whether the text is pro- or anti-enslavement. In her analysis, Méndez Rodenas focuses largely on the ways in which Merlin conforms to and rebels against prior texts about enslavement by two writers with differing approaches to emancipation, José Antonio Saco and David Turnbull (144–72). Méndez Rodenas characterizes Merlin's position on enslavement as conflicted, and attributes this to gender difference and anxiety of authorship: "the obvious ambivalence of her position is due, in part, to the constant 'slippage' between 'original' text and source document; in short, to her dependency on the male book" (146). Méndez Rodenas reveals concern for the writer's contemporary reception in her reference to Domingo Figarola Caneda's defense of *La Havane*'s dedication to Capitán General Leopoldo O'Donnell: "It is helpful to quote Figarola Caneda's defense in full, for it helps to put the Creole countess in a more *positive light*, hence *tempering the accusations* as to her procolonialist and proslavery stance" (emphasis added; 145).[11] Finally, Méndez Rodenas defends Merlin's positions on race and enslavement by characterizing them as being similar to those held by Saco (147–48). While Saco and Merlin might each be accused of racism, this critic proposes that this charge is "balanced" by the fact that each also promoted the gradual termination of enslavement (163). However, where Saco's "Mi primera pregunta" presents arguments in favor of ending both the human traffic from Africa and also enslavement in Cuba, Merlin both begins and concludes her treatise with an expression of support for enslavement in Cuba as a civilizing institution. The female author's work broke boundaries by engaging with international debates over enslavement that were dominated by male voices at the time, yet the race and class privileges that facilitated her literary career and travels are also reinscribed in her text.

Daylet Domínguez identifies additional contrasting source material for Merlin's text, the works of Francisco Arango y Parreño and those of the largely female writers contributing to English- and Spanish-language Atlantic antislavery discourse throughout the nineteenth century ("En los límites" 253). As such, she characterizes Merlin as inserting herself into "una doble tradición" of Cuban pro-enslavement arguments and international antislavery rhetoric, which overlap in their abyssal assessment of Afro-descendants (253; 269). In contrast to Méndez Rodenas, however, Domínguez characterizes *Los esclavos* as a pro-enslavement tract: The text is "probablemente la única defensa proesclavista escrita por una mujer en la tradición cubana y caribeña" (probably the only proslavery defense written by a woman in Cuban and Caribbean traditions; "En los límites" 252). Domínguez demonstrates that Merlin's support for enslavement draws from Arango's casting of the Cuban institution as patriarchal and pacific in his appeals to the Spanish monarchy to end its monopoly on the transatlantic traffic from Africa shortly after the outbreak of the Haitian Revolution (258–59). At the same time, Domínguez argues, Merlin also relies upon the two strains of rhetoric employed by Atlantic antislavery writers to pass moral judgment on enslavement and to sway readers: "los derechos naturales del hombre y la retórica sentimental" (the natural rights of man and sentimental rhetoric; "En los límites" 263). Although Domínguez associates this writing with female antislavery writers, her characterization of these two rhetorical resources is also a very apt descriptor of Tocqueville and Beaumont's strategies in addressing enslavement, particularly as seen in the combination sentimental novel and antislavery treatise *Marie*. Likewise, Domínguez's identification of *microhistorias* in Merlin's work to narrate brief but illustrative episodes of enslavement also describes a strategy employed by Tocqueville and Beaumont in their analyses of enslavement ("En los límites" 254). However, Domínguez does not address the French antislavery movement beyond a brief reference to Charles Dupin, to whom "Lettre XX" of *La Havane* is dedicated and who belonged to the same antislavery society as Tocqueville and Beaumont (254).

Merlin's proslavery case opens with a simultaneous invocation and negation of liberal political concepts, continuing the same line of thought from the US letters that casts liberty and equality as equally to blame for creating dangerous tyrannies of the majority. The author pronounces and then immediately decries the word *libertad*, arguing that it is not a magic word but rather is a trap that has fooled and upended many (*Los esclavos* 1).[12] In a view that recalls her earlier characterization of the Haitian Revolution, as well as Tocqueville and Beaumont's racialized predictions for the future of the US, Merlin proposes that the purportedly philanthropic desire to free the enslaved would in fact mean violent death for whites and ruination for Blacks: "[L]a filantropía concluye por hacer degollar á los blancos para sumergir en la miseria á los negros" (Philanthropy concludes by causing the whites' throats to be slit just to submerge the Blacks into misery; 1). Thus, the stage is set to characterize the quest for liberty through emancipation as resulting in violent and ruinous mob rule throughout the treatise.

Merlin clearly states her support for ending the traffic from Africa but not for abolition by appealing to justice in each case. There is "[n]ada mas justo que la abolición de la trata de negros; nada mas injusto que la emancipación de los esclavos" (nothing more just than the abolition of the trade in Blacks; nothing more unjust than the emancipation of the slaves; 2).[13] Whereas Saco's argument against the trade from Africa is presented in racialized economic terms, Merlin argues that it must stop because it is an affront to universal human rights (un atentado contra el derecho natural; 2). However, she also argues that emancipation must not be allowed because it would unjustly violate property rights and, in a concern shared by Tocqueville but not Saco, it would require costly indemnities to be paid to slaveholders (Saco, "Mi primera pregunta" 38; Merlin, *Los esclavos* 2–3; Bhambra and Woodholm 75–76). Using liberal terminology to make a colonializing argument, Merlin turns the human traffic from Africa into subhuman property in Cuba and prioritizes the protection of the private property of the slaveholding class over the right to freedom of the enslaved (Domínguez, "En los límites" 257–58). Like Tocqueville, Merlin characterizes the introduction of enslavement into

Cuba as the planting of "una semilla deplorable" (an evil seed; 18). Echoing Tocqueville's assertion that enslavement must be maintained with all its rigor once it is in place, Merlin continues the metaphor to argue that the seed has grown into a tree too big to cut down without taking everyone else down with it (18). Over the course of the treatise, Merlin presents a series of arguments in favor of Cuban enslavement and against the promotion of liberty and equality amongst enslaved people of color.

Merlin's initial reliance on the language of political liberalism and support for universal human rights gives way to the original phrasing of the discourse of coloniality through the text's abyssal presentation of Afro-descendants and the colonialist view of Africa as a place of barbarity. Before the European traffic began, Merlin proposes, prisoners of war in Africa would either be cannibalized or sacrificed (4); sold to Europeans, they are removed from a barbaric land to civilized places where they are better treated (5). Merlin supports her argument with a quotation that she attributes to the eighteenth-century explorer Mungo Park, who proposes that Africans are better off as slaves of Europeans than of Africans: "'Lejos de ser una desgracia, es una fortuna para la humanidad la esportacion de los esclavos africanos á las Antillas,' dice el célebre Mungo Park" ("Far from being a disgrace, the exportation of African slaves to the Antilles is fortunate for humanity," says the famous Mungo Park; 6).[14] Throughout the treatise, Merlin repeats the negative and contradictory stereotypes of Afro-descendants that appear in both pro- and antislavery writings, referring to them variously as indolent, faithful, stupid, superstitious, and savage beneficiaries of enlightened treatment by civilized, white Europeans (Domínguez, "En los límites" 269).

As Méndez Rodenas points out, Merlin's abyssal view of Afro-descendants mirrors that expressed by Saco. In fact, the negative terms that Saco uses to argue that free white labor is superior to enslaved Afro-descendant labor appear almost word for word in *Los esclavos*, although they are employed for a different purpose. Saco writes that, unfit for disciplined work, the uncivilized Afro-descendant "á la manera de otros salvajes, sabe correr y saltar, y vencer también en los combates a su semejante y á las fieras" (in the same manner as other savages, knows how to run and jump, and also defeat those like him in combat and also wild beasts; 7). Merlin similarly states that "[é]l es apto para correr, saltar, domar animales salvajes; pero resiste al trabajo regular" (he is fit to run, jump, tame wild animals; but he resists regular work; *Los esclavos* 59). In the latter case, however, this characterization justifies the harsh treatment that the enslaved receive from the overseers (60). In another example of the reinscription of the original discourse of coloniality in the text, Merlin defines *bozal* in the following way: "Denominación que se da á los africanos sin instrucion y todavia salvajes" (Term used for Africans without education and still savage; 19).

To further strengthen her case against abolition, Merlin follows Arango's late eighteenth-century characterization of Cuban enslavement as a patriarchal and beneficent institution. As Domínguez explains, Arango had presented this argument to allay fears of uprisings when lobbying the Spanish government to end the crown's monopoly on the traffic from Africa shortly after the outbreak of the Haitian Revolution ("En los límites" 258–59). In this regard, Merlin's text presents a significant departure from Tocqueville and Beaumont's overt criticism of enslavement as an immoral and brutalizing institution. Following Arango's lead, Merlin proposes that *criollo* slaveholders provide more humane treatment than newly arrived Europeans do because of their paternal outlook: The Cuban is more compassionate "porque su vida patriarcal le llev[a] à [sic] estender à [sic] los negros la piedad paternal del hogar doméstico" (because his patriarchal life leads him to extend to the Blacks the paternal piety of the family home; 23). On this point, Merlin also differs from the reformist writers of the Del Monte group, who often portray the slave-owning class as being deeply corrupted by their proximity to slavery. Examples of villainous slaveholders abound in Cuban literature of the era, as exemplified by Suárez y Romero's Ricardo, Villaverde's Cándido and Leonardo Gamboa, and the Marquesa de Prado Ameno in Manzano's autobiographical account.[15] Finally, in a familiar apology for the institution of enslavement, the author argues that, unlike paid workers who cannot afford to miss a day of back-breaking labor, enslaved people are free of worry and will be cared for their whole lives: The enslaved person is "libre de porvenir y de ambición, tranquilo, indiferente, vive con el dia, abandona á su amo el cuidado de su conservación" (free of the future and ambition, peaceful, indifferent, lives for the day, abandons to the master all concern for his keep; 49).

Like both Arango and Tocqueville, Merlin references the practice of slavery in the ancient world to characterize the modern institution in Christian societies. Tocqueville concludes that the primary difference between ancient and modern enslavement is the indelible racial difference between Europeans and Africans existing in the latter, leading him to propose that race-based enslavement is the more difficult to eradicate (*Democracy* 327). However, without recognition of the Roman origins of Cuba's codes, Arango and Merlin contrast ancient enslavement with the Cuban version in order to demonstrate the supposedly "humane" character of Cuban slave laws (Domínguez, "En los límites" 259). Merlin argues that the enslaved in Cuba have a variety of legal rights and recourses not available in other slaveholding areas: "Si alguno de estos puntos no es observado, el esclavo tiene derecho à presentar su queja al síndico procurador" (If any of these points is not observed, the slave has the right to present his complaint to the protector of the slaves; 41). Merlin recounts many of the same legal rights that were denied to Juan Francisco Manzano, such as those of changing slaveholders, hiring out, *coartación*, and owning property (Manzano's case is discussed in chapter 1 above).

Merlin relies upon religious conversion as a justification for colonization when attributing the humane treatment of the enslaved on the island to religion: Catholicism "ha producido la piadosa humanidad de nuestros colonos [h]acia sus esclavos" (has produced the merciful humanity of our colonists towards their slaves; 39). Her warnings against African "superstition" further reinscribe the evangelizing pretext for enslavement of early Spanish colonialism. Again echoing Saco, Merlin equates Afro-Cuban religious practices with the mortal illnesses that threaten the well-being of enslaved Afro-descendants: unsupervised, African arrivals "sucumben à las prácticas secretas é infernales exijidas por los misterios de su *Obeah*" (succumb to the secret and hellish practices demanded by the mysteries of their *Obeah* sorcery; 65; Saco 15). In Merlin's case, however, this argument aids in counteracting her own initial stance in favor of abolishing the traffic from Africa as it points out the problems related to the failure to protect the enslaved in the illegal trade. Saco and Merlin's efforts to characterize African and Afro-Cuban beliefs as deadly blights indicate the extent to which they were perceived as threatening by the elite class and thereby demonstrates their empowering capacity for practitioners.

As Merlin's treatise progresses, the author turns to sentimental rhetoric when recounting what Domínguez terms *microhistorias*, brief anecdotes that narrate the bonds that tie the enslaved to slaveholders and strengthen Merlin's position as an authority on the topic of enslavement ("En los límites" 263). I argue that Merlin's use of micronarratives is remarkably similar to that of both Tocqueville and Beaumont, who present brief, first-person encounters with enslavement and prejudice in the US to authorize their assertions. In the "Three Races" chapter, for example, Tocqueville describes an interlude with a white slaveholder who fathered children born into enslavement to illustrate the cruelties of the institution (*Democracy* 347). In the foreword to *Marie*, Beaumont briefly narrates his experience of segregation in a theater in the US to paint a clearer picture for the reader (4–5). Additionally, Beaumont justifies his decision to write a sentimental novel rather than a more serious text by explaining that he wanted to reach both hearts and minds: "I have tried to clothe my work in less severe garb in order to attract that portion of the public which seeks in a book ideas for the intellect and emotions for the heart" (3). Adopting the same method and returning to the language of the Enlightenment, Merlin employs micronarratives to illustrate her argument that the enslaved generally do not want to be free, that the few who do seek liberty later regret it, and that devotion to white *amos* is extreme. Describing a young prince from Africa enslaved in Cuba who refuses to go back when the opportunity rather fantastically arises, the narrator concludes that "el estado de príncipe en África no equivale al de esclavo en nuestras colonias" (the status of prince in Africa does not equal that of slave in our colonies; *Los esclavos* 57–58). In another micronarrative, Merlin describes a person formerly enslaved by her uncle bitterly weeping while describing the fine treatment he received when he was not free, outlining his current difficulties, and calling himself a *caballo* (horse) for seeking liberty (51). Finally, Merlin asserts that the "sweet" treatment that the enslaved receive in Cuba produces a devotion so intense that the rare uprising, usually provoked by outsiders, can be quelled by the mere appearance of the white slaveholder (68–73).

As occurs in the treatises on enslavement by a number of Merlin's Cuban and French contemporaries, the Haitian Revolution appears as a negative example throughout Merlin's pamphlet and is characterized along the same lines as it is presented in the US letters. The incendiary ideas of universal human rights, rather than the cruelties of enslavement and colonial institutions, are to blame for violent uprisings that would not otherwise occur. Early in the treatise, for example, Merlin proposes that the same liberal ideals that upended both France and Haiti brought unrest and a military government to a previously peaceful Cuba: "[L]a palabra *libertad* resonó en la colonia y varias sublevaciones respondieron á ella" (The word *liberty* resounded in the colony and various uprisings answered it; 26–27). Echoing Tocqueville's abyssal characterization, Merlin proposes that enslaved Afro-descendants do not comprehend the abstract concept of liberty: "El negro no comprende el sentido de la palabra *libertad*, él estima el bienestar material mas que la independencia" (The Black man does not understand the meaning of the word *liberty*, he values material well-being more than independence; 34). Again, like her French contemporary, the author states that enslaved Afro-descendants are "felices en su estado imperfecto de hombres salvajes" (happy in their imperfect state as savage men; 82).

Even if a peaceful process of emancipation were somehow forced upon Cuba, the author argues, the example of "la revolución de Santo Domingo" would be followed one way or another (79–80). Firstly, she argues that the economy would quickly be ruined by the freedman's aversion to regular work (80). Moreover, should they "por un milagro" (by a miracle) be educated within a constitutional political system, formerly enslaved people of color would aspire to equality with whites. Recalling the disdain for racial equality and miscegenation displayed in the US letters, Merlin assumes that such an eventuality would disturb her white readers: "¿Hareis de ellos vuestros jueces, vuestros jenerales y vuestros ministros? ¿Les dareis vuestras hijas en matrimonio?" (Will you make them your judges, your generals and your ministers? Will you give them your daughters in marriage?; 82). The author proposes that not even "los amigos de los negros," those who promote abolition and liberty, desire racial equality (82). She then rather apocalyptically returns to the idea that emancipation followed by enlightenment is the real problem and also to the racial logic of settlerism: "[E]l dia en que luzca para ellos la luz de la intelijencia conocerán que son hombres como vosotros, y el campo de batalla quedará por el mas fuerte. Reflexionad que no habrá cuartel entre dos razas incompatibles desde que se dé la señal de combate" (The day that for them the light of intelligence begins to shine they will know that they are men like you, and the field of battle will go to the strongest. Reflect upon the fact that there will be no mercy between the two incompatible races once the combat begins; 82–83). Having previously proposed that the Black race is the stronger of the two, the implication is that the whites will be annihilated in a race war (59).

As her pro-enslavement argument nears its conclusion, Merlin somewhat incongruously addresses the New York City race riots of July 1834, which are also discussed by both Tocqueville and Beaumont. The riots are especially relevant for the latter's *Marie*; the author explains that these events provided the inspiration for chapter 13 of the novel, and they are discussed at length in appendix L (243–52). In addition to referencing the riots, Merlin also includes a footnote with demographic statistics taken directly from *Marie* without attribution (*Los esclavos* 83n1; Beaumont, *Marie* 378).[16] Historians explain that the violence in New York City in 1834 resulted from multiple social, economic, and political pressures, including the spread of rumors in sensationalist newspapers that abolitionist groups were presiding over interracial marriages (Kerber 30). In appendix L of *Marie*, Beaumont reports that the violence was caused by white prejudice in response to Black efforts to achieve fair treatment and to the celebration of mixed marriages (245).[17] Promoting amalgamation as the only way to achieve equality, Beaumont characterizes interracial marriage as "the best . . . means of fusing the white and the black races" (245). In contrast, Merlin references the riot as an example of the dangers of liberty and equality. She writes, "Apenas los negros se vieron libres, aspiraron á la igualdad; ¿y cómo respondió á esta pretension el orgullo de los blancos? Con el fuego y con el hierro" (As soon as they found themselves free, they aspired to equality; and how did the pride of the whites respond to this pretension? With fire and with iron; 83). Merlin then follows Tocqueville and Beaumont's proposal that Blacks escape the tyranny and violent mobs of the north by fleeing south, where they find refuge in the midst of enslavement (Merlin 83; Tocqueville 339; Beaumont 252). After his description of the riot, Beaumont suggests that it is the tyranny of the majority, the fatal flaw in US democracy, that has chastened the Anti-Slavery Society into disavowal of interracial marriage (251). In contrast, Merlin writes that it is the Black escape from the north to the south that has "calmado mucho la exaltación de los abolicionistas y de la sociedad anti-slavery" (greatly calmed the exaltation of the abolitionists and of the Anti-Slavery Society; 84), who now turn their attention to the impractical program of "la esportación de negros á Africa" (the exportation of Blacks to Africa; 84). Finally, in wording that echoes Tocqueville's dire predictions of race war in the US while also responding in the negative to Saco's question, Merlin argues that emancipation always leads to ruin: "Así en todas partes donde se ha puesto en planta la emancipacion ha tenido por resultado la cesacion de trabajo y la ruína de los colonos, ó el trastorno y desorden social" (Thus everywhere that emancipation has taken place the result has been the end of work and the ruin of the colonists, or social disruption and disorder; 84).

Merlin cements her position as a supporter of colonization and its institutions as the treatise enters its final pages. Despite having characterized Cuban enslavement as a gentler form of the institution, the author mirrors the position held by white *criollo* reformists by calling for amendments rather than emancipation: Revised laws would be "mas sabios, mas justos, [y] mas humanos" (wiser, more just, [and] more humane; 85). Improved treatment, she argues, would be the best option for the enslaved: Reformed codes would make "mejor la suerte de los negros de lo que sería con la emancipación" (better the luck of the Blacks than it would be with emancipation; 86). Restating her opposition to the traffic from Africa on humanitarian grounds, Merlin again reinscribes subhuman status for enslaved people: Greater demand for enslaved labor would mean that "los amos cuidarán mas al esclavo, propiedad cuyo valor se aumentará" (owners will take better care of the slave, property whose value will increase; 86). To end enslavement itself, she argues, would provoke widespread destructive forces. Reform, rather than liberty and equality for all, would "absteneros de arruinar á vuestros colonos y de trastornar el mundo" (save you from ruining your colonists and from disrupting the world; 86). Merlin concludes by appealing to a series of abstract values associated with liberal political discourse and, finally, proposes that even God's justice is moderated by what is fair (87–88).

CONCLUSION: COMBINED DISCOURSES OF COLONIALITY IN *LA HAVANE*

The early letters in *La Havane* dedicated to the author's travels in the US and to her reflections on the necessity of enslavement demonstrate significant reliance on concepts and terminology employed by Tocqueville and Beaumont. However, Merlin does not simply echo the writings of her French compatriots, but rather adapts them to her purposes. Where Tocqueville and Beaumont express concerns about what they perceive as the tyranny of equality, they also identify the aristocratic privilege of individual liberty as a check on the power of the proletarian masses. Merlin, in contrast, entirely rejects the two concepts as equally destructive forces empowering the criminal majority in representative government. The author continues to employ the terminology of liberal thought in sections of the treatise on enslavement, arguing against the traffic from Africa as well as emancipation by appealing to different concepts related to human and individual rights. The language of the Enlightenment gives way to the original discourse of coloniality when the author proposes that Cuban enslavement is a civilizing institution for savage Africans.

While the frameworks of the sixteenth and eighteenth centuries have been conceived as contradictory in Northern and Western scholarship, the arguments put forward by decolonial thought reveal that each one operates in support of the colonial matrix of power. In other words, Merlin's concurrent use of both the language of political liberalism and also the terms of the original discourse of coloniality does not represent a contradiction in her thought. Rather, I argue that Merlin invokes the language of Enlightenment values only to reject these concepts in her arguments against democratic forms of government, emancipation, and racial equality. In presenting liberty and equality as causes of violent uprisings along with an abyssal view of Afro-descendants and by characterizing Cuban enslavement as benevolent, Merlin establishes the discourse of coloniality in the early letters of *La Havane*, which thus informs the portrayal of colonial Cuban culture and institutions that follow in this work.

PART II
WRITING FROM OUTSIDE CUBA

CHAPTER FOUR

MANIFEST COLONIALITY

Maturin Murray Ballou and the "Africanization" of Cuba

In the mid-nineteenth century in the US, Cuba was a controversial focus of attention, particularly as the national debate over enslavement was reaching a critical point. The sugar-producing island promised wealth, a strategic location, and strengthening of slaveholding interests for some, while others objected to increasing slaveholding territory and to adulterating the perceived Anglo-Saxon identity of the US. Capitalizing on this public interest, Maturin Murray Ballou (1820–1895) published *History of Cuba; or, Notes of a Traveller in the Tropics: Being a Political, Historical, and Statistical Account of the Island, from Its First Discovery to the Present Time* (1854) at this critical juncture. Despite the author's claims to neutrality, Ballou's narrative is an expression of Manifest Destiny, which is understood here as rhetoric that rearticulates the discourse of coloniality using the terms of Protestant and liberal values and of white, Anglo-Saxon racial supremacy to justify rapid expansion by any means. The text correspondingly promotes a Hispanophobic characterization of Spain and Cuba that makes clear that several modes of racialized discourse, especially those of Orientalism and anti-Blackness, are inherent to this rhetoric of coloniality. In a discussion of Cuban enslavement that I propose is indebted to the Condesa de Merlin's, Ballou's account nonetheless also points to strategies of resistance that challenge the discourse of power. Finally, the sensationalist Ballou adds urgency to his agenda by promoting racialized fears that a program of emancipation, pejoratively referred to in this period as "Africanization," was pushing Cuba towards an apocalyptic race war. To save a Cuba that he claims for the US, Ballou again follows previous writers in advancing whitening as the solution for the island's perceived

99

problems. However, rather than promote racial mixing, the author envisions a flood of Anglo immigration from the US that would providentially overtake the rest of the population in a program of settler colonialism.

Ballou was born in Boston to a family of Protestant clergymen that claimed a long residency in North America. His ancestor and namesake, Maturin Ballou, "had shared ownership of the Providence Plantation with Roger Williams in 1646" (Everett 45). Ballou learned about journalism from his father, who was himself a prolific writer, editor, and founder of several Universalist publications. In the 1840s, partnering with Frederick Gleason, Ballou began to write and publish sensational stories with nautical and revolutionary motifs. His early novelettes *Fanny Campbell, The Female Pirate Captain: A Tale of the Revolution* (1844), *Red Rupert; or the American Buccaneer* (1845), and *The Naval Officer; or the Pirate's Cave* (1845) were, according to Peter Benson, "phenomenally successful" in terms of sales volume (139). Satisfying the public demand for more outlandish tales, Ballou and Gleason established several highly successful periodicals, including the *Flag of Our Union* (1846), *Gleason's Pictorial Drawing-Room Companion* (1851), which was the first illustrated periodical published in the US, and *Ballou's Dollar Monthly*, the self-proclaimed "cheapest magazine in the world," in 1855. As an editor, Ballou sought outlandish stories like the ones that he often wrote himself. *Flag of Our Union* solicited "such contributions as shall be strictly moral in their tone, highly interesting in their plot, replete throughout with incident, well filled with exciting yet truthful description, and, in short, highly readable and entertaining" (cited in Everett 45). With an eye to selling copy, Ballou did not necessarily stick to the facts when reporting on the news of the day: "He did not hesitate to write fanciful tales and present them to a gullible public as fact" (Everett 49). While his sojourn at the paper was short, Ballou was also the original editor of *The Boston Globe*. Despite his career as a best-selling author and his impact on journalism, the author is little studied today. Among the few critics who analyze his output, some point to Ballou's work as an indicator of prevailing tastes; others further argue that he also helped shape popular culture and public demand for certain types of publications (Anderson 99; Everett 49; P. Benson 144–45).

In addition to his prolific career as an author of dramatic tales, Ballou penned multiple narratives about his frequent, far-flung sojourns. The titles of several of his books, *Due West; or, Round the World in Ten Months* (1884), *Under the Southern Cross; or, Travels in Australia, Tasmania, New Zealand, Samoa, and Other Pacific Islands* (1887), and *Aztec Land: Central America, The West Indies and South America* (1890), give an indication of the extent of his travels. While several of his works focus on Spanish America, Ballou wrote two narratives about Cuba in particular at key moments in the development of relations between the US and its island neighbor.[1] The earlier text, *History of Cuba* (1854), was published at the height of the 1853–1855 annexation debate. The latter of the author's two works dedicated to Cuba, *Due South; or, Cuba Past and Present* (1885), also characterizes itself as a history rather than as a travel narrative.[2] *Due South* was published nearly a decade after La Guerra de los Diez Años (Ten Years' War, 1868–78) and shortly before the war between Cuba, Spain, and the US. An astute editor and writer, Ballou would have understood precisely which aspects of the Cuba debates would enthrall US readers.

TRAVEL NARRATIVES THAT SHAPED THE HISPANOPHOBIC DISCOURSE ABOUT CUBA

Little in-depth information about the island from Cuban perspectives was available to the English-language reading public in the nineteenth-century US despite the high level of public interest. The texts that were at hand primarily took the form of travel accounts written by North Americans and Northern Europeans (Wexler 117; Guevara, "Geographies of Travel" 14). The volume of publication about Cuba in English in the US increased at the moments of greatest political and economic concern regarding the island on the part of Anglo-Americans. Alice R. Wexler describes similar patterns of publication about Cuba for both magazine articles and books: "A trickle of magazine articles in the 1820s and 1830s swelled somewhat during the 1840s and reached a peak during the expansionist 1850s, reflecting not only growing annexationist sentiment but also fascination with the filibustering expeditions of mysterious Narciso López between 1849 and 1851" (Wexler 117). Publication increased again during La Guerra de los Diez Años and then once more in 1895.[3] Wexler states that she found only one historical article about the island that referenced Cuban cultural accomplishments, although dismissively, and few Cuban-authored works were translated into English, with José María Heredia's "Niágara" being a noteworthy exception (118). The sizeable Cuban exile communities and their Spanish-language publications in the US during the nineteenth century were on the whole neglected by mainstream English-language culture. As Wexler puts it, "[d]espite some limited contact between Cuban and North American writers, and the large and growing communities of Cuban exiles in New York and Key West, Florida, Cuba remained culturally more remote from the United States than the geographically more distant lands of England, France and Italy" (118).

Wexler points out that most of the travel writers read by Anglo-Americans were themselves typically limited in ability to communicate effectively in Spanish (119). Potential travelers relied on such narratives as Alexander von Humboldt's *Essai politique sur l'île de Cuba* (1826), David Turnbull's *Travels in the West* (1840), Fredrika Bremer's *The Homes of the New World* (1853), and the Condesa de Merlin's *La Havane* (1844) (discussed above in chapter 3). The first texts authored by North Americans that would inform the perspectives and expectations of later US travelers were the Congregational minister Abiel Abbot's *Letters Written in the Interior of Cuba* (1829) and John G. Wurdemann's *Notes on Cuba* (1844). Travelers also perused texts about Spain or translations of Spanish literature to prepare themselves to visit the island colony. For example, Samuel Hazard, author of *Cuba with Pen and Pencil* (1871), recounts thinking of Washington Irving's *A Chronicle of the Conquest of Granada* (1829) and *Tales of the Alhambra* (1832) while in Cuba (Wexler 119). Mary and Sophia Peabody, later to become Mary Mann and Sophia Hawthorne, read Miguel de Cervantes's *Don Quijote* (1605; 1615) in preparation for their journey to Cuba, which resulted in Mann's novel, *Juanita: A Romance of Real Life in Cuba Fifty Years Ago* (1887) and Hawthorne's *Cuba Journal* (1835) (Masiello 32).[4] Just as some contemporary travelers to Latin America confuse language with nationality, many of these writers indicate little to no distinction between Spaniards and Cubans. In summary, Wexler concludes that many of the travel narratives written in English about the island at the time reflect "the dominant American cultural ethos": "As portraits of Cuba, the nineteenth century travel accounts were significant because they helped to establish a vocabulary, a set of images, a way of imagining Cuba and the Cubans which fed into the rhetoric of imperialism" (129). Writing in 1978, Wexler's conclusions about travel writing devoted to Cuba anticipate theories of such narratives as imperial constructions as forwarded by Mary Louise Pratt's *Imperial Eyes: Travel Writing and Transculturation*, discussions of the representations of Spaniards and their Spanish American descendants in US literature by contemporary critics María DeGuzmán and John C. Havard, and the decolonial explanation of the continuity of the discourse of coloniality.

ABYSSAL FEARS OF THE "AFRICANIZATION" OF CUBA

Ballou published *History of Cuba* during a brief period of heightened domestic and international turmoil that raised annexationist ambitions and anxieties over potential US expansion into the Caribbean. Although politicians had previously taken note of Cuba's strategic location and abundant resources, the late 1840s and early 1850s saw the most concerted efforts by the northern country to obtain control of the island thus far. Following the Mexican-American War (1846–1848), which cut Mexico's territory in half, continuing westward settlement increased debates over whether enslavement should be allowed in new territories occupied by the US, and adherents of Manifest Destiny began to look beyond continental borders for more areas of expansion. Moreover, as Tom Chaffin illustrates, the US had considerable national, rather than sectional, economic interests in enslavement-powered Cuba: "Urban mercantile interests in both the North and South sought and enjoyed profit from the island's economy" (93). President James K. Polk tried to purchase Cuba from Spain in 1848, and President Franklin Pierce's administration tried again without success in 1853.[5] When this latter effort appeared to be floundering, three US diplomats meeting in Belgium authored the unofficial Ostend Manifesto (1854), which justified military seizure of the island in case the purchase failed. The potential addition of Cuba as a state added fuel to the national controversy over enslavement that had been intensified by the Compromise of 1850 and the debates preceding passage of the Kansas-Nebraska Act (1854).

In addition to official efforts to purchase Cuba, now-infamous filibusters launched private expeditions to establish US colonies, many of which were envisioned as slaveholding, around the Caribbean at the midcentury. The adventurers leading such campaigns were the subjects of widespread fascination in the popular press: "Hailed for their colorful, derring-do swagger, filibusters such as [Narciso] López, William Walker, Henry A. Crabb, Joseph Morehead, and others became fixtures of the nation's new penny press during the mid-nineteenth century" (Chaffin 81). As Piero Gleijeses explains, US annexationists interested in Cuba understood the filibustering expeditions as a means of bypassing both political debate and the expense of purchasing the island (220). This view held that, once provoked into independence, Cuba would follow the precedent set by Texas and request admittance into the US. Narciso López launched four expeditions from 1850 to 1851, with only two reaching Cuba. Despite the illegality of his actions, the press often romanticized López's commitment to democracy and to US expansionism, as well as his bravery (Chaffin 82–84). John O'Sullivan, the originator of the term *Manifest Destiny*, and Moses Beach, who published both the New York *Sun* and the Cuban exile newspaper *La Verdad*, were among the journalists who openly supported López's efforts.[6] As an indicator of his own interest in the filibusters, Ballou references Louis Schlesinger's account of the second López attempt, *Personal Narrative of Louis Schlesinger, of Adventures in Cuba and Ceuta* (1852), in *History of Cuba*.

During the years between 1853 and 1855, Spanish officials believed that their hold on Cuba was particularly at risk from US aggression (see C. Stanley Urban; Tom Chaffin; and Piero Gleijeses). While the northern country had expressed interest in Cuba for decades, the British naval presence in the Caribbean had prevented any possible invasions. When Britain and France went to war against Russia in 1854, however, Spanish officials feared that their Caribbean colonies might be more vulnerable to US incursions and requested assurances from Britain that were not immediately granted. Spanish diplomats determined that the only way to ensure British protection for Cuba was to finally enforce the treaties signed between the two countries in 1817 and 1835 to end the human traffic from Africa to Cuba. A reformist captain general, Juan de la Pezuela, was installed and instructed to put a stop to the traffic that had previously guaranteed the loyalty of Cuban slaveholders to Spain. Pezuela, considered "a friend of the blacks," instituted a number of reforms designed to stop the importation of enslaved people into Cuba and established a militia of free Afro-descendants (Gleijeses 225–26). These actions alarmed slaveholders and investors in both Cuba and the US, who feared that the next step would be widespread emancipation, race war, and economic ruin that would also provoke uprisings in the southern US. Although these are the same racialized fears that were associated with the memory of the Haitian Revolution after 1790, the English-language press began to employ a sensationalistic new term for this—"Africanization"—that appears designed to stoke abyssal fears of Blackness.[7] Further, wealthy Cuban *criollos* and US investors alike perceived abolition as a means by which Spain could maintain its foothold in the Caribbean: It was widely believed that the US would have no interest in annexing an island dominated by free rather than enslaved Afro-descendants (Urban 29–32). At the same time that the US was moving closer to an internal war over the enslavement of people of color, the certainty of the "Africanization" of Cuba was projected in newspapers from New York to New Orleans.

BALLOU'S *HISTORY OF CUBA*: THE MODES OF HISPANOPHOBIC COLONIALITY

While limited information is available about Ballou's stay in Cuba, it was probably no longer than a few months. Further, like many of the travel writers who preceded him, Ballou had limited ability to speak Spanish (Guevara, "Geographies" 15). As a result, he relies heavily on other sources, many of which are the same North Atlantic texts that Wexler names. While Ballou does cite authorities throughout, there are also instances in which *History of*

Cuba is remarkably close in content and word choice to source texts without any citation. However, there do not appear to have been any accusations of plagiarism of the type faced by Merlin after the publication of *La Havane*. Among the informants and authors that Ballou directly names are Merlin, Francisco de Arango y Parreño (referred to as "Arranjo"), Ramón de la Sagra, Senator Edward Everett, Alexander Everett, Louis Schlesinger, Fredrika Bremer, Reverend Abiel Abbot, Alexander von Humboldt, and William Cullen Bryant.[8] Together with an anonymous "gentleman in Cuba," Merlin and Arango are the only Cuban-born authors that Ballou acknowledges in the narrative (58–59). As my analysis of his text indicates, important aspects of the Bostonian Ballou's assessment of Cuba and its institutions appear indebted to Merlin's *La Havane*, which in turn draw upon the writings of José Antonio Saco, Alexis de Tocqueville, Gustave de Beaumont, and Arango. While coinciding with the coloniality of these earlier writers, however, Ballou's evaluation of Cuba is expressed from a Northern US perspective.

History of Cuba engages throughout with Hispanophobic rhetoric and representations of Spain and Cuba. Through its reliance on multiple racialized modes of expression, Ballou's text illustrates that the Hispanophobic rhetoric propagated by North Atlantic powers is a redirecting of Spain's earlier discourse of coloniality, which Walter D. Mignolo and the theorists of decoloniality identify as the source for the logic of Western racialized discourses today (Mignolo, "*Islamophobia / Hispanophobia,*" 20). I use the term *Hispanophobic discourse of coloniality* to characterize Ballou's racialized representations of Spaniards and of all of Cuba's inhabitants in *History of Cuba* and, building on María DeGuzmán and John C. Havard's assessment of US national identity, propose that it is fundamental to the text's expression of Manifest Destiny. In other words, Hispanophobia and Manifest Destiny are mutually informing facets of Ballou's expression of the ongoing discourse of coloniality. Additionally, following Mignolo's characterization of the Black Legend as the labelling of Spaniards as "Moors, Jews, Indians, and Blacks," I argue that Orientalism is central to rather than distinct from the Hispanophobic discourse of coloniality ("*Islamophobia / Hispanophobia*" 20). I largely follow Edward W. Said's formulation of Orientalism as it is commonly understood in Western literary criticism, but refer to the sixteenth-century Spanish Conquista in the American Hemisphere as the chronological starting point for the modern European discourse of coloniality as posited by decolonial thought (Castro-Gómez 276–77).[9] This is an important point of departure between my analysis and the treatment of this topic in the works of other critics addressing this aspect of US national rhetoric (DeGuzmán xxix; Havard 10). It is Hispanophobia's Orientalist mode that categorizes

Spaniards and their colonial descendants as exotic, morally deficient and, to use DeGuzmán's useful term, racially "off-white" (4). While it maintains the anti-Black rhetoric of the original discourse of coloniality, the Hispanophobic iteration also suggests that Cuba's Afro-descendants, under the care of Spaniards and Cubans perceived as off-white, are too close to their African origins to be rational humans and therefore are content to remain enslaved. Ballou's account of Cuban enslavement appears to be heavily influenced by the colonialized defense of enslavement expressed in "Lettre XX" of Merlin's *La Havane*, which was available in English translation (see chapter 3 above). Ballou's text cycles through several modes of the racialized Hispanophobic discourse of coloniality as it builds the case for the inevitable annexation of Cuba by the purportedly white and Anglo-Saxon US.

MODES OF HISPANOPHOBIC COLONIALITY: THE SPANIARD AS VIOLENT CONQUEROR

The preface to *History of Cuba* begins by signaling that Cuba was at that time the subject of "interest expressed on all sides" (1). Ballou himself remarks on the dearth of published information available (in English) regarding Cuba: "In preparing the volume for the press, the author has felt the want of books of reference, bearing a late date. *Indeed, there are none*" (emphasis added; *History of Cuba* 1). Despite his restricted language ability, the author explains that he has relied on "Spanish books and pamphlets" made available to him by Edward Everett, who was at that time a US senator and had formerly served as president of Harvard University and as US secretary of state.[10] Becoming again the author of sensational, attention-grabbing tales, Ballou creates a strong sense of urgency by predicting an upcoming apocalypse for Cuba at the conclusion of the first paragraph: "So critically is the island now situated, in a political point of view, that ere this book shall have passed through an edition, it may be no longer a dependency of Spain, or may have become the theatre of scenes to which its former convulsions shall bear no parallel" (1). For Ballou's readers, it would be clear that the author refers to the "Africanization of Cuba," which relies upon the racialized fears of another Haitian Revolution and recalls the catastrophic predictions seen in Merlin's *La Havane* and in two of her source texts, Tocqueville's *Democracy in America* (1835–1840) and Beaumont's *Marie; or Slavery in the United States* (1835). Fear of such a devastating rebellion was also common among both Cuban and US slaveholders. By promoting his book simultaneously as a "political history," a dire account of the racialized threat facing the neighboring island, and a pleasant relation of tropical travel, Ballou fashions his text to appeal to a wide range of readers with a strong dose of sensationalist, Hispanophobic excitement.

Ballou commences the text proper by invoking the names and deeds of the first Spanish conquerors to arrive in the Caribbean, thereby further inscribing his text into very long-standing colonial narrative practices. Cristóbal Colón, often referred to in Spanish colonial texts by his title, "el Almirante" (the Admiral), inaugurated the literary model of navigator and conqueror of "new" realms in the diaries that he composed during his voyages. As Daylet Domínguez points out, the influential Alexander von Humboldt writes himself into the tradition inaugurated by Colón. In *Essai politique sur l'île de Cuba*, the German naturalist follows this model to establish his textual authority: "Humboldt se legitima en la tradición de los conquistadores españoles, invocando los nombres y las travesías de Cristóbal Colón y Hernán Cortés por el mar Caribe" (Humboldt legitimizes himself in the tradition of the Spanish conquistadors, invoking the names and voyages of Cristóbal Colón and Hernán Cortés through the Caribbean Sea; "Alexander von Humboldt y Ramón de la Sagra," 144). Ballou, who identifies Humboldt as a source, likewise calls upon the image of "the great admiral" in the very first sentence of his history and, shortly after that, he refers to Cortés's expedition to a Mexico "thronged with savage tribes" and to Pizarro's conquest of Peru by way of "perfidy and sword" (Ballou, *History of Cuba* 11–13). Even while stating that the Indigenous peoples of North America did not "fare much better at the hands of men *professing a purer faith*," Spain is nonetheless characterized in these Hispanophobic terms as a brutal, retrograde nation deserving of celestial justice (emphasis added, 12). Ballou legitimates this depiction by citing the words of Whig Senator Edward Everett in his text: "The horrid atrocities practiced at home and abroad . . . cried to Heaven for vengeance upon Spain; nor could she escape it. . . . The wrongs of both hemispheres were avenged by her degeneracy and fall" (14). The nation's divinely ordained rapid loss of empire, Ballou claims, "is almost without a parallel in the history of the world" (14). The final act of justice in "the great drama of historical retribution," the liberation of Spain's few remaining island colonies, will surely come soon (14).

Alternation between the extremes of Hispanophilia and Hispanophobia in *History of Cuba* leads to an ambiguous and vacillating characterization of Spain, Spaniards, and Cubans, among whom Ballou does not consider Afro-descendants. At times the author expresses admiration for the Spanish conquerors, as is seen in his portrayal of Cortés as a medieval knight: The conquistador's actions in Mexico are characterized as a "romantic adventure, worthy of the palmiest days of chivalry" (11). Concurrently, however, "the

Spaniard" is inherently flawed: "[T]he threads of courage and ferocity are inseparably blended in the woof and warp of Spanish character" (11). Reflecting the view that Havard largely associates with colonial-era US literature, Ballou proposes that the soldiers who fought for the Spanish displayed "discipline, courage, ferocity, fanaticism and avarice" (11; Havard 4–5). At the same time, Ballou also regularly describes the nation of Spain as a weak, degenerate, and duplicitous fallen power: the metropole is an "enfeebled, distracted and despotic parent monarchy" (*History* 38). Ballou invokes Spain's most celebrated medieval *caballero* to serve as a reminder of how far the country had lapsed in character and in courage: "[I]t must be remembered that Spanish valor is but a feeble shadow of what it was in the days of the Cid" (97). Miguel Tacón y Rosique, the notorious captain general, is presented as a despot, yet Spain continues to display "imbecile weakness" that means the metropole will not be able to hold Cuba for much longer (34; 191).

MODES OF HISPANOPHOBIC COLONIALITY: ORIENTALIST PORTRAYALS OF SPAIN AND CUBA

Ballou's portrayals of Cuba, its landscape, and its inhabitants continue the author's alternation between attraction to and revulsion for his narrative subjects, all of which is filtered through Hispanophobia's Orientalist mode. This characterization extends even to the island's geography, which Ballou compares to that of a "Turkish scimiter [*sic*]" (66). Cuba is exotic, different, and uncivilized: "Indeed, it is impossible to express fully how *everything* differs in Cuba from our own country, so near at hand. . . . [T]he visitor seems to have been transported into another quarter of the globe, the first impression being, as we have said, decidedly of an Oriental character. But little effort of the imagination would be required to believe oneself in distant Syria, or some remote part of Asia" (ellipses added, 193). Further adhering to the discourse of coloniality, Ballou finds much of Cuban culture morally suspect or even repellent, and attributes this to the inherited Spanish character of off-white Cubans. (I use DeGuzmán's term *off-white* here to indicate that when he refers to Cubans and Creoles, Ballou means light-skinned inhabitants of the island whom the author perceives as racially distinct from Anglo-Saxons.) The lottery and the cockfight, both of which were indeed popular in Cuba at the time, confirm for the author the tendencies towards vice and violence inherited from the mother country (117, 143). Ballou's judgment of another practice, the burial of the dead, is unreservedly critical: Cuban interment does not match that of "semi-civilized or even savage nations. We all know the sacredness that is attached by the Turks to their burial grounds" (106). Finally, corresponding to the North Atlantic Protestant view articulated in the Hispanophobic discourse of coloniality, Catholicism is characterized as a suspect sect that has outlived its usefulness: "Whether the Catholic church has accomplished its mission, and exhausted its means of good, is a question open to discussion" (82). For Ballou, masses are primarily carnivalesque spectacles with little to no lasting effects (81); he quotes Rev. Abiel Abbot's *Letters* to further bolster these characterizations of religion in the colony (81n).

Ballou's characterization of off-white Cubans indicates the continuity of the discourse of coloniality from Spain to Northern Europe to the US as he combines views that Havard generally associates with different eras of US literature. Havard largely connects the belief that the tropical climate produced torpor with colonial-era discourse and characterizes the belief in the racial inferiority of Latin Americans as arising later, but Ballou relies on both of these colonialized concepts at once in his mid-century narrative (Havard 4–7). Moreover, as Mignolo argues, the logic of coloniality is maintained even while the terms evolve from a religious to a racialized taxonomy (*"Islamophobia / Hispanophobia"* 20). The island's more alluring exotic charms derive from Spain's Moorish heritage, yet shortcomings are further attributed to a belief in the negative effects of the tropical climate and possible mixing with the Indigenous population. Off-white Cuban women are presented in sensual, Orientalized terms: "Beautiful as eastern houris, there is a striking and endearing charm about the Cuban ladies" (78). Citing William Cullen Bryant, Ballou celebrates the "languor" of off-white *criollas'* eyes and their "rich, liquid, and sweet" voices (139). The equestran skill of the countryside *montero*, or cowboy, arises from his "Old World" ancestry: "The Montero inherits all the love of his Moorish ancestors for the horse" (155). Wondering why Cubans have not successfully rebelled against Spain, Ballou remarks that "[i]t would seem that the softness of the unrivalled climate of those skies beneath which it is luxury only to exist has unnerved them, and that the effeminate spirit of the original inhabitants has descended in retribution to the posterity of the *conquistadores*" (37). Male slaveholders in Cuba, Ballou argues, are small and light, weakened by their environment and lifestyle: "The lazy life that is so universally led by them tends to make them less manly in physical development than a life of activity would do" (139). Kept in a life of leisure by the labor of enslaved people in this "genial clime," off-white *criollos* can freely dedicate themselves to frequent romantic adventures: "[T]he West Indies seem peculiarly adapted for romance and love" (140). Ballou's characterization of Cuban men conforms to "the tendency of the American travelers, most of them men, to describe the alleged submissiveness, idleness, narcissism of Cuban men in ways suggesting lack of masculinity or effeminacy" (Wexler 123). Thus, Ballou's text simultaneously inscribes the characterization of the Spaniard as the bloodthirsty, fanatical conqueror and as the exotic Moor alongside the image of the languid, effeminate, tropical Cuban; each of these modes of representation forwards the logic of coloniality.

Just as the inhabitants of Cuba are portrayed as unfit to govern themselves, they are also characterized as unable to be productive and to adapt to modern technologies, despite Cuba's status as the world's largest producer of sugar. As Gema R. Guevara argues, Ballou utilizes a rhetorical strategy of "innocence while asserting cultural hegemony over colonial peoples" in his Cuba narratives ("Geographies of Travel" 13). In his discussion of the bias in texts that present themselves as objective, Santiago Castro-Gómez refers to this as "the hubris of zero degrees" (278). While overtly stating that he is not proposing the annexation of Cuba, Ballou peppers *History of Cuba* throughout with references to the failure to realize Cuba's latent potential for productivity and for power in the region. Ballou proposes that the land is so fertile that the *monteros* of the countryside have little to do; they need only gather up and sell what the land produces. Further, these rural inhabitants are not habituated to planning for the future: [T]hey live "'from hand to mouth'—that is, they lay in no stores whatever, and trust to the coming day to supply its own necessities" (102). Rather than the Turkish scimitar, here Cuba becomes an exotic Garden of Eden waiting for the proper cultivation of Providential bounty. Instead of a place of innocence, however, Ballou's Orientalized characterization of the landscape is one of "a feminized and sexualized nature longing for capitalist development" (Guevara, "Geographies of Travel" 12). Citing diplomat Alexander Hill Everett, the author expounds upon what the island could produce in the hands of more industrious people:

> On treading the fertile soil, and on beholding the clustering fruits offered on all sides, the delicious oranges, the perfumed pine-apples, the luscious bananas, the cooling cocoanuts, and other fruits for which our language has no name, we are struck with the thought of how much Providence, and how little man, has done for this Eden of the Gulf. We long to see it peopled by men who can appreciate the gifts of nature, men who are willing to do their part in reward for her bounty, men who will meet her half way and second her spontaneous efforts. (127–28)

The potential productivity of feminized Cuban soil in particular is a fascination for Ballou: "The virgin soil of Cuba is so rich that a touch of the hoe prepares it for the plant, or, as Douglass Jerrold says of Australia, 'just tickle her with a hoe and she laughs with a harvest'" (195). Moreover, the author pays rather symbolic attention to the variations in the color of Cuban soil: "The richest soil of the island is the black, which is best adapted to the purpose of the sugar-planter" (195). The darkest soil is so nutritious that it does not need to be turned or even replanted "for years" (195). The "red soil" he describes as being less fertile and better for coffee, while the "mulatto-colored earth" is considered inferior but can be improved for tobacco planting (196). He also notes the "mineral wealth" of island, which contains coal, copper, iron, and lodestone (196). What Cuba needs, Ballou argues, is "the infusion of a sterner, more self-denying and enterprising race" to realize the island's full potential (128–29).

MODES OF HISPANOPHOBIC COLONIALITY: ANTI-BLACK FEARS OF "AFRICANIZATION"

Like the Cuban theorists José Antonio Saco and Domingo del Monte, Ballou's understanding of what is meant by "Cuban" refers to light-skinned descendants of Spaniards and excludes both free and enslaved Afro-descendants. Moreover, Ballou does not address the range of racial identities available at the time in Cuban culture, nor does he devote much narrative attention to free Cubans of color, who made up a sizeable portion of the island's population. Rather, Ballou's warnings regarding Cuba recall the predictions by Tocqueville and Beaumont, which are reiterated in Merlin's text, of the inevitable and destructive race war that will be provoked by emancipation. Tocqueville writes, "[T]he most dreadful of all the evils that threaten the future of the United States arises from the presence of blacks on its soil" (Tocqueville, *Democracy in America* 326). Likewise, Merlin proclaims that emancipation and the resulting desire for equality would destroy Cuba's white population and productivity. While white fears of a devastating uprising were constant where enslavement was practiced after the Haitian Revolution, the early 1850s saw Spanish reforms that increased international rumors of the colony's "Africanization." Like the earlier critics of US democracy, Ballou's presentation of the "Africanization" of Cuba presents Black liberty and equality as threats not only to the lives of off-white Cubans but also to residents of the nearby US.

Despite reinforcing the fearmongering beliefs surrounding violent "Africanization," Ballou nonetheless presents Cuban enslavement as a paternalistic institution that benefits enslaved people in much the way that Merlin, who is regularly cited as a source in *History of Cuba*, does in her defense of enslavement (discussed in chapter 3 above). Ballou, like Tocqueville and Merlin, insists on the contentment of enslaved people and the benefits that they receive when enslaved, discounts the intensity and productivity of their labor, and reinforces the idea of racial difference while at the same time pointing out the aggressive control systems in place to terrorize enslaved people into submission. This provides a point of contrast with Saco and Del Monte, who feared that violent rebellion could occur at any moment.

Ballou abyssally proposes that enslaved African-born people newly arrived on the island have "dull natures requiring a vast deal of watchful training" (181). In accordance with the civilizing mission of the discourse of coloniality, the author proposes that contact with Western culture brings about generational change: Afro-descendants born in Cuba are "more intelligent than their parents, from mingling with civilization" and become stronger and healthier (181). Again sounding very much like Merlin and contrasting notably with the first-hand accounts written by Juan Francisco Manzano and Esteban Montejo, Ballou proposes that enslaved people in Cuba have a good lot in life: "The slaves upon the plantations in all outward circumstances seem quite thoughtless and happy" (182).[11] He remarks that they are "comparatively free to roam about the plantation," even while devoting considerable attention to the ways in which mastiffs are trained to hunt runaways (178). Contradicting Manzano's accounts of constant hunger, Ballou proposes that enslaved people, like the *monteros*, have plenty to eat in the island paradise: "[T]hey always eat freely of the fruits about them, so ripe and inviting, and so plentiful, too, that half the crop and more, usually rots upon the ground" (182; Manzano 305).[12] Even during the sugar harvest, when forced laborers are allowed only five hours of sleep per night, "the slaves do not seem to dread [the harvest season], as they are granted more privileges at this period, and are better fed" (146n43). The author acknowledges that oxen die from overwork at this time of the year, but unlike Anselmo Suárez y Romero in his meditation on the plantation cemetery, Ballou does not recognize the high price paid by enslaved people (146) (Suárez y Romero's response to the cemetery is discussed above in chapter 2).

Ballou's characterization of Cuban enslavement as beneficent and the slaveholders as benign reiterates Merlin's proslavery position. Like Merlin, Ballou proposes that the purportedly generous Cuban slave code "is never widely departed from," and that, improving upon US enslavement, these "laws favor emancipation" (182). By keeping pigs and managing a small plot of land, "an industrious slave can accomplish [self-emancipation] at farthest in seven years" (183). Quoting the Reverend Abbot, who attests to the same experience, Ballou states that he did not witness a single act of cruelty towards an enslaved person during his visit, particularly since it is in the slaveholder's interest to treat his property with care (183). Not only does Juan Francisco Manzano's account of his treatment at the hands of the Marquesa de Prado Ameno contradict this characterization, writings by white members of the Del Monte *tertulia* also make clear that brutal violence and corruption were endemic to enslavement on the island. Having commented on the perceived mildness of Cuban enslavement, Ballou importunes his reader not to think that he is in favor of the institution: "Let no ingenious person distort these remarks into a pro-slavery argument. God forbid!" (184). As Ballou characterizes it, however, enslavement in and of itself does not appear to be the source of Cuba's difficulties.

Even while proposing that enslaved Afro-descendants are unenlightened, Ballou's efforts at abyssal characterization also reference elements of African and Afro-Cuban cultures that signal political and ethnic identity, sources of solidarity, and resistance to power. Echoing the Reverend Abbot, Ballou mentions that those born in Africa can be recognized by their "tattooed faces, bodies and limbs" (Ballou 181; Abbot 7). For authors like Abbot and Ballou, body markings are a sign of the primitive nature of Africans and contribute to Cuba's exotic Otherness. However, tattooing and scarification conveyed a variety of meanings in West African cultures, including ethnic identity and citizenship, individual accomplishments, and spirituality.[13] Ballou also reinscribes the associations between African tribal or national identities and personality types that also appear in Cuban-authored literature of time, such as Anselmo Suárez y Romero's characterization of *minas* as being particularly musical in "Ingenios" (313). As Rafael Ocasio explains, "References to African ethnicities were often at the center of debates among plantation owners about the best or worst type of personality to endure the physical and mental impositions of slavery" (45). Suggesting the scientific racism of the era, Ballou proposes that personality and nationality are externally discernable among enslaved Afro-descendants: "[T]heir characteristics are visibly marked, so that their nationality is discernable, even to a casual observer" (180). As he outlines the traits that are associated with different nationalities, Ballou reinscribes stereotypes and methods that were used to control enslaved persons. For example, traffickers and slaveholders made efforts to mix Africans from different language groups on board ships and on plantations to prevent uprisings (Castellanos and Castellanos 26). Reinscribing the stereotypes that served the purposes of enslavement, Ballou proposes that "Congos" are smaller and make good workers and that "Ashantees" are "prized for their strength" (180–81).

At the same time, the terms for ethnic, tribal, and national groups that were used in Cuba were not only the result of efforts to categorize and control but also arose from self-identification (Castellanos and Castellanos 28). As Jorge Castellanos and Isabel Castellanos explain, African nationalities expressed in Cuba, such as *arará-sabalú*, indicate "no sólo los nombres tribales, étnicos o lingüísticos sino los geográficos y politicos" (not only the tribal, ethnic, or linguistic names but also the geographic and political ones; 31). Ballou reveals signs of resistance contained within this taxonomy when reiterating such Cuban stereotypes as that associated with the "Fantee," who he states are considered "revengeful" (180–81). He further explains that the most recently arrived "Carrobalees" are avoided by planters; their belief that they would return home after death made them prone to suicide, an act that today is considered one of both resistance and sabotage (Barcía 51). Finally, even when separated from others of their nation or language group, Ballou reminds the reader that enslaved Africans and Afro-descendants have the opportunity to join together to dance to the beat of the drum, which the author describes as a "rude" and "monotonous" instrument (194). Failing to recognize it as an act of spirituality, resistance, and solidarity, Ballou nonetheless signals the importance of this practice for the dancers when he remarks that "they perform grotesque dances, with unwearying feet, really surprising the looker-on by their power of endurance in sustaining themselves in vigorous dancing" (194).

Like Merlin, Ballou adapts Tocqueville and Beaumont's racialized warnings for the future of the US to Cuba when he presents the island's majority population of color as a dangerous threat to the puportedly off-white population: "Cuba is at present politically in a critical and alarming condition, and the most intelligent natives and resident foreigners live in constant dread of a convulsion more terrific and sanguinary than that which darkened the annals of St. Domingo" (54). If there were any doubt, the reference to "St. Domingo" clarifies that Ballou is foreshadowing another Haitian Revolution and its destruction of the white, slaveholding class. Repeating the rumors in circulation at the time, the author argues that imperial Spain not only would not prevent such events but that the metropole is promoting them in order to maintain her hold on the colony: "Those best informed of the temper, designs, and position of Spain, believe in the existence of a secret treaty between that country, France and England, by which the two latter powers guarantee to Spain her perpetual possession of the island, on condition of her carrying out the favorite abolition schemes of the British government, and Africanizing the island" (54). Whereas Ballou has elsewhere proposed that the enslaved are "thoughtless and happy," an emancipated population of color on the road to political and social equality is dangerous. Ballou cites as evidence Captain General Juan Manuel González de la Pezuela's efforts to emancipate illegally enslaved workers and employ free laborers from Africa: "All the recent measures of the Captain-General Pezuela are calculated to produce the conviction that the Africanization of Cuba has been resolved upon" (55).[14] Rumored reforms being made on behalf of this free population, such as schools for Black students and the legalization of intermarriage, demonstrate to Ballou that Spain is bent on establishing "social equalization of the colored and white population [that will lead to] a war of races, which could only terminate in the extinction of the whites" (57). The prospect of enlistment of free men of color in the army intended to promote the metropole's cause "is a deadly insult offered to the white population of a slave-holding country" (96). This behavior on the part of the colonial administration is for Ballou and his unnamed informant, "a gentleman in Cuba," a clear sign of "Spanish duplicity" (58–59). According to the anonymous source, no action by a captain general has caused more indignation than the rumored authorization of legal intermarriage, although permitting students of color into the university and training them for religious orders follow closely behind (60). Echoing Merlin's tone of outrage when confronted by the concept of racial equality, the author's unnamed informant is quoted as stating that annointing Black clergy members and instituting other possible reforms "will lead to bad consequences.... The indignation of the Creoles has been difficult to restrain,—at which you cannot be surprised, when their daughters, wives and sisters, are daily insulted, particularly by those in uniform. I fear a collision may take place. Once commenced, it will be terrific" (60).

MODES OF HISPANOPHOBIC COLONIALITY:
THE SETTLER COLONIALISM OF MANIFEST DESTINY

As Ballou's narrative progresses, the US acquisition of Cuba is increasingly described as the inevitable and best outcome in accordance with the discourse of coloniality in its Manifest Destiny iteration. Given the Hispanophobic characterizations of the island's inhabitants, the narrative proposes that only white Anglo-Saxons from the US can carry out the modernizing and civilizing mission that Cuba requires. Stating that Cubans "fear innovation," Ballou suggests that the US-led process of modernization is already underway when he writes that "the introduction of railroads, telegraphs, and even the lighting of the city of Havana by gas,—[has all been] done by Americans" (192). Train travel is jingoistically characterized as all-American: "On all the

Cuban railroads you ride in American-built cars, drawn by American-built engines, and conducted by American engineers" (70). Modern transport and communications between Havana and the US cities of New York and New Orleans are "revolutionizing all business relations and the course of trade" (198). The steamship line connecting Havana to the two US cities is "one of the best in the world," and a telegram from New York could reach Cuba in three days' time (198). According to Ballou, plantations wanting to innovate will also require the costly importation of machinery and operators from the northern country (145). Ballou argues that neither Spaniard nor Cuban nor enslaved Afro-descendant should or would operate these engines: "A Spaniard or Creole would as soon attempt to fly as he would endeavor to learn how properly to run a steam-engine, . . . a duty that it is not safe to entrust to even a faithful slave" (146). As a reminder of the relevance of the commercial gaze that Ballou directs towards Cuba, the North American engineer reappears in twentieth-century Cuban revolutionary films such as Sergio Giral's *El otro Francisco* (1975) as a capitalist enabler of racist oppression.

Ballou's strategy of innocence is upheld when he appears to reject the idea of occupying Cuba by force, but the narrative ultimately gives way to an accounting of the benefits of US occupation of the island. While admiring the gallantry and courage of the filibusters, Ballou initially argues that their actions must nonetheless be condemned: "No amount of sympathy with the sufferings of an oppressed people, no combination of circumstances, no possible results, can excuse the fitting out of a warlike expedition in the ports of a nation against the possessions of a friendly power" (39–40). However, the author nonetheless presents strong arguments in favor of annexation that go beyond capitalist production to the protection of US security and the expansion of US naval power. Echoing John Quincy Adams, Ballou proposes that the island's "political position all concede to be of the most vital importance to the United States" (67). The author soon becomes explicit about Havana's strategic significance for the Caribbean and Gulf of Mexico: "[T]he possessors of this stronghold command the whole Spanish West Indies" (73). Citing Alexander Hill Everett, Ballou extols the quality of the Havana harbor as one of the best in the world and capable of protecting "a thousand ships of war" (73). This line of thought clearly anticipates future actions of the US in Cuba both during and after the war of 1898.

Ballou continues to inscribe Manifest Destiny into his text as *History of Cuba* draws to a close when returning to the idea that the separation of Cuba from an inept, cruel Spain is divinely predetermined. The metropole's efforts to alienate enslaved workers from planters and to "Africanize" the island is dangerous for off-white Cuban colonists and, by implication, for the US

(190). For all its perceived moral, economic, and political failures, Ballou argues that "Spain deserves to lose Cuba because of her perfidy" (190). That the US should be the nation to free Cuba is divinely ordained: "The time has come when the progress of civilization demands that the island shall pass into the hands of some power possessed of the ability and the will to crush out this remnant of barbarism. That power is clearly designated by the hand of Providence; no European nation can dream of obtaining Cuba" (190). Later, Ballou more explicitly proposes that "Cuba naturally belongs to the US and will soon be ours" (199). The author begins to lay the groundwork for ideological acceptance of Cuba into the northern nation by pointing out shared historical origins in a return to his initial invocation of the "great admiral": The US also exists because of Colón's explorations (191).[15] Further, Ballou points out that absorption of "a foreign population" into the northern nation has precedents: "Louisiana, with her French and Spanish Creoles, is one of the most reliable states of the Union" (228). Ballou also reminds his reader of the recent acquisition of what had been the northern half of Mexico when pointing out that the "gallant Creoles" fought at the Rio Grande (228–29).

In Ballou's account, US occupation of the island would be easily accomplished and, inscribing the genocidal logic of white settlerism, allow for a repopulation of the island through an inundation of Anglo-Saxon immigration that would have miraculous effects. Despite Spain's efforts to conceal information about Havana's harbor through "Japan-like" secrecy, the author proposes that the federal government in Washington already has detailed information about Cuba's harbors and defenses (158). Referring to an idea expressed by Alexander Everett that also recalls Tocqueville's colonialism, the author states that the island could easily be taken, "like the French took Algiers" (198). Ballou proposes that incorporation of Cuba is merely a matter of time when stating that "the US will move to protect national interests" when threatened by the "Africanization" of Cuba (223). Finally, he argues that such actions would be welcomed by a Cuba already "longing for annexation" (223, 229). In the liberal language of North Atlantic coloniality, Ballou argues that a military takeover would liberate Cuba: "Her home is in the bosom of the North American confederacy. . . . Cuba will be free" (229–30). Once liberated from Spain, Cuba would be overcome and magically renewed by a flood of Anglo immigration from the US: "A tide of emigration from the States will pour into the island, the waste lands will be reclaimed, and their hidden wealth disclosed; a new system of agricultural economy will be introduced; the woods of the island will furnish material for splendid ships; towns and villages will rise with magical celerity, and the whole surface of the 'garden of the world' will blossom like the rose" (229).

Recalling the racialized dangers of race war raised by Saco, Del Monte, Merlin, Tocqueville, and Beaumont, Ballou identifies the colony's enslaved Afro-descendant population as the major threat facing not only the island but also the slaveholding nation to the north. Moreover, he abyssally characterizes the island's off-white residents as impediments to the moral and economic progress of the island's providential bounty. Unlike Saco, Del Monte, Tocqueville, and Beaumont, however, Ballou does not appear to propose whitening through racial mixing as a solution, but rather upholds the exterminationist logic of white settlerism when he calls for a displacement of the island's existing population by a flood of Anglo-Saxon immigrants into the country.

CONCLUSION: THE HISPANOPHOBIC DISCOURSE OF COLONIALITY / MANIFEST DESTINY

Ballou's *History of Cuba* clearly expresses the tenets of Manifest Destiny—which is inseparable from a Hispanophobic presentation of Spain and Cuba—to justify the vision of territorial expansion. An analysis of the author's employment of Hispanophobia reveals it to be a redeployment of Spain's sixteenth-century discourse of coloniality by that country's political and economic rivals, as is posited by Mignolo and decolonial thought. What began as a Christian taxonomy opposing the purported heresies of Muslims and Jews that was then extended to Indigenous peoples and Africans during the conquest and colonization in the American Hemisphere becomes a racialized one by the mid-nineteenth century. Operating in support of US hegemony in the hemisphere, Ballou's text relies on the multiple modes of racialized representation that are contained within the Hispanophobic iteration of the discourse of coloniality. Racially, morally, and temperamentally distinct from the model of the white Anglo-Saxon, off-white and Orientalized Spain is variously presented as violent, vengeful, intolerant, incompetent, and morally decadent. Off-white Cubans are also Orientalized as tropical "natives" who are voluptuous, weak, lazy, and sinful. Finally, as residents of an Orientalized island and thus removed from exposure to true whiteness, Cuba's African and Afro-descendant population is presented as more exotic and thus less civilized than that of the US. While one might suppose that Ballou would have chafed at Merlin's characterization of the US as an illustration of the failures of democracy, he reinscribes her defense of Cuban enslavement as a patriarchal and beneficent institution and, like Tocqueville and Beaumont as well, her position that liberty and equality make Afro-descendants dangerous to those considered white. Finally, the author posits the genocidal logic of white settlerism when proposing that the moral and economic regeneration of the island is destined by Providence to be carried out by an inundation of Anglo-Saxons from the US.

History of Cuba claims to be articulated from a position of neutrality, yet it nonetheless reinscribes the discourse of coloniality from a US perspective. As a discourse of power, this rhetoric also contains inconsistencies and points to strategies of resistance employed by those most disempowered by coloniality in Cuba. The characterizations of Spaniards and Cubans vacillate in contradictory ways within Hispanophobic discourse according to the intent of the messages being delivered by the text. Spaniards are bloodthirsty tyrants who are nonetheless unable to keep their colonies; Cubans are lazy and unproductive despite living in the world's most lucrative sugar colony. Afro-descendants are presented as being content and "dull-natured" when enslaved, yet dangerous threats to civilization when free. Further, while attributing subhumanity and primitive development to Africans and Afro-Cubans, Ballou's discussion of aspects of Afro-descendant life on the island reveals elements of African and Afro-Cuban cultures that belie that characterization. Moreover, even while reinscribing a defense of Cuban enslavement as benign, he also reveals signs and strategies of resistance when referring to the vengeance, suicide, religious beliefs and practices, and acts of solidarity by Afro-descendants that confront coloniality on the island.

CHAPTER FIVE

BLACKFACE, PLANTATIONS, AND TROPICAL SPACES

Julia Ward Howe's *A Trip to Cuba*

Julia Ward Howe and her spouse, Samuel "Chev" Gridley Howe, travelled to Cuba in early 1859 seeking the benefits of the island's mild winter climate. The journey provided an important stepping stone for Howe's literary career when she received a commission from *The Atlantic Monthly* to document the trip in a series of letters to be published in the magazine and later in book form as *A Trip to Cuba* (1860), a text that is little studied today. While Howe has been mythologized in popular US history as the progressive author of "Battle Hymn of the Republic," *A Trip to Cuba* nonetheless relies upon the Hispanophobic discourse of coloniality in its presentation of Spain, Cuba, and the wider Caribbean, which by opposition constructs a white, upper-class, Anglo-Saxon, and female identity for the author. Rather than an abolitionist critique of enslavement, Howe's Cuba narrative follows the example of blackface performance in presenting plantations as entertaining diversions and enslavement as a civilizing institution that is even more necessary in the Orientalized Caribbean than it is in the US. Likewise, Howe's defense of women's rights in this narrative further demonstrates the coloniality of race and gender because those rights are not to be extended to the off- and non-white women of Spain and the Caribbean.[1] Finally, *A Trip to Cuba* exposes the role of the Hispanophobic discourse of coloniality in shaping the rhetoric of US national identity, Manifest Destiny, and Anglo-US racial identity in the work of a writer traditionally associated with progressive thought.

The most recent literary study of Howe's life, Elaine Showalter's *The Civil Wars of Julia Ward Howe: A Biography* offers an extensive look at Howe's private and public lives, at times strongly critiquing the author's racism while at others exemplifying what María Lugones terms as the "persistent absence of a deep imbrication of race into the analysis that takes gender and sexuality as central in much white feminist theory and practice" (187). For example, making a comparison that occludes the double burden placed on women of color, Showalter proposes that the writer's turbulent and confining marriage can be seen not only as a paradigm for the "clash of nineteenth-century male and female ambitions" but also as an allegory for "that other civil war of emancipation" (xiv).[2]

Howe was born into a position of social privilege in 1819 as the daughter of a banker in New York, who provided her with a more thorough education than was typical for white women at the time. Nonetheless, she struggled as an adult against her spouse's intense opposition to her efforts to write, publish, and lecture in public venues. Exercising his legal rights as the head of the family, Chev Howe insisted that the couple have numerous children and expected his wife to dedicate herself solely to the care of the children and the household. Howe secretly prepared and anonymously published her first volume of poetry for publication, *Passion-Flowers* (1853), although her identity as the author of the controversial text was quickly leaked. One of five volumes of poetry that Howe authored, *Passion-Flowers* caused her spouse considerable discomfort upon publication and is still interpreted as critique of his domineering approach to marriage (Showalter 115–21; W. Johnson 17–18).

Howe considered *A Trip to Cuba* to be important in establishing her career as a writer (Briggs 19). She remarks in *Reminiscences* that the "publication of my Cuban notes brought me an invitation to chronicle the events of the season at Newport for the 'New York Tribune.' This was the beginning of a correspondence which lasted well into the time of the civil war" (*Reminiscences* 236). Shortly after *A Trip to Cuba* was published, the Union Army song "John Brown's Body" inspired Howe to write "Battle Hymn of the Republic," which cemented her position as a public figure celebrated for progressive views. Having established her reputation as a writer, Howe considered the decade from 1860 to 1870 as "mark[ing] a new epoch in my intellectual life" (*Reminiscences* 304). Before the war ended, she undertook public speaking in defiance of social norms and of her spouse: "Women speakers were few in those days, and were frowned upon by general society. [My husband] would have been doubly sensitive to such undesirable publicity on my account" (*Reminiscences* 305). She began lecturing in philosophy but found even greater inspiration in leadership roles in numerous women's associations, including the New England Suffrage Association and the American Woman's Suffrage Association (Showalter xii). In her later years, Howe tirelessly travelled the country as a feminist lecturer, continued to write, and became increasingly celebrated as a symbol of "the triumphant spirit of a nation that had survived a terrible test" (231). By the time of her death in 1910, Howe's fame had eclipsed that of her late husband and, as Showalter writes, she had become "an international icon" in the form of a matronly, black-clad spokesperson for female suffrage and racial equality (235, 243). In the 1950s, Howe's granddaughter donated her family's papers to Harvard University, thereby uncovering new dimensions of the author's personal and creative life. Letters, journals, and unpublished creative works reveal the intensity of the author's frustration with her marriage and the restrictions placed upon her because of her gender and social position. The most recent scholarly articles on Howe's literary work focus on *The Hermaphrodite*, an incomplete novel about an intersex character that was discovered in fragments among her writings. As Showalter concludes, "In the twenty-first century, [Howe] is a new woman" (243).

While Howe identified both her spouse and motherhood as obstacles to her intellectual life, her partner's interests also put her in contact with progressives, scientists, and intellectuals in Boston with whom she might not otherwise have had long-term connections. Reformers, activists, and writers were among Chev Howe's closest friends, particularly Horace Mann, Charles Sumner, Henry Wadsworth Longfellow, and Theodore Parker. According to both Mary H. Grant and Showalter, Chev was the first of the couple to genuinely oppose enslavement (Grant 129–30; Showalter 104, 140–41). He was a Free Soiler and a member of the Secret Six that provided funds for John Brown's doomed raid on the federal arsenal at Harper's Ferry.[3] However, the often-cited problem of abyssal beliefs among white opponents of the institution of slavery were a factor even for a group that supported radical action against enslavement. As Showalter phrases it, "Their antislavery beliefs did not preclude racism. Like Emerson, Thoreau, and Bronson Alcott, each of them regarded black slaves as an inferior race. Abolitionism and white supremacy were not contradictions" (144).

Despite the popularly held image of the author as an opponent of enslavement, Howe's support for abolition did not take shape until shortly before the outbreak of the US Civil War (1861–1865). Grant comments that "Julia was not an enthusiastic abolitionist" and "was not an activist" for the antislavery cause for most of the 1850s (130). Antislavery came into her life with her spouse, and Grant proposes that her "coolness" towards the movement may have been in part a means of rebellion against him (133). Her negative opinion of abolitionists themselves also reflects her class bias. Showalter remarks that "Julia had indeed looked down snobbishly on the abolitionists, believing them to be 'men and women of rather coarse fibre'" (140). She was reluctant to meet William Lloyd Garrison because of his outspoken, radical discourse but then found him "sincere and benevolent" in person. Nonetheless, as Grant comments, "Julia held out against the cause. It was one area where she could exercise her intellectual freedom and let Chev know it" (133). Grant further argues that Howe participated in some historical revisionism regarding the timeline of her engagement with abolitionism: "Later, in her various memoirs, Julia attempted to shine up her reform credentials by dating her commitment to abolitionism vaguely. . . . [S]he always implied that she had been an early supporter. In fact she was not" (133). Grant dates Howe's committed opposition to enslavement from late 1859, after the trip to Cuba and the raid at Harper's Ferry, the latter an event that polarized the country even further over the institution and accelerated the onset of war. Howe's alarm at the proslavery faction's push to see Chev hanged for treason once his identity was known as a member of the Secret Six, along with her admiration for John Brown's conviction that he was on a holy crusade, finally pushed Howe into the abolitionist camp: "From now on, Julia would be an abolitionist without stint" (Grant 134). However, *A Trip to Cuba* not only makes it clear that the author was not an abolitionist in early 1859 but also that she held the deeply ingrained, colonialized conceptions of race, gender, and class that were embraced in much US national discourse at the time.

A Trip to Cuba, the third of six books the author published, traces her journey from Boston to New York, the Bahamas, and Cuba. Like Maturin Murray Ballou, Howe also inscribes herself into the tradition of travel writing and refers to the authors of previous narratives about Cuba. At the same time, however, she rarely characterizes her book as anything other than a travel narrative. The author's style is notably marked by ironic and self-deprecating humor that appears intended to deflect criticism that could be aimed at a female author for writing for the public. In contrast to Ballou's lofty invocation of Spanish explorers and conquistadores, Howe begins her text by interrogating the reasons for travel in the first place: "Why one leaves home at all is a question that travelers are sure, sooner or later, to ask themselves" (*Trip* 1). However, she quickly inserts herself into long-standing Western literary conventions by referring not to Colón and Cortés but rather to classical Greece in an ironic use of epic style: Describing the journey by train to New York, Howe remarks that "under the guidance of our fiery Mercury, we pass [the icebound trees] as safely as ancient Priam passed the outposts of the Greeks,—and New York, hospitable as Achilles, receives us in its mighty tent" (2). Having begun with a lament for leaving behind the routines, familiarity, and comforts of home, Howe claims with more sincerity a patriotic feeling of loss upon her departure from New York: "[T]he anchor is weighed, the gun is fired, and we take leave of our native land with a patriotic pang, which soon gives place to severer spasms" (2). This start to the text indicates Howe's establishment of New England as an ideal place with which spaces to the south can only negatively contrast. Writing for *The Atlantic Monthly*, Howe's literary and cultural references as well as her brand of humor suggest that she imagines a reader with sensibilities very similar to her own and also shed light on the expectations of her audience.

COLONIALITY IN NASSAU: BLACKFACE, ENSLAVEMENT, AND TROPICAL DEGENERATION

The ship's first port of call is in Nassau, and Howe's description of her brief visit to shore establishes the colonialized framework through which she views residents of the Caribbean throughout *A Trip to Cuba*. Likewise, Showalter states that Howe's narrative contains "scathing and uncensored descriptions of the Nassauese, Cubans, Creoles, and slaves. . . . Her most offensive comments were about race and slavery" (153). Colonized by the British, the Bahamas are obviously not part of the Spanish-speaking world, but Howe nonetheless characterizes what she sees by employing the logic of the discourse of coloniality. Her conception of the British colony largely prefigures her use of the Hispanophobic discourse of coloniality in narrating her stay in Cuba, but without invoking Orientalism. The author's characterization of the white residents of Nassau reflects her adherence to the belief in the racially degenerative effects of the tropical climate and suggests that the white inhabitants are no longer fully English because of their altered complexions and behavior. Viewing the "pale children and languid women" of the island, the author asks herself "what epidemic has visited the island and swept the rose from every cheek" (15). She further adds that the "Nassauese" are "a pallid race [who] retain little of the vigor of their English ancestry. One English trait they exhibit,—the hospitality which has passed into a proverb" (15). Recounting a visit to the barracks of the West India Regiments, Howe's description of a British colonel is suggestive of Hispanophobia: She refers to him as "a lean Don Quixote on a leaner Rosinante, [who] dashes up to us with a weak attempt at a canter" (16). Only one of the white residents of Nassau presented by Howe appears to have maintained his combined national and racial identity while his family has not: an English physician who has retained "his robust form and color in spite of a twenty-years' residence," while his family members are "without a shade of pink in lips or cheeks" (18). Concluding her visit to Nassau, Howe is overt in explaining that the tropical climate and diet alters the white racial makeup: "Physically, the race suffers and degenerates under the influence of the warm climate" (26).

Howe likewise demonstrates reliance on the discourse of coloniality in her anti-Black representation of people of African descent in the Bahamas, characterizing them as existing in an unenlightened state of nature in the uncivilized tropics and as conforming to the reductive stereotypes of blackface performance. Howe describes her initial approach to land in the Bahamas in a way that suggests equivalence between the island's tropical flora and people of African descent: The "earliest feature discernible was a group of tall cocoa-nut trees...; the second was a group of negroes in a small boat, steering towards us with open-mouthed and white-toothed wonder" (11). Howe then compares the Bahamians rowing the vessel to blackface performers, who were popular at that time in the US. The full quotation is as follows: "The negroes, as they came nearer suggested only Christy's Minstrels, of whom they were a tolerably faithful imitation,—while the cocoa-nut trees transported us to the Boston in Ravel-time, and we strained our eyes to see the wonderful ape, Jocko, whose pathetic death, nightly repeated, used to cheat the credulous Bostonians of time, tears, and treasure" (11).

While the allusion to blackface is brief, it offers important insights into Howe's ideas about race and identity, as well as those of the readers of *The Atlantic Monthly*. While this reference appears to be an attempt at humor, it nonetheless illustrates the ways in which the author perceives new places and people through ingrained ideological frameworks. Rather than present the white performers wearing blackface makeup and fake palm trees in Boston as imitations of Black people, Howe presents them as the authentic, original versions without fully convincing today's reader of ironic intent. Rather, this comparison indicates that both the author and her audience have established ideas of Black racial identity deriving from subhuman caricatures, and Howe proposes that actual people of color do not quite conform to the reductive model.

As Brian Roberts describes in *Blackface Nation*, Christy's Minstrels was the most popular company of its type in the 1850s, particularly because of their perennially celebrated composer, Stephen Foster (182). The company, founded by Edwin P. Christy and his stepson, George, had a decade-long run on Broadway and an international following. Unlike the earlier, rowdier characters, such as Jim Crow and Zip Coon, who initiated the demand for blackface performance, Christy's Minstrels appealed more to middle-class than to working-class sensibilities. As an 1847 *New York Daily Tribune* description of Christy's Minstrels indicates, their shows were considered a "'pleasing relief' from fashionable music and 'high-toned opera, for 'Negro melodies are the very democracy of music'" (cited in Roberts 184). Blackface companies like Christy's made claims to representational legitimacy, stating that they performed studied recreations of plantation songs and dances as well as those of "black riverboat workers and stevedores along the Mississippi" (95); their performances were accepted as being authentic and genuine expressions of Blackness (161). Nonetheless, these were "nearly always spurious versions of African American song, dance, and expression" (15).

Further, Roberts argues that many of the features of the early blackface characters originate from the stereotyped stage Irishman (95). This assertion is based on the career of Thomas Rice, the white performer who created the popular Jim Crow character after considerable stage experience in the role of the stereotyped Irishman. The parodic Irish stage character presents many of the stereotypes also associated with invented African Americans: "For artists, they were simian-like creatures, all receding brow, beady eye, and jutting jaw. For pamphleteers and novelists, they were mired in Catholic superstition and bizarre ritual. For Americans everywhere, it seems, they were regarded through the lens of old Anglo hostilities, as uncivilized and undisciplined, as very close in essence to African Americans" (96). Referring to "Catholic superstition and bizarre ritual" as well as "old Anglo hostilities," Roberts's discussion of the Irish stage character points to the North Atlantic discourse of coloniality as the source for this model of representation. Rice's adaptation of the Irishman model into the blackface Jim Crow resounded greatly with working-class audiences in New York who felt threatened by the changes that they were experiencing as white US citizens and workers (98). Further modifying the blackface figure on the stage for middle-class audiences, Christy's Minstrels intended "to play to the tastes of 'refined people'" by highlighting sentimentality (182). The addition of Foster's popular, nostalgic melodies added to the appeal for wealthier audiences. As Roberts explains, "By the 1850s, the American middle class embraced blackface" (18).

The transition of the stereotyped stage Irishman into the blackface character drives home the point that this figure is a signifier of negative characteristics with a changeable exterior that serves the coloniality of power. As Roberts puts it, the blackface character is essentially a medium for the expression of desires: "Blackface performance depicted black characters as bodies without minds" (20). As Roberts argues, these caricatured performances served to strengthen the coloniality that has shaped US society: Blackface "produced a form of racism that meshed well with the modern racial state" (Roberts 20). Howe's text takes the same images that operate to maintain the internal matrix of power to characterize identity in the Caribbean as uncivilized and nonwhite. Blackface-inspired types appear throughout *A Trip to Cuba*, such as the vengeful "imp of a black boy" on a sugar plantation and the "hateful black servants [who] flit past you like a dream" on her departing steamer (74, 247).

In addition to the reference to blackface performance, Howe declares that the "negro" of Nassau represents black "raw material," by which she means he has not been exposed to what she considers to be white values and culture. Not only does Howe's depiction here recall the Jim Crow blackface character but it also overtly invokes coloniality through the reference to Caliban: "[T]he negro among negroes is a coarse, grinning, flat-footed, thick-skulled creature, ugly as Caliban, lazy as the laziest of brutes, chiefly ambitious to be of no use to any in the world" (12). In order to be of service, this instinct-driven creature "must go to school to the white race, and his discipline must be long and laborious" (12–13). By way of comparison, Howe presents Afro-descendants from the US as being much improved, although still abyssally subhuman, by having lived among those whom she considers white and Anglo-Saxon: "The negro of the North is an ideal negro; it is the negro refined by white culture, elevated by white blood, instructed even by white iniquity" (12). This understanding of people of African descent as primitive causes Howe to make what later she refers to as the "heretical whisper" for which William Lloyd Garrison strongly criticized *A Trip to Cuba* when it was published (*Reminiscences* 236). The perceived condition of "the negro among negroes" in the Bahamas precedes Howe's proposal that enslavement of Afro-descendants by whites is necessary as a civilizing force: "Nassau, and all that we saw of it, suggested to us the unwelcome question whether compulsory labor be not better than none" (13).

Writing *Reminiscences* decades later, Howe unsuccessfully tries to alter the meaning suggested by her original statement. Rather, she reinscribes her colonialized viewpoint in the later book: "[S]peaking of the natural indolence of negroes in tropical countries, I had ventured to express the opinion that compulsory labor is better than none. Good Mr. Garrison seized upon this sentence and impaled it in a column of 'The Liberator' headed, 'The Refuge of Oppression.' I certainly did not intend it as an argument in favor of negro slavery. As an abstract proposition, and without reference to color,

I still think it true" (*Reminiscences* 236).[4] However, the appearance of the original declaration supporting forced labor in the context of a discussion of the subhumanity of "the negro among negroes" undermines Howe's later attempt at correction as well as her contemporary reputation as a proponent of racial equality and abolition. Moreover, she reiterates the idea that enslavement by whites "improves" Afro-descendant people several times in *A Trip to Cuba*.

Howe's additional comments on Afro-Bahamians continue in the same vein. She speaks positively of the infantrymen of the colonial West India Regiments while nonetheless reinscribing their savage nature: "[T]hese men, well drilled and disciplined, seemed of a different sort than the sprawling, screaming creatures in the other boats" (13). Her description of their North-African-inspired "costumes" marks them as "Oriental" and suggests that they are satisfying childish vanity in their military uniforms: "Their Zouave costume is very becoming, with the Oriental turban, caftan, and loose trousers; the Philosopher of our party remarks that the African requires costume" (17). Observing the men at their barracks, Howe returns to the idea that Afro-descendants in the US have visibly mixed with the white population to their betterment while those in the Bahamas have not in a characteristic effort at humor: In Nassau, "[t]he soldiers are black, and very black,—none of your dubious American shades, ranging from clear salmon to *café au lait* or even to *café noir*. These are your good, satisfactory, African sables, warranted not to change in the washing" (17). Howe soon reverts to the notion that Bahamians of color are not "of use to anyone": Reminiscent of Cuban proponents of whitening, she suggests that Europe should send "buxom Irish girls to outwork the idle negro women" (27).

Howe's description of women of color selling goods in the harbor particularly reveals the coloniality of race and gender at work in the narrative: "These may be termed, in general, as ugly a set of wenches as one could wish not to see. . . . [T]heir clothes are so ill-made that you cannot help thinking that each has borrowed somebody else's dress, until you see that ill-fitting garments are the rule" (23). Despite her later acclaim as a promoter of women's rights, she demonstrates little empathy in this narrative for the women of the Caribbean and thus exposes the myth that North Atlantic white feminism universally serves all women (Espinosa Miñoso 143–44). Anticipating her proposals for Cuba, Howe argues that what Nassau needs to become civilized and efficient can be brought upon the steamer ship from the US: "All these good things, and more, the States have for the Nassauese" (28). After their short stay in the Bahamas, the Howes proceed to Cuba.

HISPANOPHOBIC PORTRAYAL OF CUBA: BLACK INSECTS AND PLEASANT PLANTATIONS

Howe's characterizations of Afro-descendant people in Cuba reinscribes the coloniality of race and gender demonstrated in her relation of Nassau. When not presenting the "natural indolence of the negroes in the tropics," Howe's portrayal of active Afro-descendant people conforms to Roberts's assessment of blackface characters as prerational "bodies without minds" (20). The narrative does this by equating Cuban Afro-descendants with the flora and fauna of the natural world, as in the account of Nassau, and also with machines. Immediately upon arrival in Havana, the author again locates Afro-descendants within the tropical landscape. Describing her last night on the steamer *Karnak* in the Havana harbor, Howe associates the sounds of animals and insects with those of people of color: "Coolness and quiet on the water to-night, and heat and mosquitoes, howling of dogs and chattering of negroes to-morrow night, in Havana" (35). When visiting a sugar plantation, Howe likens the bustling quarters for the enslaved to an apiary: "All within the court swarmed the black bees of the hive" (76).

When not animalized as insects or other creatures, Howe often presents Afro-descendant workers as unthinking automatons. When complaining of feeling imprisoned in the hotel because a woman of her class and race is not allowed to walk unescorted in the street, Howe refers to the saving grace of the carriage rather than that of the seemingly mechanized driver: The "Angel of deliverance is the *volante*, with its tireless horses and *calesero*, who seems fitted and screwed to the saddle, which he never leaves. He does not even turn his head for orders. . . . [T]he black machine moves on, without look, word, or sign of intelligence. . . . [I]n the Cuban negro of service, dumbness is the complement of darkness" (44). Unlike the Condesa de Merlin, Howe does not attempt a portrait of the Afro-descendant women who proudly claim the Havana streets as their territory (*La Havane*, 330).

Whereas Ballou packages his Cuba text as a history, Howe's has more of the generic features of a travel guide: She provides information about roads, transportation, lodgings, and shopping for her audience. Having read other accounts of visits to the island, she arrives with the expectation that she will be able to witness such cultural events as a cockfight (157) or a "Negro ball" (126), both of which "Miss Bremer" was able to experience.[5] She reacts with frustration when she is not allowed either by Cuban custom or by her spouse to witness these events because she is white, female, married, and from Boston (157). Although he prevents her from seeing cockfights, her abolitionist husband does consider sugar and coffee plantations in Cuba to be acceptable destinations for his spouse. Thus, Howe visits multiple *ingenios* and *cafetales* available for touring during her stay. In describing them for the readers of *The Atlantic Monthly*, she generally does not take the reformist approach of Mary Louise Pratt's *exploratrice sociale* but rather that of a travel writer providing information for future visitors and, recalling the faux-plantation-style entertainment of blackface performance, a pleasant diversion for her readers (Pratt 155–71). When describing the town of San Antonio de los Baños, for example, Howe characterizes a local plantation as a top destination for visitors: "[The resources for travelers] of the neighborhood are various. Foremost among them is the *cafetal*, or coffee-plantation of Don Juan Torres" (70). Howe's visits to Cuban plantations offer little suggestion that she would be associated with opposition to enslavement within two years of her return to the US. Rather, recalling Alexis de Tocqueville's argument that the enslaved are unenlightened and thus contented, she subscribes to the view that enslaved Afro-descendants are ignorant, lacking self-awareness, and at ease (Tocqueville's attitudes are discussed above in chapter 3). Howe consistently remarks that the only sensibilities injured by the conditions of forced labor that she observes are her own.

Howe also provides a lengthy account of a sugar mill in the vicinity of San Antonio de los Baños. Unlike *cafetales*, which need the shade of various trees, sugar plantations require full sunlight and thus provide views that Suárez y Romero considered both monotonous and sad (see chapter 2 above). Likewise, Howe explains that the "points of interest here are the machinery, the negroes, and the work" (74). Her visit falls on a Sunday, so she is not able to observe the sugar-making process, although she does describe, as promised, the workers and the machinery. The Spanish engineer operating the steam engine meets with Howe's approval as being "kind and obliging," whereas the heavily armed overseer does not: "We found him a powerful, thick-set man, of surly and uncivil manners, girded with a sword, and further armed with a pistol, a dagger, and a stout whip. He was much too important a person to waste his words on us" (74–75). In contrast to Cuban writers like Del Monte and Merlin, Howe makes no mention of slave rebellions in Cuba, nor does she indicate a sense of imminent danger despite the numerous weapons carried by the overseer. Indeed, Howe appears curiously unafraid of apocalyptic uprisings compared to the other writers studied in the present book.

When she arrives at the "Negro quarter," Howe employs the previously mentioned bee metaphor to characterize the inhabitants (76). Unlike Suárez y Romero, who conceals himself in order to spy on enslaved Afro-Cubans and Africans during their few moments of leisure, Howe does not demonstrate any awareness either that her presence might impact those whom she observes or that she might be invading their privacy. The author comes closer to the attitude of the *exploratrice sociale* when describing the conditions of the quarters for the enslaved, yet she also positively assesses certain aspects of life there. She communicates a sense of confinement in describing the buildings: "We now entered the Negro quarter, a solid range of low buildings, formed around a hollow square, whose strong entrance is closed at nightfall, and its inmates kept in strict confinement till the morning" (75). Howe's tone changes to one of appreciation for cozy domesticity when describing individual cooking facilities: "All had their little charcoal fires, with pots boiling over them" (76). Nonetheless, the windowless rooms "looked dismally dark, close, and dirty" (76). The only privacy some captive workers can find for themselves consists of "a screen of dried palm-leaf," although they do not prevent the author from peeking in at the "board[s] with a blanket or coverlet" that serve as beds (76).

Howe next describes the nursery and the sugar-making facilities, presenting some of the most extreme examples of her abyssal understanding of enslaved Afro-descendants. Turning her attention to the nursery, the writer focuses on the lack of clothing and offers qualified admiration for the children: "The babies are quite naked, and sometimes very handsome in their way, black and shining, with bright eyes" (76). Reverting to animalization, she also remarks that when they are offered bits of fruit, the babies "scramble like so many monkeys" (77) to reach them. As a travel guide author, Howe warns that visitors to the plantation are frequently asked for handouts, but that travelers should not give in or their own sensibilities may be harmed: "[I]f you give to one, the others close about you with frantic gesticulation, and you have to break your way through them with some violence, which hurts your own feelings more than it does theirs" (77). After viewing the quarters and the nursery, Howe's group visits the "Sugar-house." Describing the sugar factory, the author makes a deeply disturbing statement apparently intended as a joke that reinscribes the perceived subhuman status of Afro-descendant people: "Above are the hogsheads of coarse, dark sugar; below is a huge pit of fermenting molasses, in which rats and small negroes occasionally commit involuntary suicide, and from which rum is made" (77–78). At last, she departs the sugar plantation with a rather frequent complaint, that of an "aching head" (78).

Howe visits another sugar plantation during her stay in Matanzas. Like the *cafetal* in San Antonio de los Baños, this too is a must-see tourist destination. Once more suggesting the stereotypes of blackface performance, the author's tone in describing this *ingenio* is lighthearted and, at times, mocking, as in the case of her lampoon of the limited English and intellectual capacities of her Afro-descendant guide (137–40). Approaching the sugar mill, Howe describes hearing joyful sounds: "A loud noise, as of cracking of whips and of hurrahs, guides you to the sugar-mill, where the crushing of the cane goes on in the jolliest fashion" (138). Howe's characterization of the work on a sugar plantation as "jolly" contrasts enormously with Manzano's reluctant descriptions of the violence, danger, and humiliation of working on the *ingenio* (discussed above in chapter 1). Following the "hurrahs" to the source, Howe observes enslaved workers perched upon the rotating wheel and whipping animals to power the machinery: The bars of the mill wheel "are dragged round by six horses, vehemently flogged by the like number of slaves, male and female. This is really a novel and picturesque sight. . . . [T]heir attitudes, as they stand, well-balanced on the revolving wheel, are rather striking" (139). Despite the considerable noise they make, these six workers "produced scarcely a tenth of the labor so silently performed by the *invisible, noiseless slave* that works the stream-engine" (emphasis added, 139). Finally, Howe briefly mentions visiting the cane fields, where "many slaves" were at work cutting cane, but without commenting on the intensity of such labor or the violence required to maintain it (139). Howe does not romanticize the sugar plantation as Eliza McHatton Ripley's plantation-fiction approach does, but she is not particularly critical of the institution beyond her lampoons of both the enslaved and the owners (Ripley's work is discussed below in chapter 6).

Cuban literature of the nineteenth century generally elevates coffee plantations over sugar mills because of their perceived greater beauty, the purportedly less barbaric workload for the enslaved, and the symbolic values associated with each type of plantation. For example, in Cirilo Villaverde's *Cecilia Valdés*, the corrupt Gamboa family embodies powerful sugar interests while the more benevolent Ilincheta family represents the liberal ideals associated with coffee growers, themselves more correlated with liberal France than with despotic Spain (Luis, *Culture* 5). A contrast in descriptions is also true for Howe's narrative, although without the suggestion of the abstract values of Villaverde's novel. The coffee plantation that Howe visits near Matanzas receives a particularly favorable review as being beautifully landscaped and supporting enslaved people who "looked in excellent condition, and had, on the whole, cheerful countenances" (167). The *cafetal* is approached by way of "a fine avenue of palms" and boasts many flowers as well as a "very pretty" plantation house (164). Howe is particularly impressed by the library, which she describes as containing "many good books in French and Spanish,—and in English, Walter Scott's Novels" (165). The author is taken to visit the plantation nursery here as well; during this account, she translates "los negros chiquitos" to English using a racial slur (165). The children and their young caretakers are kept enclosed in a structure that Howe refers to as essentially a well-ventilated cage: "[I]t is a house with a large piazza completely inclosed [sic] in coarse lattice-work, so that the *pequeñuelos* cannot tumble out, nor the nurses desert their charge" (165). She is convinced that the enslaved people are treated well on this plantation based on the "good proportion of their increase" (167).

Although she rejects a purely domestic role for herself, Howe again tends towards sentimental portrayals of cozy domesticity associated with women when describing the "the negro-houses" on this *cafetal*, and she does not shy from observing private scenes. In contrast to the previous plantation's system, the food here is prepared collectively for the enslaved people. Even with this service provided, many also cook for themselves: "We found little fires in most of the houses, and the inmates employed in concocting some tidbit or other" (166). During the time designated for rest or their personal chores, Howe observes "some of the men enjoying a nap between a board and a blanket" and, in an echo of Suárez y Romero's comment that enslaved women never get a chance to rest, notes that most of "the women seemed busy about their household operations" (167). Observing that the daily schedule allows for breaks at noon and at the end of the workday, the author notes that during these periods enslaved people "improve mostly in planting and watering their little gardens, which are their only source of revenue" (167). She remarks with admiration that the enslaved workers here formed a cooperative savings society and had amassed a sum of two thousand dollars (167).

The conception of the plantation as a place for entertainment is further highlighted during this visit as enslaved children are made to perform music and dance for the foreigners. While touring the nursery, Howe reports that "[o]n our arrival, African drums, formed of logs hollowed out, and covered with skin at the end, were produced" (165). The drums are played by two young girls, while two others perform a dance: "Two little girls proceeded to belabor these primitive instruments, and made a sort of rhythmic strumming, which kept time to a monotonous chant. Two other girls executed a dance to this, which for its slowness, might be considered an African minuet" (165–66). Howe's description of the music and dance is not quite as negative as Francisco Baralt's, but she nonetheless agrees with him that the music is "monotonous" and "primitive" (Baralt's views are discussed above in chapter 2). Howe offers reserved admiration for the performers: "The dancing children were bright-looking, and not ungraceful" (166). Just as she does not appear to recognize the multiple weapons wielded by the overseer as an indicator that the enslaved are not content to remain so, the author does not acknowledge the empowering functions of drumming, singing, and dancing as expressions of religious devotion, solidarity, and resistance on the plantation.

Whereas Howe relies on the imagery of blackface performance to describe Afro-descendants, she characterizes an episode of abuse of an indentured Chinese worker as comedic yellowface during her first visit to a coffee plantation near San Antonio de los Baños.[6] The appearance of an indentured East Asian worker in Howe's narrative is noteworthy in part because this labor force rarely appears in Cuban-authored fiction of the mid-nineteenth century despite their relatively large numbers in the second half of the century. Between 1847 and 1874, an estimated 125,000 Chinese indentured servants were brought to Cuba as a means of circumventing British efforts to stop the traffic from Africa, and the indentured Chinese suffered under much the same conditions as did enslaved Afro-descendants (Corbitt 130).[7] During Howe's visit to the *cafetal*, Don Juan Torres orders his "sightless Samson of a Cooly" to sing, dance, and fight off an attacking dog with a broomstick to entertain his visitors (71–72). Howe is upset by the mistreatment of a blind person, but again proposes that only her own sensibilities are affected: "The Chino laughs, the master laughs, but the visitor feels more inclined to cry, having been bred in those Northern habits which respect infirmity" (72). As Lisa Yun points out in *The Coolie Speaks*, being forced to imitate animal sounds to entertain contract holders and overseers is a form of dehumanization that is frequently mentioned in the testimonies given by indentured Chinese to the Cuba Commission in 1873 (153).[8]

HISPANOPHOBIC ORIENTALISM AND THE COLONIALITY OF RACE AND GENDER

Howe's perception of Afro-descendants in Cuba must also be located within her understanding of Spain and Cuba as uncivilized, uncultured, and immoral spaces. Like Ballou and other US writers of the era, Howe considers Spaniards and lighter-skinned Cubans to be racially different from herself, and she relies on the Orientalist mode of Hispanophobia to describe both the metropole and the colony. However, Howe's characterization of Spaniards is considerably more negative than Ballou's: Howe employs such terms as "oily" and "villainous" throughout the text to characterize them. Upon arrival in Havana, for example, she calls the customs officials "Spanish flies" that invade the ship: "As soon as we had dropped anchor, a swarm of dark creatures came on board, with gloomy brows, mulish noses, and suspicious eyes" (30). She proposes that the Spaniards view the fair "Saxon" passengers "with all the hatred of race in their rayless eyes" (30). Again like Ballou, Howe also summons the Hispanophobic discourse of coloniality in presenting Spain as the most fanatical and violent of the European colonizers: "[T]he first glance at this historical race makes clear to us the Inquisition, the Conquest of Granada, and the ancient butcheries of Alva and Pizarro" (30–31).

Near the conclusion of *A Trip to Cuba*, Howe offers a summary assessment of Cuba and concludes that the island exists in an earlier state of civilization than do Northern Europe and the US. The author claims that the upper-class islanders have no skill in the arts save one that appears in all underdeveloped societies: "One art remains to them, common to all early civilizations, first in history, first too in rank,—they are Poets" (232). Howe is additionally clear that she perceives off-white Cubans as belonging to an inferior racial category distinct not only from her own but also from that of Spaniards: On the island, "[t]he Spanish race is in the saddle, and rides the Creole, its derivative, with hands reeking with plunder" (225).[9] Moreover, Howe is critical of what she identifies as much greater racial mixing in Cuba than in the US, despite her earlier assessment that mixing with whiteness has improved "the negro of the north." The author states, "I have not seen in Cuba anything that corresponds to our ideal separation of the two sets of human beings" (216). The coloring and "tastes" of Cubans suggest to the author "their indebtedness to the African race" (230). Cuban "Creoles" have neither the "clear olive of the Spaniard, nor the white of the Saxon,—it is an *indescribable* clouded hue, neither fair nor brown" (emphasis added, 230). If they were to live "in the North," they would be considered "mulattoes" (230). Reflecting her own limited understanding of both the language and the culture in Cuba, she questions the use of the term *criollo* to describe a group of "coffee-colored" school children: "[T]hose whom we interrogated them called them 'Criollos,' as if the word had a distinct meaning" (231; see the introduction above for the definition of *criollo* in Cuban Spanish).

Scholars studying nineteenth-century female-authored travel narratives often propose that greater ease of travel offered an increased sense of freedom for middle- and upper-class white women (Alvarado 22; Schriber 264). In writing about Cuba, the liberty that Howe discovers is textual rather than physical: She delves into topics that were not then considered appropriate for the female domain. While claiming written space for herself, Howe chafes at the physical restrictions placed upon her as a white, female, and upper-class visitor to Cuba while nonetheless reinscribing the Hispanophobic coloniality of race and gender. As demonstrated above, the author does not attribute human awareness to Afro-descendants, and her discussion of female oppression by patriarchal society excludes Afro-descendant women. Howe additionally suggests that the upper-class and, in her view, off-white women of the colony are insensible to their treatment: "The Creole and Spanish women are born and bred to this" (43; DeGuzmán 4). For Howe, the cloistering of such women in Cuba is a sign of the island's Oriental nature: "They of the lovely sex meanwhile undergo, with what patience they may, an Oriental imprisonment" (*Trip* 43). Female travelers like herself who do not have male escorts or carriages at their disposal must remain in the hotel like prisoners: "[T]hey look a good deal through the bars of the windows, and remember the free North" (46). When she and her fellow female tourists are denied entry to the university because male students are present, they are told that it is for their own benefit (83); invoking another common stereotype, she writes that having women among them would apparently drive the "saucy little Cubans" to misbehave (83). The author finds that this episode explains why women are sequestered in uncivilized, Orientalized places: "Let me say here that a few days in Havana make clear to one the seclusion of women in the East, and its causes. Wherever the animal vigor of men is so large in proportion to their moral power as in those countries, women must be glad to forego their liberties" (85). For Howe, this behavior is "barbarous" and tyrannical. Hewing to the Hispanophobic equation of Catholicism with Islam, the author proposes that Christianity is the solution for the oppression of women in Catholic Cuba: "The Christian religion should change this, which is justifiable only in a Mohammedan country" (85).

Rather than express a sense of shared patriarchal oppression, Howe tends to mock the cultural and social practices of the upper-class off-white women that she observes. For example, Howe derides their use of white powder to lighten their faces without recognizing that colorism motivates such practices: Their *cascarilla* face powder "is formed by the trituration of egg-shells; and the oval faces whitened with it resemble a larger egg, with features drawn on it in black and red. In spite of this, they are handsome; but one feels a natural desire to rush in amongst them with a feather duster, and lay about one a little, before giving an available opinion of their good looks" (146). Howe portrays mass in Matanzas as an opportunity for dressing up, flirting, and exaggeratedly performing suspect and Orientalized religious gestures. The women in attendance appear to be dressed in gowns from "the ball of the night before" (141) and perform the sign of the cross multiple times, "conclud[ing] by kissing the thumb-nail, in honor of what or whom we could not imagine" (142). When the mass concludes, "[l]adies and lovers look their last, flounces rise in pyramids, the prayer-carpets are rolled up, and with a silken sweep and rush, Youth, Beauty, and Fashion forsake the church, where Piety has hardly been" (144).

HISPANOPHOBIC MANIFEST DESTINY: "FROM THE NORTH THE IMPULSE MUST COME"

Howe inserts political commentary throughout the text, although much of it is presented in her typically ironic tone. Departing the mass at Matanzas, for example, the author's consideration of the Spanish soldiers in attendance produces thoughts of US intervention: "[You are] musing on the small heads and villainous low foreheads of the Spanish soldiery, and wondering how long it would take a handful of resolute Yankees to knock them all into—But you are not a Filibuster, you know" (144). At the end of the text, however, the author leaves behind mockery and some self-deprecation in what she refers to as her "Chapter of philosophizing" to engage in a sustained commentary on enslavement, primarily as practiced in Cuba but also in the US South (237). Addressing the institution in the US, Howe's position is one of very gradual emancipation. She overtly states that enslavement must end, while again expressing a belief that Africans and Afro-descendants are not ready for liberty. Enslavement, she argues, will ready them for freedom: "Looking at realities and their indications, we see a future for the African race, educated by the enslavement which must gradually ameliorate, and slowly die out" (214). Although she does not subscribe to the extreme predictions of apocalyptic race war promoted by others, Howe nonetheless presents the same argument for racial incompatibility: "We see that in countries where the black men are many, and the white few, the white will one day disappear, and the black govern. In South Carolina, for example, the tide of emigration has carried westward the flower of the white population" (214). Ultimately, she proposes the logic of white colonial settlerism as an eventual resolution for the US South. Suggesting that racial mixing "is an indication of changes which will work themselves slowly" (215), the author also argues that the traffic from Africa must be fully halted: "Let the wounds of Africa first be stopped,—let her lifeblood stay to enrich her own veins" (216). While writing that she does not anticipate a quick end to enslavement, Howe points to the national rather than the regional responsibility for having allowed the institution to continue: Speaking as a New Englander, she writes that "the calm satisfaction with which some of us divide our national moral inheritance, giving them all the vices, and ourselves all the virtues, is at once mournful and ridiculous" (213).

Turning her attention to the island, Howe at times sounds like an apologist for Cuban enslavement. She proposes that the colony's laws are "far more humane" than those of the US and that treatment of enslaved Afro-descendants has improved somewhat on the island because of the pressure to end the international traffic from Africa (218–24). That Cuba should have better enslavement laws ought to embarrass the northern country: "Americans should feel a pang in acknowledging that even in the dark article of slave laws they are surpassed by a nation which they contemn" (224). However, she writes, the realities of the institution do not correspond to the "humane" nature of the laws. In addition to the corruption of officials, which perpetuates the institution, Howe also shares rumors of plantations "in the interior of the Island" that correspond more closely to those described by historians of Cuban enslavement than what she has previously related of her plantation excursions: These are "horrible places . . . , where the crack of the whip pauses only during four hours in the twenty-four, where . . . there are no women . . . not even the mutilated semblance of family ties" (220). In this passage, Howe indicates the greatest level of sincerity and sympathy to the plight of enslaved people in the whole narrative: "How can human creatures endure, how inflict this? Let God remember them, as we do in our hearts, with tears and supplication" (221). She further points to the high rate of suicide among indentured Chinese workers as evidence of the abusive treatment on plantations (219). While reverting to the animalization of racialized forced workers by proclaiming that she wished workhorses could protest in the same way, Howe nonetheless recognizes here the rebellion of suicide: "Self-assassination is, surely, the most available alleviation of despotism. When Death is no longer terrible to the Enslaved, then let the Enslaver look to it" (220).

Ultimately, Howe concludes that the inherent deficiencies of off-white Spaniards and Cubans make them incapable of ending enslavement. The colonists will not take action against the institution themselves: "It does not seem likely that the Cubans will ever by their own act abolish slavery. The indolence and mechanical ineptitude which enter into their characters will make them always a people to be waited on" (233). Moreover, she reiterates her belief in the degenerative effects of the tropics when proposing that the island's location is part of the problem: "Perhaps no nation, living below a certain parallel, would be capable of such a deed" (233). Finally, Cuba is governed by the tyrannical Spain of Hispanophobic discourse: "The past history of Spain shows to what a point that nation can carry insensibility to the torment of others" (221). Reverting to the notions that Cuban enslavement is mild and that the enslaved are insensible, the author claims that off-white Cubans suffer more at the hands of Spaniards than do enslaved people on the island: "[T]he Creoles seem an amiable set of people, enduring from the Spanish government much more than they in turn inflict on those beneath them" (221). Howe concludes her chapter of philosophizing with an expression of Manifest Destiny as the solution for Cuban enslavement and colonial status. She argues that only northern intervention will rescue those enslaved in southern spaces once they are enlightened by forced proximity to whiteness: "From the North the impulse must come. . . . The enslaved race too, gradually conquering the finer arts of its masters, will rise up to meet the hand of deliverance, having in due course of time reached that spiritual level at which enslavement becomes impossible" (234). However, this miraculous event will happen only when God wills it: "God has in His power swift miracles of redemption. . . . But we cannot call down these wonders, nor foretell their appointed time" (236).

CONCLUSION: BLACKFACE SENSIBILITY SUPPORTS MANIFEST DESTINY

Julia Ward Howe continues to be mythologized today as a social reformer who campaigned for abolition and for women's right to vote. Although it was criticized in the nineteenth century by activists such as Frances Ellen Watkins Harper, the white supremacy that infused much of the US suffragism movement is under increasing scrutiny by contemporary historians.[10] However, published scholarship on Howe's work still tends to overlook the coloniality of race and gender in her belated abolitionism and in her feminism, and to ignore *A Trip to Cuba* almost entirely. The success of Howe's Cuba letters among the readers of *The Atlantic Monthly* bolstered her long career as a writer and lecturer, which indicates that her sense of self as a white, female New Englander and her Hispanophobic perceptions of the Caribbean were shared by a wide audience. Further, the narrative characterizes Afro-descendants using the abyssal stereotypes of blackface performance and promotes enslavement as a necessary civilizing institution shortly before the author wrote the famous lyrics to "Battle Hymn of the Republic." Howe's proposals for resolving enslavement and the coexistence of purportedly incompatible races in both the US and Cuba endorses imperialism and the logic of settlerism by promoting the erasure of Blackness through racial mixing and increased white immigration.

Howe anticipates, yet does not prevent, abolitionist criticism of her commentary on enslavement in the penultimate chapter of *A Trip to Cuba*: "I feel that any one in the North who gives a mild, perhaps palliative view of slavery, will be subject to bitter and severe censure. But this should surely make no difference to us in the sincere and simple statement of our impressions" (236). The writer's attempt decades later to recast her remarks on compulsory labor suggests that, at a minimum, she was aware that her 1859 support for enslavement as a civilizing institution for Afro-descendants was damaging to her reputation. However, her promotion of the various modes of the Hispanophobic discourse of coloniality—particularly anti-Black racism and Orientalism—to characterize the Bahamas and Cuba does not undergo the same revisionist process. In *Reminiscences*, which was published during the first US occupation of Cuba, the author does not repudiate her abyssal assessments of the island's residents. Moreover, she also writes fondly about Chev's participation in the venture to annex the Dominican Republic to the US and in the colonizing Samaná Bay Company in the 1870s (*Reminiscences* 345–71; Showalter 193–95). Written for the readers of *The Atlantic Monthly*, *A Trip to Cuba* perpetuates the Hispanophobic discourse of coloniality through blackface-inspired characterization of plantations as places providing light-hearted entertainment, through the coloniality of race and gender, and through adherence to the belief that the US has been chosen by Providence to intervene in inherently degenerate tropical spaces.

CHAPTER SIX

LA GUERRA DE LOS DIEZ AÑOS AND THE LOST CAUSE

Eliza Ripley's Desengaño

Eliza Chinn McHatton Ripley's memoir, *From Flag to Flag: A Woman's Adventures and Experiences in the South During the War, in Mexico, and in Cuba* (1889), is a little-studied account of the author's Civil War–era flight from the Arlington sugar plantation in Louisiana to the Desengaño sugar plantation in Cuba, where the McHatton family attempted to prolong their antebellum lifestyle for nearly a decade.[1] Employing many of the tropes of US postbellum plantation narratives, Ripley's memoir projects a nostalgic version of a past plantation operating harmoniously under her benevolent guidance. As such, it engages with Reconstruction-era contentions in the US over national identity and the devaluation of racialized labor. Moreover, Ripley's account reinscribes Hispanophobia into its discourse of coloniality through its focus on a Cuban rather than a US plantation. Ripley's portrayal of an unfree workforce stratified by both race and place of birth as well as her recasting of major events on the island together reflect the hemispheric aspirations of former Confederates during Reconstruction while also propagating the Hispanophobia that was widely expressed by US writers. Suggesting that Cuba has been laid to waste by war in the same way that the US South was, Ripley leaves her reader with a vision of an exotic island in need of benevolent white supervision. Simultaneously addressing racialized labor in the US and in Cuba, Ripley's plantation narrative illustrates the continuity of the discourse of coloniality between Reconstruction-era formulations of white national identity and the hemispheric ambitions of the US in the late nineteenth century.

Although it is regularly mentioned in literary studies of nineteenth-century Cuba travelogues, *From Flag to Flag* has remained nearly unstudied within literary and cultural criticism. Only one scholar, Edlie L. Wong, provides an analysis of Ripley's text as part of her exploration of Chinese exclusion in US cultural production in *Racial Reconstruction: Black Inclusion, Chinese Exclusion, and the Fictions of Citizenship*. Contextualizing Ripley's memoir in Asian American studies and Chinese diaspora studies demonstrates that this late nineteenth-century text represents the intersection of multiple national dialogues over race in the US at a key moment (Wong 42). In the 1880's, apologists for enslavement were recuperating the image of the antebellum South as a place of romance and chivalry while undermining Reconstruction's efforts to establish racial equality (37). Concurrently, exclusion laws associating citizenship with perceived Anglo-Saxon whiteness were being passed to prevent both naturalization of Chinese living in the US and also further immigration from East Asia (Wong 4–5). Reading Ripley's text as an entrée into inward-facing debates over labor, race, and immigration in the late nineteenth-century US, Wong's study is strongest when it addresses Ripley's reliance on the tropes of plantation narratives and on the racialized exclusion of the Chinese in US discourse (42).

Wong's analysis would benefit from further consideration of the fact that the larger part of Ripley's memoir takes place in Cuba rather than in the US. *From Flag to Flag* does employ the devices of US plantation narratives, but it is also informed by the Hispanophobia that appears in many US texts about Cuba and by events that occurred on the island. Where Wong reads Ripley's text as a counternarrative to critiques of enslavement and forced labor in Cuba by such authors as Richard Henry Dana and Maturin Murray Ballou, I argue that this pro-enslavement and pro-indenture text notably overlaps with those by opponents of forced labor in its Hispanophobic understanding of colonial Cuba (36). Ripley's characterization of indentured Chinese workers, which is Wong's primary interest, is also affected by the distinction that the author perceives between US Black Americans and Cuba's Afro-descendant population. Additionally, Wong does not credit Ripley with a full understanding of the implications of La Guerra de los Diez Años (1868–1878). However, the size of the war, its significance for forced labor institutions on the island, and cues from the narrative itself indicate that Ripley intentionally relegates this major conflict to the background of her text. I build upon the work begun by Wong in Asian American studies by further analyzing Ripley's text with greater attention to its reliance on the Hispanophobic discourse of coloniality, its intersections with debates over Cuba following the US Civil

War, and the author's alteration of Cuban events to echo the mythology of the Lost Cause of the Confederacy.

Limited information has been published about Eliza McHatton Ripley's life aside from that which is included in her two memoirs, *From Flag to Flag* and *Social Life in Old New Orleans* (posthumous, 1912). The biographical note found at the conclusion of *Social Life* indicates that Ripley was born into the wealthy Chinn family in Lexington, Kentucky, in 1832, but was raised in New Orleans (E. R. N. 331). In 1852, she married James Alexander McHatton, also from an affluent Southern family. They began their married life together at Arlington, a Louisiana sugar plantation, where they lived until the Union Army invaded the area around Baton Rouge during the Civil War. Although while in Cuba Ripley was primarily occupied in the work required as the married co-owner of the Desengaño sugar plantation, Ripley wrote a series of articles that were published in *Hearth and Home Magazine* using the pseudonym Siempre Fiel (Ever Faithful) (Wong 41). Ripley's adoption of a pen name derived from proclamations of Cuba's fidelity to Spain calls attention to the question of the author's loyalties and foreshadows her shaping of Cuban concerns to her own purposes in *From Flag to Flag*.

After being widowed in 1872, the author remarried and relocated with her new spouse, Dwight Ripley, to New York in 1873. Along with her brother, Ripley was a co-owner of Desengaño from the mid-1860s until 1877, during which time the human trades from both Africa and China to Cuba were halted and not long before enslavement was definitively abolished in Cuba.[2] Ripley remained in New York until the time of her death in 1912. The author made arrangements for the publication of her second memoir, *Social Life in Old New Orleans*, the day before she died at the age of eighty-one.

US PLANTATION NARRATIVES: DOMESTIC AND INTERNATIONAL COLONIALITY

Ripley published her memoir of life as an international plantation "mistress" during an upsurge in the production of plantation narratives and of national readership of such works in the US during and after Reconstruction (Wong 37). As Jeremy Wells outlines, plantation narratives first appeared in US literature in 1832 with the publication of John Pendleton Kennedy's *Swallow Barn; or, A Sojourn in the Old Dominion*, which established a model for literary idealization of the plantation and that sought to locate this institution within a network of "nationalisms" making it at once "Southern" and "[US] American" (49). Plantation narratives continued in this vein until the Civil War brought an end to enslavement and Southern secession (50). While postbellum plantation narratives capitulated to the need to end the institution, they nonetheless persisted in reinscribing coloniality by romanticizing life amidst enslavement and in positing that the formerly enslaved, unprepared for freedom, posed a "problem" that needed to be solved. The paternalistic plantation master and mistress are represented in these memorializing works as offering the best model for the management of this perceived challenge. As Wells puts it, this renewed plantation narrative "still sought to romanticize and indeed to preserve the old plantation as a set of *relations*, a social order whose racial hierarchies were said to be better for everyone since they promoted happiness and harmony and since, in any event, they were natural" (original emphasis, 50). Writing about Joel Chandler Harris's Uncle Remus stories, Jennifer Ritterhouse similarly proposes that Southern writers and their readers in the 1880s were in the process of "developing memories of a plantation past" that in turn became instruments of white supremacy maintaining the colonial matrix of power (587–88). Not only did nostalgic representations of a seemingly benign version of enslavement aid in disenfranchising Black Southerners, they also served to strengthen and consolidate a conception of white identity at a national level (591).

As the century progressed, the US saw increasing immigration from Southern Europe and Asia, particularly from China, along with rising debates over national identity and belonging. Late-century plantation narratives modeled the ways in which the "burden" of managing a multiracial reality was carried out by white men and women "of character" (Wells 52). Although Caroline H. Yang does not use the term "coloniality" in her analysis of Harris's work, she nevertheless demonstrates the continuity of the discourse of coloniality from antebellum blackface performance to later plantation narratives in her analysis of a Harris tale in which the logic of blackface is applied to the Chinese. Whereas Harris claimed that minstrelsy did not represent the "genuine plantation negro," Yang argues that "[o]f course, it is preposterous to read Harris's Uncle Remus stories featuring Black *and animal* characters speaking in a 'Black' dialect as *not* participating in the tradition of blackface minstrelsy" (original emphasis, 2). In accordance with coloniality's devaluation of racialized labor, blackface sensibility approaches the Chinese with a similar racial logic. Discussing Harris's "Why the Negro Is Black," Yang writes that "the story's climax, which explains how some Black people became *Chinese*, allows us to see how one of the ways that the antiblack minstrel form lived on was in and through the racialization of Chinese workers" (original emphasis, 4). By proposing that they are mulattos with straight hair, the story discursively relegates the Chinese to the same devalued status held by enslaved Black workers before the war (10).

Ripley's text additionally engages with foreign policy debates in the US over southward expansion that were reignited shortly after the Civil War's conclusion by such events as the outbreak of Cuba's first war of independence in 1868.[3] Just as Cubans closely followed the US Civil War, the colony's own war was an event of significant US national interest.[4] La Guerra de los Diez Años (1868-1878) gave rise to extensive US debates over the possibility of intervening on behalf of the Cuban rebels and annexing the island, with arguments that tended to interpret the foreign war as correlating to domestic concerns. As Jay Sexton proposes, "American statesmen viewed the Cuban rebellion through a lens tinted by Reconstruction, the meaning of the Civil War, and an evolving and contested idea of national mission" (cited in Fleche 29). In a bid to further their causes internationally, numerous veterans of the two opposing armies of the US Civil war enlisted to fight on the same side, against Spain, in the Cuban conflict (Fleche 33). Viewing the issue of forced labor as unsettled in the wider hemisphere and reflecting their antebellum designs on the island, former Confederates determined to fight in Cuba for what they had lost in the US Civil War (28). For committed abolitionists, including President Ulysses S. Grant, the annexation of Cuba was understood as a means of promoting emancipation in the wider Caribbean (32). Divided over forced labor amongst themselves, exiled Cubans in the US supported all efforts to end the colonial regime on the island (34).

Although hundreds of US Americans fought in La Guerra de los Diez Años, Secretary of State Hamilton Fish convinced Grant not to act to annex the island (Fleche 28; French 76). Fish was motivated in no small part by his Hispanophobic conviction that the island's population was racially unsuitable for incorporation into the US (Fleche 43; French 75). Not only did he believe that no Cuban qualified as white, Fish also thought that there was a disparity between Afro-descendant populations in the US and in Cuba: "He believed the black Cuban to be inferior to the black American and therefore rejected the idea that Cuba could be brought into the union" (Priest 547). He appears to share with Julia Ward Howe the idea that "[t]he negro of the North is ... refined by white culture, elevated by white blood, instructed even by white iniquity" (*A Trip to Cuba* 12). Sharing this Hispanophobic view of Cuba's inhabitants, Ripley's text suggests that, while not ideal, Cuba's stratified and multinational workforce can be productive under proper management. Her narrative of Cuban plantation life downplays La Guerra de los Diez Años and suppresses its early connection to abolition, thereby illustrating the shared coloniality of domestic Reconstruction-era white supremacy and of the image of the US as the racially and morally superior power in the American Hemisphere.

COLONIALITY IDEALIZED: THE LOUISIANA PLANTATION

From Flag to Flag opens with nostalgic scenes of idyllic life on the Arlington plantation, named after Robert E. Lee's famous home, that establish the plantation of the US South as the ideal model. Ripley's memories of Arlington are those of a bucolic utopia: "Turning back a quarter of a century, I see a picture of peace, happiness, and the loveliest surroundings. . . . The roses that arched the gateways, the honeysuckles and jasmines that climbed in profusion over the trellises, the delicate-foliaged crape myrtle with its wealth of fairy pink blossoms, all contributed perfume to the breeze" (8). Ripley's romanticized portrayal depends upon the colonialized conception of enslavement as a beneficial and patriarchal institution for the childlike enslaved, who are abyssally characterized along the lines of blackface stereotypes. The appearance of enslaved people in Ripley's introduction to the plantation contributes to rather than disrupts the sense of peace and happiness that the author attributes to Arlington: During the autumn sugar harvest, "the fields were dotted with groups of busy and contented slaves, and their cabins resounded with the merry voices of playing children" (8).

Reminiscent of Alexis de Tocqueville's assertion that the enslaved are contented to remain so until introduced to the concept of liberty, the author implies that it is the approach of the Union Army rather than the conditions of forced labor that cause unrest among the enslaved population on Arlington and surrounding plantations. In Ripley's characterization, the effects of liberation do more harm than good for the unprepared Black population. For example, when many of the enslaved liberate themselves to follow the federal forces to New Orleans, Ripley suggests that their unsupervised behavior is immoral, irresponsible, and even unnatural: "Some went from Arlington, too; several women, in their eagerness, and desiring to be unencumbered, left their sleeping babies in the cabin beds" (45). Thus, the family's illegal transfer of enslaved people from Arlington to Texas is presented as a service to the enslaved, rather than as a means of preserving wealth that was also undertaken by other Confederates (Ferrer, *Cuba* 122). By sending them to Texas "in direct violation of military orders," the enslaved are saved from dangerous idleness and need: "[A] number of our negroes were sent to my brother's plantation, where work was provided for them, by which they could at least earn their food, and at the same time partially relieve us of an element of querulous discontent that was fast becoming dangerous" (51). Ripley later imagines them as happy to be put to work in the cotton fields: "[O]ur slaves were there at peaceful work on land cultivated on shares" (66). While pleasant memories of life on Desengaño, the family's Cuban plantation, appear in the memoir, they do not match the perfect beauty and peace of Arlington.

ORIENTALIZED BORDERS AND ISLANDS

Ripley presents her escape from Louisiana to Texas, Mexico, and Cuba as occurring without apparent forethought. However, the route they follow was also undertaken by other Confederates who fled across Texas with the eventual goal of reaching Cuba via northern Mexico, both of which were places that provided financial and other lifelines to the Confederacy during the Civil War (Ferrer, *Cuba* 121). Ripley's Orientalization of peoples in Spanish-speaking regions, which is central to the Hispanophobic discourse of coloniality, begins with her description of her experiences as a blockade runner moving cotton into Mexico. Revealing her conception that whiteness is represented only by English-speaking Protestants like herself, Ripley claims to be the first white woman seen by the inhabitants of Laredo, Texas: As they enter town, the "numberless little, half-naked *muchachos* . . . hung on to the traces, ran by the wheels, and caught on behind . . . for I was the first *white* woman and my attendant [Delia] the first *black* one the generation had seen" (original emphasis, 83). When she goes to collect milk from the public goat pen, Ripley is treated to "a courteous, deep *salaam*" from men "wrapped in blankets like Indians" (emphasis added, 84). Throughout the narrative, Ripley proposes that only whites speak what can properly be called a language and that they alone can intelligibly communicate rational thought. Moreover, only English is identified as a language; all others are referred to as "jargon," "foreign lingo," "mixture," and "dialects" (83; 142; 155; 171). In an example of this, Ripley acknowledges the mestizo identity of many in West Texas through a disparaging reference to their speech: "Daily I went to the pen . . . because I could ask for it in their mixture of Spanish and Indian" (84).

Narrating her family's relocation to the port city of Matamoros, Mexico, Ripley briefly refers to one of several events that revived US American expansionism after the Civil War—the French occupation of Mexico (1861–1867). During the Civil War, Confederate leaders unsuccessfully attempted to convince France to recognize the Confederacy by expressing support for

Emperor Maximillian I (Kelly 73). Writing well after the French were forced out of Mexico, Ripley nonetheless characterizes their presence in Matamoros as civilizing and welcome, especially after her experiences in the wilds of Texas. Describing a military review, Ripley celebrates the French while denigrating the Mexican soldiers: The gathered crowd "gazed upon company after company of brilliantly uniformed French soldiers, with the no small contingent of swarthy natives" (116). The author additionally savors the memory of "delicious French confections and wines . . . delicacies of which we had so long been deprived" that were offered by her hosts (116). Despite the "civilizing" French presence, Mexico proves to be a place of resistance for at least two of the enslaved workers that the McHattons had illegally transported from Louisiana. Delia and the family's cook and wagon driver, Humphrey, quickly liberate themselves from Ripley's control once they cross the border. Humphrey additionally tries to prevent the author from illegally taking Martha, who was also an enslaved domestic worker transported from Arlington, out of Mexico (112, 123). The McHattons next follow their cotton to Cuba.

Narrating her arrival in Havana, Ripley invokes a nostalgic tone when describing an Orientalized Cuba that echoes her idealization of Arlington, yet nonetheless highlights the otherness of the island: "The rising ground beyond, the *cerro* (hill) crowned all with its Oriental *quintas* and pleasure-gardens, and gradually faded away into the ethereal distance of the loveliest skies. . . . Church spires and belfries, very Moorish in design, diversified the whole landscape" (126). As with Arlington, this period of economic prosperity fueled by forced and racialized labor is presented as idyllic, but with an exotic twist: "How prosperous and rich Cuba was in those days! How happy the people! how animated and gay! We arrived when it was at the very acme of its opulence, when fairly drunk with the excess of wealth and abundance" (126). As Ada Ferrer explains, Cuba's slaveholders saw the Civil War as a far-reaching threat to enslavement and supported the Southern cause by facilitating trade in such goods as cotton, armaments, and rum for Confederate ships in the island's ports (*Cuba* 120–21). Confederate representatives, traders, and planters like the McHattons received a warm welcome. The family stayed for some time at the Hotel Cubano, which was "the Confederates' headquarters in the Cuban capital" (Ripley 126; Ferrer, *Cuba* 123). Ripley's portrait of escaped Confederates regrouping in Havana during and after the war is not one of desperation and defeat, but rather suggests a return to an elegant and abundant way of life (126–29). Like other Southerners who fled to various parts of Latin America, the McHattons attempt to recreate their antebellum lifestyle through the purchase of a sugar plantation, Desengaño (Ferrer, *Cuba* 123–24).

HISPANOPHOBIC HIERARCHIES ON DESENGAÑO

Wong reads Ripley's Desengaño as "a microcosm of the struggles over race, labor, and immigration that engulfed the US in the 1870s and 1880s," particularly as Ripley describes her efforts to control a multiracial labor force in Cuba (42). I argue that Ripley's formulation additionally incorporates the Hispanophobic conception of the island's inhabitants as racially and morally inferior to those of her own country. Where Wong reads the narrative as a "spirited defense of Chinese contract labor," I argue that it is a defense of racialized forced labor generally that reinscribes the discourse of coloniality. Ripley's embrace of Chinese labor is amplified by her disparagement of Cuba's enslaved Afro-descendant population as inferior to Black US Americans. The author's Hispanophobic logic is the same as that deployed by such opponents of enslavement as Ballou, Howe, Fish, and others. *From Flag to Flag* establishes a hierarchy of trustworthiness and capacity among Desengaño's unfree laborers according to their place of origin, as well as according to their perceived racial identity. Illegally taken from Louisiana to Mexico and then to Cuba as enslaved workers, Martha and Zell are outlined along the lines of blackface and plantation narrative caricatures as childlike yet faithful and useful family retainers (Wong 40). In contrast, the enslaved Africans and Afro-Cubans on Desengaño are characterized as abyssally subhuman, incompetent, and incomprehensible by the author. Chinese laborers, in conformity with the promotion of the international trade in indentured East Asian workers as a modernizing yet not fully human workforce, are characterized as being technologically apt, yet nonetheless neither white nor endowed with rational thought.

Throughout the narrative, Ripley reveals her dependence on Martha and Zell while nonetheless undercutting suggestions that they are fully rational humans. Before explicitly introducing them to the reader, she presents them as possessions: "[I]n May [we] moved our little belongings, Martha and Zell included, to '*Desengaño*'" (149–50). The author characterizes Zell as a Louisiana "creole," which indicates cultural rather than racial identity, and underscores his having been born in the US: He is "a full-blooded creole negro, black as ebony" (150). While portraying Martha as a faithful and steady servant, Ripley largely presents Zell as a farcical figure in the mode of blackface humor. The author regularly recounts the ways in which the young man's abilities prove to be essential for the family's well-being, but then typically counters this with an episode of comic relief that casts him as an object of derision. For example, Zell acts as a much-needed interpreter throughout the narrative. Travelling through Texas, Mexico, and Cuba, he learns to speak Spanish: "as the darky readily acquires a foreign lingo, it was not long before he could master enough Spanish for any occasion" (142). Having referred to her reliance on his linguistic abilities, however, Ripley then mocks Zell's pretensions to teach English: "He was considered such a *savant* that he applied for permission to give English lessons at the corner *bodega*: 'Dey'll give me four dollars a month jist to go dar and talk evenings'" (original emphasis, 142).

While she claims to have a maternalistic relationship of intimacy central to plantation narratives with Zell and Martha, Ripley does not suggest that she has a similarly close and caring connection with the Africans and Afro-Cubans enslaved on the plantation. The author does not present any of those previously enslaved on Desengaño as named individuals, and she attributes almost entirely negative and animalistic qualities to them. The only enslaved Afro-descendant in Cuba whom the author describes in any detail is the unnamed housekeeper and cook in residence upon their arrival at Desengaño: "Never can I forget the horrors of the early days at Desengaño. When the black woman, in a dirty, low-necked, sleeveless, trailing dress, a cigar in her mouth, and a naked, sick, and whining child on one arm, went about spreading the table, scrupulously wiping Royo's plates with an exceedingly suspicious-looking ghost of a towel, the prospect for dinner was not inviting" (151). Whereas nineteenth-century Cuban fiction often portrays enslaved women in domestic work as appealing in one way or another, Ripley textually associates the housekeeper with the grime and insects found in their newly purchased residence.[5] Ripley banishes the housekeeper from the house and the text after her initial appearance: "Until a tidy Chinaman was installed in the kitchen I was very dainty" (52). This provides a notable contrast to her stereotyped embrace of Humphrey's culinary skill in Texas: "The Southern negro is a born cook" (119).

For the remainder of the narrative, enslaved Africans and Afro-Cubans forced to labor on Desengaño are presented as a nameless, frustrating, and alien mass by the writer. Ripley appears to share with Howe, Fish, and others a belief that the Afro-descendants of the Caribbean are further removed from civilization, humanity, and whiteness than those in the US. Contrasting with her introduction of Zell as a Louisiana-born Creole, Ripley accentuates African origins when communicating the animal nature she perceives in the enslaved in Cuba: "The negroes, direct descendants of imported Africans, were more or less stupid and stolid, like 'dumb-driven cattle'" (180). Unlike her use of nostalgic scenes of enslaved people happily at work on Arlington in the opening of *From Flag to Flag*, the author does not provide quaint images of contented productivity featuring the Afro-descendants on Desengaño. Rather, they are presented as incomprehensible and incompetent workers useful only for their physical strength. She blames the enslaved for the difficulty that she has communicating with them: "The mixture of bad Spanish and African jargon of the negroes I never did understand" (155). Ripley claims that her husband, to whom she refers in the text as "Lamo" from *el amo* (the master), has to teach the enslaved workers what to do: "[H]e was in the field teaching the stupid negroes and dazed Chinese to dig and plow" (155). The author attributes the Afro-descendants' lack of productivity to mental incapacity rather than to resistance to the plantation owner's authority. Instead of suggesting a plantation narrative relationship of mutual affection, Ripley proposes that the "strange" enslaved Afro-descendants in Cuba "feared and distrusted" the McHattons and, unlike the many Cuban slaveholders who were afraid of uprisings, not the reverse (165).

Ripley is also witness to Sunday performances of dancing to the drums, without evident acknowledgement of the resistance and solidarity inherent in this activity. The author describes the music and dancing at some length, although she refers to the drums as *tombos* rather than as *tumbas* or *tambores*. Echoing Francisco Baralt and Julia Ward Howe, Ripley categorizes the beat as "monotonous thrumming," yet also recognizes its powerful effect: "The two *tombos* make a mournful, monotonous thrumming, beating time in regular cadence, and are accompanied by a dry bladder containing a few shells or stones, which is rattled by an old, tattooed African woman, whose cracked voice adds a melancholy wail, peculiarly penetrating repetition of the same dull sound, that lingers in the ear long after the vibrations have ceased" (187). The drums are played by "hard black hands, occasionally scratching variations with the tough thumbnail" (187). The author uses more positive adjectives to describe the dancing, using such terms as "deftly," "amazing," and "wonderful" to characterize the dancers' movements and ability to follow the rhythms. Despite this brief moment of positivity, however, she reverts to the discourse of coloniality when demonizing the drum: "[T]he diabolical *tombo* beat a devil's tattoo in my head" (188). Given that drums were not permitted on US plantations, Ripley's inclusion of dancing to the drum in her book suggests that it appears as exotic local color in the narrative and also reinscribes the perception of Cuba's Afro-descendants as uncivilized heathens.

CHINESE LABOR AND THE COLONIALIZED NARRATIVE OF TRANSITION

Although it is not mentioned in *From Flag to Flag*, the McHattons discovered in 1867 that Spain had finally ended the centuries-old human traffic from Africa to the island. A confluence of economic and political forces meant that the end of the institution was in sight from that point onward (see Scott). However, the search for alternative labor sources in Cuba had begun earlier in the century as part of the move to "whiten" the island and to cut labor costs. In 1847, Spain began the practice of importing to Cuba contract laborers, euphemistically called *colonos* or *colonos contratados* (colonists, contracted colonists), primarily from China.[6] As Lisa Yun describes in *The Coolie Speaks: Chinese Indentured Laborers and African Slaves in Cuba*, Spain did not initially have to contend with British efforts to end the Asian traffic as they did with the trade from Africa at the mid-century, and Chinese indentured servants "were easier to procure and cheaper to produce" at that time (14–18).[7] When the human traffic across the Atlantic was reduced, the trade across the Pacific to the island was still going strong. The notable Chinese presence in Cuba after the mid-century is much more apparent in travelers' accounts of the island, like Howe's *A Trip to Cuba* and Ripley's *From Flag to Flag*, than it is in Cuban fiction of the same era.[8] In this regard, texts by foreign authors become valuable sources of information about Cuba, perhaps despite expectations and even when taking the Hispanophobic coloniality of their approaches to the island into account.

As Wong points out, Ripley's presentation of both overt and de facto forms of enslavement was formulated for a late-century US readership that was "facing its own 'Chinese Question'" (Wong 42). The migration of free workers from East Asia to the US began when indentured Chinese were first being trafficked to Cuba, and increased over the course of the century. As the population grew, however, the US ratified racialized exclusion laws to prevent both further entry and also the naturalization of Chinese laborers, as exemplified by the 1875 Page Act and the 1882 Chinese Exclusion Act (6). Participating in what Yun refers to as the "narrative of transition" that was used to describe Chinese contract labor as more modern and less objectionable than overt enslavement, Ripley's memoir likewise promotes the use of Chinese indentured labor as "an efficient alternative to and modern improvement on the now out-moded system of black chattel slavery" (Yun 1–5; Wong 42). At the same time, however, Ripley's narrative seeks to "shore up shifting ideologies of race and slavery" at a time of intensified debate over race and labor in the post-Reconstruction US, which occurred simultaneously with heightened interest in imperial expansion based on the idea of moral and racial supremacy (Wong 20). Ripley's portrayal of the indentured Chinese supports what Yang refers to as "the false equivalence between the Chinese labor question and U.S. racial slavery" in US discourse, particularly as it illustrates the state-sanctioned means by which legally free Chinese were maintained in conditions of unfree labor on Cuba's sugar plantations (13).

The representation of Chinese workers in *From Flag to Flag* relies on a colonialized understanding of racialized labor that claims them as a more capable labor source that is nonetheless abyssally subhuman and that requires the type of white care and oversight that the McHattons can provide (Wong 43). The author proposes that the Chinese are quick to learn, although she refers to this as copying rather than understanding: "It is surprising how quickly and accurately the Chinese imitate" (Ripley 182). She presents Ciriaco, their cook, as the model Chinese worker. He is easily trained by Martha to reproduce necessary actions: "I never saw any servant so systematic, so methodical, so quiet, so solemn, so intent, so clean" (184). Ciriaco appears to be more automaton than human: "He was like a machine wound up when he kindled the morning fire, and run down when he turned the key in the court at night" (184). In accordance with the racialized discourse of labor at the time, the indentured workers are presented as being smarter yet physically weaker than Afro-descendants: "The Chinese . . . could not stand the same amount of exposure as an African, but they were intelligent and ingenious" (177).

As Wong points out, Ripley reiterates the discussions of Asian labor in the US at the time by associating the use of Chinese labor on Desengaño with the family's technological advances and modernization in sugar production (41). Even though Chinese labor was not new either to Cuba or even to their plantation, the narrative implies that the McHattons were the first to bring Chinese workers to Desengaño.[9] These workers play an important role in narrating the family's innovations in using farming methods and technology superior to those of their Cuban neighbors. For example, the staves and heads that the family imports to make hogsheads are "put together by Chinese in our cooper-shop" (257).[10] In contrast to "[g]eneration after generation of thriftless Cubans" who did not properly rest, fertilize, or plow their fields, the McHattons yield bumper crops of sugar cane by employing North American agricultural methods (253–54). At the same time, the author promotes the concept that the greatest productivity is achieved by combining the perceived greater competence of the Chinese together with the strength and hardiness of Africans and Afro-Cubans. As Yun explains, "contract labor did not *necessarily* shorten the course to abolition" (original emphasis, 4); rather, enslavement endured in Cuba even when combined with other forms of labor such as indenture. Ripley's presentation of work on Desengaño proposes that a distribution of duties among similarly coerced yet differentiated laborers could be managed efficaciously.

Even while deploying the language of modernization associated with Chinese contract labor, Ripley presents matriarchal relationships with specific individuals that mirror those she claims to have with Martha and Zell but not with the anonymous mass of enslaved Africans and Afro-Cubans on Desengaño. As Wong describes, Ripley's narrative treatment of Chinese workers "allows Ripley to portray herself as an idealized plantation mistress whose careful custodianship secures the coolie's undying fidelity" (49). The case of Epifanio, who suffers from a severe depression that Ripley refers to as "nostalgia," serves a particular case in point (Ripley 158–59). Epifanio is so miserable after his arrival that he appears to be quickly headed for an early grave. Under Ripley's supervision, which includes spoon-feeding, he revives "little by little" and eventually develops a talent for sugar-boiling as well as a devotion to Desengaño and the McHattons. Recalling her portrayal of enslaved workers as contented when occupied, the author writes, "Epifanio voluntarily remained at Desengaño long after his term of service had expired, though he had the option of returning to the home for which he had suffered and pined so long" (179). Not only does Ripley present herself as a maternal figure for the indentured Chinese but she also suggests that return to China was simply a matter of choice (Wong 50). However, Wong writes that the McHattons in fact forcibly recontract Chinese indentured workers just like many of their Cuban peers: "In the final years of Ripley's ownership of Desengaño, her son Henry increasingly relied on coercion to secure the recontracting of their Chinese laborers, especially in the case of their cook Ciriaco" (62).

While discursively equated with unfree labor in the US, the indentured Chinese in Cuba were legally free but were in fact held in unfree conditions. Ripley's account of colonial Spanish contract labor laws is reminiscent of apologies for the enslavement code in Cuba as altruistic and favoring the unfree workers: "The Spanish law, in regard to the management and treatment of Chinese coolies by the contractors for their labor, was very explicit and generous to the laborers" (176). Likewise, her presentation of the terms of and careful adherence to the contract suggests that the McHattons' employment and treatment of Chinese laborers was entirely within the bounds of fair laws. Describing a serious revolt of hungry Chinese workers on Desengaño, Ripley explains that reading the contract aloud, in both Spanish and Chinese, was an important feature of quelling the rebellion (174). After some use of violence, the local captain "then read their contract to them, Ramón repeating it sentence by sentence in Chinese" (174).[11] Elsewhere, Ripley explains the importance of the contract to the workers as well: Each worker "carried his contract on his person, and never hesitated to assert his rights" (177).

Despite the reliance on language suggesting modernization, Ripley makes clear that she considers the Chinese to be both nonwhite and uncivilized when describing their appearances during their rebellion: "[S]tripped to the middles, their *swarthy* bodies glistening in the hot sun, they rushed with *savage* impetuosity up the road, . . . brandishing their hoes in a most threatening manner, and yelling like *demons*" (emphasis added, 172). Ripley expresses amazement at the reaction of the workers upon having their queues forcibly removed following the uprising: "The soldiers with drawn swords, at the order of *el capitan*, walked up the ranks, taking each by the long pig-tail and with one blow severing it close to the head. How quickly they wilted! How cowed they looked!" (original emphasis; 174). In China, this alteration would be considered an act of treason and a capital offense: Losing the queue "forever severed the Chinese subject from China" (Wong 47). Noting the value of the shorn braids, Ripley feminizes and commodifies their hair by comparing it to that of a young Cuban woman's: "Black as is the hair of a señorita, that of a Chinaman is many shades blacker. Chinese hair besides, was a drug in the market" and was collected by Martha to sell (175).[12] Finally, she suggests that moral failings are a feature of the Chinese character: "In their own barracoon they were inveterate gamblers, and if two or more were seen squatting together, they were surely at their besetting vice" (189).

From Flag to Flag consistently reinforces episodes of racialized difference among the subjugated populations on the plantation, suggesting that a rebellious alliance among them would not be possible. One particular anecdote that Ripley shares is indicative of several features of the narrative's coloniality: mockery of non-Christian religious beliefs, a hierarchy of power and capacity that is informed by birthplace and race, and the use of humor to ease the racial tensions present on the plantation (Wong 46). In this case, the author ridicules the fear of ghosts held by both the Afro-descendant enslaved in Cuba and by the indentured Chinese workers while placing Zell in the role of comic buffoon unable to fully exert his limited authority over the other two groups. The motive for the episode is the apparent problem of the Chinese taking fruit at night from a garden that is forbidden to them. The enslaved Afro-descendants avoid the garden because they believe it is haunted: "[T]he negroes had a superstition that the [former] señora's ghost visited the garden every night . . . [and they] were mortally afraid of seeing her again" (193). Not having known the previous mistress, the author jokes, the Chinese were not afraid to enter the garden. Zell, wanting to eat oranges himself, decides to cover himself in a white sheet to scare away the unwanted visitors. According to the narrator, he succeeds in terrifying them: "The brave [Chinese] band broke ranks and fled with woful [*sic*] yells and shrieks" (196). However, Zell is unable to contain his own hilarity and becomes a comic display himself: "The overwhelming success of the pantomime so convulsed him with laughter that he rolled over and over on the ground, trailing the winding-sheet after him.... [T]he good-natured negro's unmistakable 'guffaw' rose above every other sound" (196). This anecdote suggests that Zell is authorized to take action against the Chinese incursion into the fruit orchard, but is not capable of fully enacting his plan. The Chinese are presented as being craftier than the enslaved Africans and Afro-Cubans, yet both groups fall victim to their superstitions in this episode, which is presented as harmless fun. The exploitation of all of these unfree workers is justified by the discourse of coloniality, and they are ranked in accordance with a Hispanophobic view of Cuba.

SPANISH TYRANNY RESEMBLES NORTHERN AGGRESSION

Ripley's narrative reframing of La Guerra de los Diez Años illustrates the role of Anglo white supremacy in US perceptions of Cuba in a way that reflects the interests of former Confederates while also conforming to the widely held Hispanophobic conception of the island. Much of the writer's residence on Desengaño overlaps with what was a significant war that attracted international attention, yet she dismisses it as a minor uprising. Wong attributes Ripley's attitude to her "low regard for Cubans" (50). While this is an accurate assessment, Wong also suggests that the author was not fully aware of what was happening: "[I]nsurgency and counterinsurgency transformed the political landscape of Cuba far beyond Ripley's imagination" (50). In contrast, I argue that Ripley intentionally reconfigures the war's size and importance because it immediately posed a threat to the institutions of forced labor memorialized by the memoir. Evidence from the narrative indicates that she very likely understood what was happening in Cuba as events unfolded. Ripley was living on the island during a long war with significant casualties, had friendships with Cuban and Spanish slaveholders, was in contact with the US consul, and received US newspapers. Moreover, *From Flag to Flag* was published in 1889, after the author's return to the US and the definitive abolition of enslavement in Cuba in 1886. Like many others of her generation who viewed La Guerra de los Diez Años through the lenses of both the US Civil War and Reconstruction, Ripley suppresses the abolitionism promoted by both sides at the outbreak of the Cuban war, diminishes the war's importance throughout the narrative, and ultimately casts Spain in the role of the abolitionist aggressor who lays waste to plantation wealth and productivity. Thus, Cuba's failed bid for independence is rewritten in an echo of the mythology of the Lost Cause of the Confederacy and in conformity with the Hispanophobic view of Spain as a tyrannical colonial power.

The clearest acknowledgement of the extent of La Guerra de los Diez Años in *From Flag to Flag* occurs in the introductory note, which connects the US Civil War with national interest in expansion into Mexico and Cuba. She promises the reader an exciting tale of international adventure:

> The years covered by this narrative were full of stirring interest. Civil war in the United States put the nation under arms from the St. Lawrence to the Rio Grande, and shattered the entire social and political fabric of the South. Mexico was conquered by the French, who, in time, were driven from the country, and the improbability of any European power obtaining a foothold there forever settled. A large portion of the Island of Cuba was for years under the control of insurgents; and not until a sea of blood and millions of treasure had been poured out, was a semblance of peace secured. (3)

The introductory note indicates the author's familiarity with these significant international events and also with the debates over expansion, national identity, and US influence in the hemisphere. Her claim that "a sea of blood and millions of treasure" were lost before peace was restored acknowledges the extent and the high costs of the Cuban war while also echoing the devastation and aftermath of the US Civil War.

Within the narrative itself, however, Ripley downplays the impact of the Cuban insurgency on her life at Desengaño. The narrative is dismissive of both sides in the conflict, and the references to the rebellion are often asides contained within other topics. For example, the first mention of the war appears within a description of the primitive nature of Cuba's rural inhabitants, especially those in Oriente, at the center of the uprising. To substantiate her characterization, Ripley relates what she was told by a Spanish army officer from his time stationed "in the extreme eastern part of the island . . . during some raids on insurgent camps" (147). The rural people observed there were "primitive, indeed, how near to Adam and Eve. . . . When they do not live in rocky caves, their abodes are rude huts. . . . '[T]hey toil not, neither do they spin'" (147). Likewise, she refers to news of skirmishes in a larger passage proposing that Cubans in general and Cuban women in particular do not read. In their censored daily newspapers, women read "simpering 'to be continued' stories" and "a paragraph relating the killing of, perhaps, one insurrectionist and the capture of two others, and a horse" (163).

The extent of the war's impact beyond Oriente becomes more apparent as the narrative progresses. Ripley and her spouse are especially disturbed by the war taxes that they are expected to pay to insistent Spanish officials. She suggests that the war is a minor event and has provided a cover for abusive practices by Spanish collectors: "The insurrection in a remote southern part of the island had furnished excuses for innumerable taxes, forced loans, and impressments of horses and cattle from the planters in every district. . . . Uniformed men lighted down upon us almost daily" (205). The former Confederates display envelopes from the US consul and a card with President Grant's name on it to bolster arguments that they are exempt from the war taxes as both US citizens and neutral parties. In a further sign of the war's effects, the Spanish colonial administration orders the disarming of all residents to close "one avenue of supply availed of by the insurgents" (207). In a reference to the ideological fight that accompanied the war, Ripley shares that the Spanish authorities claim that the rebel army is made up of career criminals (217). Adding to this her own disparagement of the freedom fighters, the author states that "[n]o doubt some did join, as affording a wider field for their daring, and others became purveyors for the rebels" (217). Ripley makes no mention of the famously multiracial make-up of the *mambí*, or rebel, army.

Ripley does not at any point acknowledge that the end of enslavement on the island was set into motion at the outbreak of La Guerra de los Diez Años or that an international inquiry condemned Chinese indenture in Cuba in 1873. In contrast, she rewrites the timeline of the end of forced labor on the island at the conclusion of her narrative. Unlike the US Civil War, the Cuban war was not fought over enslavement.[13] Rather, both sides promised abolition early in the conflict. Some belligerents genuinely desired full and immediate emancipation, yet others rhetorically promoted abolition as a means to an end. Leadership on each side of the conflict sought the participation and labor of Cuba's large Afro-descendant population, both free and unfree. Moreover, potential support for either Spain or the rebelling *criollos* from President Grant required definitive action against enslavement. The insurgents declared immediate abolition for the enslaved in 1869, and Spain passed the Ley Moret, or Law of the Free Womb, in 1870 (Scott 47, 65). Many enslaved Afro-descendants and indentured Chinese availed themselves of a variety of pathways of resistance that the war presented, which included joining the insurgent *mambí* army in significant numbers, seeking out maroon communities, and taking legal avenues to exercise the rights promised by the opposing sides in the war. Immediate abolition was not achieved during La Guerra de los Diez Años, but the effects of the war, resistance to forced labor, and an increase in abolitionist sentiment in Spain combined to produce the intermediary law of *patronato* in 1880 and then the suppression of the same in 1886. With Britain's support, China halted the traffic in indentured Chinese workers to Cuba in 1874; forced recontracting of unfree workers was also banned at that time.

Just as Lost Cause Confederates later erased enslavement as the cause of the US Civil War, Ripley divorces the outbreak of La Guerra de los Diez Años from the initial stages of abolition and from the additional pathways of resistance that the conflict presented for unfree workers. Rather, she suggests that "military exactions and ruinous taxation" were the only challenges to her final years on Desengaño (293). The author narrates her departure from the island before offering a condensed version of the decades-long emancipation process and the end of the traffic from China, incorrectly implying that these events postdated her ownership of the plantation. Her use of the passive voice suggests that the end of forced labor was imposed upon the island and not triggered by the rebellion: "The gradual emancipation of slaves was enforced, the importation of coolies prohibited, and, as an inevitable sequence, an untold number of valuable estates were abandoned by their impoverished owners" (293). Likewise, her account of the destruction of Cuba's plantations mirrors that of the US South during and after the Civil War.[14] Once beautiful and productive sugar mills have been destroyed by emancipation and pitiless taxation. Brito's plantation, Ripley writes, "is to-day a forsaken wilderness" (293). Don José's "magnificent" Josefita has become "little else than a waste of weeds and choked cane" (294). Corresponding at once to Hispanophobic representations of Spain and to postbellum characterizations of the North as the merciless aggressor, Spanish greed is blamed for the destruction of plantation wealth and productivity: "That superb province, whose natural resources are almost inexhaustible, has been bled to death by the leeches and parasites to whom her welfare and government were intrusted [*sic*]" (294). The final image of the island that Ripley presents suppresses *criollo* rebellion and abolitionism by blaming the devastation of a loyal island colony on the metropolis alone: "If Spain had ravaged her '*siempre fiel isla de Cuba*' with fire and pestilence, the destruction could scarcely have been more rapid and complete" (294).

Where plantation narratives typically conclude with a romantic reunification of North and South by way of marriage, Ripley's narrative ends with accounts of her ushering Zell and Martha into their postslavery accommodations under her continued benevolent guidance (Wong 51). Ripley describes her efforts to settle each into their own families and the ongoing relationships that she enjoys with them. Zell becomes a husband and father in Cuba and, with help that Ripley claims to have provided, obtains his documentation as a US citizen, is awarded his savings in the amount of "several hundred dollars," and remains on Desengaño as a contract worker (294–95). Likewise, she proposes that a loving Martha accompanies her back to the US and has enough in savings to buy land and build a house once she is married (295). As Wong outlines, however, there is a considerable amount of invention regarding the author's departure from Cuba and in her final accounts, especially regarding Martha (51–56). Ripley fails to mention that Martha had two children while living in Cuba, did not return to the US with the author, and threatened to sue over her illegal enslavement. Rather, with what appear to be loving eulogies and claims to friendship, Ripley textually reinscribes both Zell and Martha into a system of racialized forced labor characterized as beneficial and paternalistic (Wong 56). As Wong writes, "Ripley's narrative is as much about the illusory nature of contract freedom as it is about memorializing a romanticized vision of the Old South that sought to mask continuing forms of racialized labor coercion—indeed, the brutality of free labor itself—in the memory of the benevolent mutualism of the bygone era of plantation slavery" (56).

The final images of Zell and Martha not only lionize enslavement in the US but also consolidate an image of Cuba as a place occupied by nonwhites who seek continued connection with benevolent whites in the US. Martha alone, without her Cuban-born children, is settled into Ripley's narrative vision of unequal, pseudofamilial relations in the US (Wong 55). Zell and his Cuban family remain on Desengaño in the unfree conditions of contract labor and "in the same capacity as in the past, viz., *mandadero*" (295). Ripley proposes that Zell himself reinscribes his unfree status by signing off his dictated correspondence as "[y]our devoted and faithful slave" (295). Through Zell's continued mediation, Ripley also claims to maintain a friendly correspondence with the Chinese and Afro-descendants remaining on Desengaño. Zell's letters provide "all the neighborhood news of interest, and messages from the Chinese and negroes, among whom we had lived and labored almost ten years" (295). This characterization notably contrasts with her earlier claims that the plantation's Afro-descendant population feared and distrusted her. Needless to say, the author does not explain that Chinese and Afro-descendants forced to labor on Cuba's sugar plantations were largely held in unfree conditions until the suppression of the *patronato* in 1886. Ripley does not overtly reference annexation, yet she leaves her reader with an image of a Cuba lacking true leadership, of bounteous natural resources waiting to be harvested, and of a stratified workforce that can easily be managed.

CONCLUSION: HISPANOPHOBIA AND PLANTATION NOSTALGIA

In Ripley's *From Flag to Flag*, the discourse of coloniality simultaneously supports the romanticization of enslavement and the reinscription of Cuba as an Orientalized, uncivilized place. Desengaño supplies material for the author's memoir, but with its insects, climate, natural disasters, and purported lack of culture, it is not able to provide the elegant life that the family enjoyed at Arlington, which appears all the more ideal for the comparison. The author avoids domestic criticism for her romanticized portraits of forced labor through a redirection that conforms with the US imperial designs on the island that existed throughout the century. Ripley additionally suppresses the multiple threats to forced labor that occurred throughout her ownership of Desengaño and from the outset of La Guerra de los Diez Años. Thus, the memoir not only operates as a microcosm of the debates over racialized labor within the US in the late nineteenth century but it also projects the macrocosms of US ambition in the American Hemisphere and of the global traffic in racialized human labor. Ripley's open support for enslavement and indenture would appear to sever her from such writers as Ballou and Howe, yet the reinscription of the Hispanophobic discourse of coloniality in the texts studied here creates a shared conception both of US whiteness and of racialized hierarchies that unites them ideologically.

CONCLUSION AND AN EPILOGUE

LEGACIES OF NINETEENTH-CENTURY COLONIALITY

In these final pages, I offer some concluding remarks and outline the ways in which nineteenth-century expressions of coloniality continue to manifest in twentieth- and twenty-first-century cultural representations of Cuba's racial identity by authors from the island and from the US. Read in conjunction, the largely overlooked nineteenth-century texts from Cuba and the US about Cuban enslavement analyzed in this book expose the continuity of the discourse of coloniality as the matrix of power passed from sixteenth-century Spain to Northern Europe to the newly formed US. Although the terminology of this discourse shifted over the centuries from a primarily religious to a racialized taxonomy, the logic of coloniality remains largely unchanged. The central difference in these articulations of the discourse of coloniality derives from the perspective of those holding power. As Walter D. Mignolo and the theorists of decoloniality argue, where Spain claimed its providential role as the Christian conqueror and civilizer of Islamic, Black, and Indigenous peoples, Northern European and then North Atlantic powers would later claim this position and redeploy the discourse of coloniality against Spain and numerous other peoples and regions across the globe. In texts about nineteenth-century Cuba, the original discourse of coloniality and the Hispanophobic iteration come into contact and reveal that the differences between the two arise from the perspective of those in power. Although they differ as to who may be considered white, these texts nonetheless reveal a constant association between modernity, morality, progress, and whiteness; nonwhite people on the other side of the abyssal line are perceived as incapable of self-governance and as existing in a more primitive condition.

Additionally, these narratives help illustrate how control over the colonial matrix of power that subjugated Cuba shifted over the course of the century from Spain to the US, as well as the key role that Cuba has played in expressions of US identity. Despite the prevalence of abyssal thinking and coloniality in these texts, they nonetheless also reveal lateral relationships of activism that challenge the colonial matrix of power. Although they were characterized by early white *criollo* authors as representing a foreign, primitive population, Africans and Afro-Cubans have been at the center of Cuban cultural production since the earliest imaginings of Cuba as a nation. They have also been central to US images of Cuba and to the self-ascribed role of the northern country as a civilizing force in the hemisphere.

EPILOGUE

THE MYTH OF RACIAL EQUALITY IN CUBA

To borrow from the title of Doris Sommer's famous text, many of the national fictions of the nineteenth century continue to inform perceptions of racial identity and belonging in Cuba and the US today as coloniality is persistently reinscribed—although not uncontested—in cultural production.[1] In the years leading to the island's final rebellion against Spain in 1895, freedom fighters looking to unify Cubans created a mythology of La Guerra de los Diez Años (1868–1878) as an event that brought about racial reconciliation, and that Cuba had become a postracial, egalitarian society (D. Benson 9–11; Ferrer, *Insurgent Cuba* 122–38). Independence leader José Martí's essays, particularly "Nuestra América" (1891) and "Mi raza" (1893), propose a "raceless" national identity for Cuba that has been embraced in official rhetoric since independence, yet results in an erasure of Blackness because of its Eurocentrism. The segregation of public spaces that arrived with independence has historically been attributed entirely to the US presence on the island, yet scholars today contest Cuba's racial equality myth, the idea that Afro-Cubans were entirely disempowered in the first half of the twentieth century, and the proposal that racialized thought did not exist before the US occupation of the island in 1898 (D. Benson 11; 13–18). For anyone familiar with Cuba's nineteenth-century literary works, the latter is clearly not the case.

Nonfiction Cuban texts of the first half of the twentieth century demonstrate a greater level of acceptance of African influence on Cuban culture while also often reinscribing racialized thought. This is exemplified by the works of one of the island's most often cited twentieth-century intellectuals, ethnographer Fernando Ortiz, whose best-known works include an early text strongly influenced by positivism and criminal anthropology, *Hampa afrocubana: Los negros brujos* (*Black Sorcerers*, 1906), and a later essay in which he elaborates his theory of transculturation, "El contrapunteo del tabaco y el azúcar" (1940). While Ortiz later apologized for the racialized thought overtly expressed in the earlier text, Edna M. Rodríguez-Mangual argues that, despite increasing incorporation of African influence in his theorization of Cuban culture as transculturated, Ortiz was ultimately not able to overcome "the ethnocentrism that characterized anthropological discourses of his time" (27).² The work of Cuba's other famous early twentieth-century ethnographer, Lydia Cabrera, is also undergoing a process of critical reevaluation. Cabrera is the author of many significant studies of Afro-Cuban culture, particularly *El monte* (1954). Recent scholars are examining the extent to which Cabrera reinforces the idea that African and Afro-Cuban cultures are neither literate nor literary in her failure to acknowledge her reliance on written *libretas* produced by practitioners of Afro-Cuban religions and her fictionalization of Afro-Cuban folktales.³ While both Cabrera and Ortiz recognized African influence as an integral part of Cuban culture, Ortiz's promotion of a unified, *mulato* national identity as a means of eliminating perceived atavism does not appear to be very far removed from the previous century's ideological programs of Black erasure, and has been incorporated into the officially promoted, Martí-inspired raceless Cuban identity.⁴ Having elected to stay in Cuba in 1959, Fernando Ortiz has long held a position of special reverence in Cuban letters. Lydia Cabrera relocated to the US in 1960.

Following the 1959 revolution, Fidel Castro's government adopted policies intended to combat racism while also embracing the late nineteenth-century mythologies of a raceless Cuban national identity in order to unify all Cubans against external threats (D. Benson 30). Martí's interpretation of La Guerra de los Diez Años plays a significant role in this understanding of Cuban identity: The first war of independence "set up a series of national myths and approaches to raceless nationalism that later solidified with the 1959 revolution" (D. Benson 6). Since 1959, the revolutionary government has embraced the vision of the *mambises* as egalitarians, promoted the idea of a raceless national identity, and perpetuated the myth of racial equality. The revolutionary iteration of Martí's raceless Cuban proposes that there are no Black or white Cubans but only Revolutionary Cubans (Casamayor-Cisneros 1). Nonetheless, racialized thought persists among Cubans both on and off the island. As Miguel de la Torre phrases it, for many Cubans, "the primary criterion of social classification ... has been, and continues to be, colour" (103). The government's 1961 declaration that racism had been abolished made public engagement with these issues on the island impossible for decades. For Castro, however, the negative example provided by the twentieth-century US long supported the myth of racial equality: "Whenever Fidel was questioned about Cuban racism, he usually answered in typical Cuban fashion, by comparing it to the U.S." (De la Torre 105).

Another significant work of Cuban ethnography was published shortly after the revolution: Miguel Barnet's *Biografía de un cimarrón* (1966). Written in the 1960s by a former student of Ortiz's, Barnet's book narrates the experiences of Esteban Montejo, who lived through the end of enslavement, the final war of independence, and the 1959 revolution.[5] This work is at the center of multiple debates over accuracy of representation due to the often cited concerns regarding *testimonios*, to Barnet being the lone witness to Montejo's reminiscences, and to the fact that the work was published during the consolidation of revolutionary ideology in the 1960s. For example, Elzbieta Sklodowska's characterization of Barnet's process of making Montejo's story legible is reminiscent of characterizations of nineteenth-century slave narratives written down by white editors: Addressing both *Biografía* and *Me llamo Rigoberta Menchú y así me nació la conciencia*, Sklodowska states that "lo que está implícito en los discursos originales puede formularse solamente por medio de una exégesis escolar y ordenación discursiva profesional. Consecuentemente, en un discurso heterólogo la mediación editorial se hace imprescindible" (what is implicit in the original discourses can be formulated only by way of scholarly exegesis and professional discursive organization. Consequently, in a heterological discourse editorial mediation becomes essential; 83). William Luis argues for the possibility that Montejo's voice is represented in the text even while it incorporates Barnet's political agenda: "The political and economic realities of the republic and the Cuban Revolution conditioned Montejo's recollection, but the ex-slave may have included ideas of his own" ("The Politics of Memory" 479–80; Maddox and Steinkampf 74). However faithful to Montejo's lived experience it may be, *Biografía* is a remarkable exception to many literary works published in Cuba since 1959 in that the central figure and speaker in the text is a Cuban who is proud of his Blackness.[6]

The economic and political changes in Cuba that followed the collapse of the Soviet Union have created conditions in which intellectuals and writers on the island have felt somewhat more empowered to critique racial inequality and the silencing of discussions about racialized thought in literary and other discourses (D. Benson 19–20). While official rhetoric blames the Special Period for reintroducing racialized thought into Cuba, some limited space may have been established for investigation into the long-standing myths of racial equality and of Cuba as a *mulato* nation. For example, Roberto Zurbano's notable 2006 essay, "El triángulo invisible del siglo XX cubano: raza, literatura y nación," argues that the topic of race has been silenced in Cuban letters for a century (112). Additionally, Marcial Gala's novel, *La catedral de los negros* (2012) perhaps inaugurates a new era in Cuban fiction through its polyvocal challenge to the myth of racial equality on the island (Kabalin Campos 897).[7] At the same time, however, Zurbano was removed from his prestigious position at Casa de las Américas after the publication of his opinion piece, "For Blacks in Cuba, the Revolution Hasn't Begun" in *The New York Times* (2013; Maddox and Steinkampf 78–79).[8] Lastly, protests of a magnitude unseen since the early 1990s broke out across the island in the summer of 2021, in which both the participants and the primary victims of reprisals were overwhelmingly Afro-Cuban.

THE MYTH OF CUBAN RACIAL EQUALITY IN THE US

The myth of Cuban racial equality dating from the late nineteenth century, combined with an awareness of the island's significant Afro-Cuban population, has been of considerable interest to Black US Americans, who have represented their conception of the island's racial identities in a variety of formats, including literary translations, memoirs, and documentaries, over the course of the twentieth and into the twenty-first century. The absence of official segregation and rhetorical promotion of mestizo identities in Latin America generally when Jim Crow laws were in place in the US helped support the idea that racialized thought had been eliminated throughout the region for opponents of racism in the northern country as well. Additionally, the occurrence of lynching and other forms of racialized violence, as well as prohibitions against racial mixing in the US and the territories it occupied were unmatched anywhere else in the hemisphere during the late nineteenth and for much of the twentieth century. As Teresa Meade and Gregory Alonso Pirio outline, Black emigrationists in the first half of the twentieth century regularly viewed Latin America as providing a more hospitable environment in which to live (90). Encouraged by favorable newspaper articles about Brazil's lack of racism and the promise of subsidized immigration in the 1920s, numerous Black US Americans applied for visas to relocate to the South American country, but were denied because of Brazil's program of whitening (97). Himself a figure of interest for Afro-Cubans, Langston Hughes saw Cuba as a land of opportunity for artists and poets of color in a way that the US was not (Leary 150). A number of scholars have recently commented upon Hughes's friendship with Nicolás Guillén and his translation of Guillén's poetry in *Cuba Libre: Poems by Nicolás Guillén*. Vera M. Kutzinski, for example, argues that Hughes's "conservative approach" to translating the linguistically and culturally complex work of his Cuban counterpart in the end masks important distinctions between the experience of people of African descent in the US and of those in Cuba (139). At the same time, the translation also marks an important moment of recognition of an Afro-Cuban writer by a wider readership in the US.

Just as they followed the news of events related to the Conspiración de la Escalera and the wars of independence in nineteenth-century Cuba, many Black US Americans have paid close attention to the events and aftermath of the 1959 revolution, as well as to the government's denunciations of racialized thought and US imperialism. As Jafari Sinclaire Allen writes, there are many different perspectives held by Black US Americans regarding revolutionary Cuba. To write about these viewpoints requires a thoughtful and informed approach: "The relationship between the Cuban Revolution and blacks in the United States—whose intellectual and political traditions include socialism and the revolution but are more centrally organized as a fight against antiblack racism and for recognition as full (increasingly liberal) citizen-subjects—is very complex and demands nuance. The way we see Cuba ... remains conditioned by our experience as black people who have experienced racialized outer-national status, political-economic degradation, and noncitizenship at home" (56). In other words, Black activists from the US represent a spectrum of views on the Cuban Revolution. For example, Ollie Johnson writes that Malcolm X positively viewed the revolution in its earliest days as part of an international wave of uprisings: "Malcolm X saw the Cuban Revolution as part of an international trend of countries in Africa, Asia, the Caribbean, and Latin America fighting against the old oppressive systems of colonialism and imperialism" (268). In contrast, Carlos Moore, who was born in Cuba to Jamaican parents and who has also lived in the US, views Castro's denunciation of the northern country's racism in the early 1960s as an effort to manipulate US Blacks into supporting the Cuban Revolution and thereby establishing a stronghold in the northern country (Dunbar 304). Moore's autobiography, *Pichón: A Memoir: Race and Revolution in Castro's Cuba* (2008), relays his radicalization in New York City and subsequent persecutions not only by US law enforcement and intelligence agencies but also by Cuban security forces after his official break with Castro's government over its failures to eradicate racialized thought.[9]

As Jessie Lafrance Dunbar writes, members of the Marxist-Leninist Black Panther Party were also drawn to the antiracist and socialist agenda proposed by Cuba's revolutionary government in the 1960s.[10] Castro encouraged members of the party to seek asylum in Cuba when they were at risk of imprisonment in the US, and a number of Panthers accepted the invitation. Among those who became disillusioned because of the regime's opposition to Black nationalism and its silencing of discussions of race were Robert Williams and Eldridge Cleaver, both of whom departed Cuba after stays of five and seven years, respectively. Two former Panthers who remained in Cuba after seeking asylum there, William Lee Brent and Assata Shakur, authored autobiographies that were published in English in the US. Dunbar characterizes these authors' accounts as presenting "a more forgiving narrative of Panthers' asylum in Havana" than those shared by Williams and Cleaver (311). While there appears to be little criticism available on Brent's *Long Time Gone: A Black Panther's True-Life Story of His Hijacking and Twenty-Five Years in Cuba* (2000), scholarship on Shakur's *Assata: An Autobiography* (1987) notes that the writer says little about her life in Cuba and attributes this to her position of vulnerability as a political refugee on the island (Dunbar 313; Rolle 167). At the same time, however, critics do not seem to recognize that Cuban revolutionary ideology and censorship also have the potential to inform what Shakur writes about the US. The same must also apply to an analysis of Brent's memoir. For example, Dunbar appears to accept at face value Brent's argument that Cleaver alone was to blame for the author's nearly two-year imprisonment in Cuba, rather than the revolutionary government (311–12).

Twentieth- and twenty-first century technologies have also provided new formats for visitors exploring Cuba's racial identities both during and after the Special Period. Henry Louis Gates Jr.'s documentary about race in contemporary Cuba, "Cuba: The Next Revolution," is the second of four episodes in his series for public television, *Black in Latin America* (2011). In this episode, Gates visits the island with the goal of exploring concepts of race and racism in Castro's Cuba. The presenter is of course a preeminent scholar, and this documentary series for public television no doubt did introduce many English-speaking viewers to the diversity of racial identities in Latin America and to the shared coloniality at work throughout the hemisphere. Gates himself acknowledges that he is a latecomer to the study of Afro-descendant people in Latin America and is thoughtful in his approach to concepts of race in Cuba. However, as John Maddox and Michael Steinkampf argue, Gates's efforts to study race and racism in Castro's Cuba reflect some lack of familiarity with Cuban culture and history, as well as with the sophistication of the government's control over information on the island (72).[11] I would add to this that Gates also appears unaware in the documentary of the long history of interest that US Americans of various racial identities have demonstrated in Cuba, often because of their understanding of Cuban racial identity and discourses on race.

The financial exigencies of the Special Period opened the island to the foreign tourism that had not been permitted for decades. Normalization of relations between Cuba and the US in 2014 meant that significant numbers of tourists from the northern country travelling for pleasure could again legally visit the island, which they quickly began to do in large numbers. The images and interpretations of Cuba put forward by recent visitors through a variety of English-language formats, ranging from social media to travel brochures, reflect the continued reinscription of the Hispanophobic discourse of coloniality in representations of the island. Louis A. Pérez Jr., proposes that twenty-first century US travelers to Cuba view the island in ways directly connected to nineteenth-century ideologies of empire, or coloniality ("The Nostalgia of Empire" 13). While the image of Cuba as an exotic, Orientalized tropical island continues, the primary mode through which many casual US visitors comprehend their travel to Cuba now is that of nostalgia (21). For example, tourists as well as tour guides provide constant images and reflections upon the classic American cars from the 1950s that Cubans have kept operational by necessity as proof that Cuba has been frozen in time. As frequently described by the visitors who pose with them for photographs, the cars evoke a yearning for a decade that is typically portrayed in US culture as a golden era and that recalls a hedonistic Cuba populated by gangsters and movie stars. As Pérez phrases it, "The 1950s as the 'good old days' is uniquely an American memory of Cuba; the Cuban memory recalls the 1950s as a time of hardship" (21). The nostalgia expressed by contemporary US visitors for a place that they have never previously visited is instead "a historically conditioned cultural memory borne of prevailing mid-century tropes of empire. . . . The Americans return to Cuba with a presumption of familiarity, principally in the form of old knowledge with antecedents deep in the colonial ethnographies of the nineteenth century" (13). Pérez argues that the "people-to-people" mode of tourism instituted in 2017 did not alter the narrative of Cuba as unchanged since 1959 (21). Tourism provided a financial lifeline to the island after the collapse of the Soviet Union, but has also revealed that little has changed in the way that many US and other foreign visitors mediate their experiences of the island and its people as premodern, exotic, and nonwhite.

The return of largely white European and North American tourism to Cuba has exacerbated problems for Afro-Cubans, who are often excluded from jobs in the industry, and for Afro-Cuban women in particular, as is illustrated in the ways that some travelers describe the experiences of

Afro-descendant women who visit Cuba now. Indeed, this is one of the major criticisms that Maddox and Steinkampf raise in their analysis of Gates's Cuba documentary (81). Realizing that he is being "minded" while in Cuba, Gates remarks that he looks for additional Black Cubans to talk to. However, as these critics point out, he does not appear to see or at least does not comment upon the *jineterismo*, which denotes both general hustling and also sex work, that is often associated with marginalized Afro-Cubans. Accounts by some recent visitors to Cuba reveal the effects of the prevailing cultural assumptions on the island that dark-skinned Afro-Cuban women, particularly when accompanied by white men, must be *jineteras*, as well as the idea that all foreigners are white. Louis Nevaer, for example, writes of the experiences of two Afro-descendant women, one Colombian and one from the US, visiting Cuba in recent years who were mistaken for sex workers by Cubans and treated with hostility ("In Cuba, Black Lives Matter to No One"). As Maddox and Steinkampf write, racialized sex work that serves white foreign tourists suggests "Cecilia Valdés brought forward in time" (81).

The relationship between Cuba and the US continues to be more adversarial than not, discussions of Cuba within the US are made more complicated by the pressure to pick a side for or against the revolution, and the critique of the continuity of racialized thought is uncomfortable for many in the US and remains publicly forbidden in Cuba. While improvements have been made in material conditions for Afro-descendant people in both Cuba and the US since the nineteenth century, the crises of recent years have made it apparent that the colonial matrix of power continues to operate within and between the nations of the American Hemisphere, and this is reflected in our cultural representations. This book has been written with the hope that greater awareness of the operations of coloniality in the hemisphere can lead to better understanding of ourselves and of the people around us across cultures and languages, enabling us to make more informed choices that enhance rather than diminish our common humanity.

NOTES

INTRODUCTION

1. See Aníbal Quijano's *Foundational Essays on the Coloniality of Power* and Walter D. Mignolo and Catherine E. Walsh's, *On Decoloniality: Concepts, Analytics, Praxis*.

2. For more information about Cuban antislavery fiction, see Ivan Schulman's "Reflections on Cuba and Its Antislavery Literature"; Mercedes Rivas's *Literatura y la esclavitud en la novela cubana del siglo XIX*; William Luis's *Literary Bondage*; and Lorna Valerie Williams's *The Representation of Slavery in Cuban Fiction*.

3. Sophia Hawthorne's *Cuba Journal* (1833–1835; see Badaracco) and Richard Henry Dana's *To Cuba and Back* (1859) are among the limited nonfiction texts about Cuba to attract some critical attention.

4. Among the few studies of US-authored travel narratives about Cuba are Gema R. Guevara's "Geographies of Travel and the Rhetoric of the Countryside: Mid-Nineteenth-Century North American and Cuban Travel Writing" and Otto Olivera's critical anthology, *Viajeros en Cuba* (1800–1850), which includes narratives from both European and North American travelers.

5. See Boaventura de Sousa Santos, *Epistemologies of the South: Justice Against Epistemicide*.

6. For critiques of hemispheric American literary approaches, see for example Ricardo D. Salvatore's "On Knowledge Asymmetries and Cognitive Maps: Reconsidering Hemispheric American Studies"; Ralph Bauer's "Hemispheric Studies"; and Stephanie Kirk's "Mapping the Hemispheric Divide: The Colonial Americas in a Collaborative Context."

7. My use of "micronarrative" and "macronarrative" is inspired by Mignolo's use of the term *micronarrative* in *On Decoloniality* 107.

8. My discussion of these aspects of the Latin American critique of postcolonial theory here is based on Ricardo D. Salvatore's discussion of Mabel Moraña, Enrique Dussel, and Carlos A. Jauregui's *Coloniality at Large: Latin America and the Postcolonial Debate*.

9. See Elise Bartosik-Vélez on Colón's use of the rhetoric of empire and colonization.

10. See Joseph E. Inikori, "Atlantic Enslavement and the Rise of the Capitalist Global Economy."

11. As Borucki, Eltis, and Wheat also note, the first Africans to arrive in the American Hemisphere landed on Hispaniola in 1501, although they had sailed from Seville rather than directly from Africa (433n1).

12. See Mignolo and Walsh, *On Decoloniality* for an extended discussion of these three concepts (especially 135–52).

13. Castro-Gómez lists the names most often associated with the "Coloniality of Power" group: "Edgardo Lander, Aníbal Quijano, Enrique Dussel, Catherine Walsh, Javier Sanjinés, Fernando Coronil, Oscar Guardiola, Ramón Grosfoguel, Freya Schiwy, and Nelson Maldonado" as well as Castro-Gómez himself (259).

14. See "Chapter 4: Beyond Abyssal Thinking: From Global Lines to Ecologies of Knowledges" of Santos's *Epistemologies of the South* for his full discussion of abyssal thinking and the abyssal line, pp. 118–35.

15. See, for example, Frantz Fanon's *Black Skin, White Masks* (1952) and *The Wretched of the Earth* (1961) as well as Aimé Césaire's *Discourse on Colonialism* (1955).

16. For a discussion of the support for the López expeditions in North and South, refer to Tom Chaffin's "'Sons of Washington': Narciso López, Filibustering, and US Nationalism, 1848–1851."

17. The war from 1895 to 1898 has several different names in Spanish. In Cuba, it is currently called *La Guerra Hispano-Cubano-Norteamericana*, more accurately reflecting the participants and order of engagement in the conflict, and in Spain it may be called *La Guerra del 98* or *El Desastre del 98*. The US appellation does not recognize Cuban agency in the war.

18. For overviews of publications by US travelers about Cuba, refer to Alice R. Wexler's "Sex, Race and Character in Nineteenth Century American Accounts of Cuba"; Gema R. Guevara's "Geographies of Travel and the Rhetoric of Countryside: Mid-Nineteenth-Century North American and Cuban Travel Writing"; Louis A. Pérez Jr.'s *Slaves, Sugar, and Colonial Society: Travel Accounts of Cuba 1801–1899*; and Otto Olivera's *Viajeros en Cuba 1800–1850*.

19. José Martí is widely known for his criticism of the US and for his words of warning, expressed in an unfinished letter of 1895, to Cuba and the rest of Latin America about the northern country's ambition: "Viví en el monstruo y le conozco las entrañas" (I lived inside the monster, and I know its insides; *Martí por Martí* 361).

20. Spain held the territory of the Louisiana Purchase from 1763 to 1803, when it briefly returned to France. At the conclusion of the war with Mexico in 1848, the US took over the northern half of Mexico.

21. See also Richard L. Kagan, *The Spanish Craze: America's Fascination with the Hispanic World, 1779–1939*.

22. The term *La leyenda negra* (the Black Legend) first appeared in print in 1914 with Julián Juderías's *La leyenda negra: Estudios acerca del concepto de España en el extranjero*, and has been in continued use since that time.

23. See G. Cristina Mora, *Making Hispanics*, for a history of this term and its importance in the US.

24. Havard defines *Hispanism* as "studying Hispanic culture in an organic framework and to that framework's conservative tendencies" (10). This is not always the case for this term, which is used in a variety of contexts. See *Ideologies of Hispanism*, edited by Mabel Moraña and Nicholas Spadaccini, for a wide variety of approaches to this term.

25. See, for example, Walter D. Mignolo's "*Islamophobia/Hispanophobia*: The (Re) Configuration of the Racial Imperial/Colonial Matrix," and Yolanda Rodríguez Pérez's *Literary Hispanophobia and Hispanophilia in Britain and the Low Countries (1550–1850)*.

26. Esteban Montejo's testimony, *Biografía de un cimarrón* (1966), also narrates Cuban enslavement, but Montejo's oral testimony was not compiled and edited by ethnographer Miguel Barnet until the 1960s.

CHAPTER ONE: THE MANY DISCOURSES OF JUAN FRANCISCO MANZANO: DISRUPTIONS TO COLONIALITY IN *AUTOBIOGRAFÍA DEL ESCLAVO POETA*

1. This is the title that William Luis adopts for *Autobiografía del esclavo poeta y otros escritos*. Manzano's original was not titled.

2. Future investigation into accounts of enslavement in Cuba will also benefit from consideration of the *Cuba Commission Report* of 1876, which records the testimonies of Chinese coolies held in de facto slavery on the island. Chapter 6 addresses coolie labor in more detail.

3. I follow the chronology for Manzano's life proposed by Schulman (Introduction 31–32). *Marquesa* is *marchioness* in English.

4. Abolitionist Richard Robert Madden served as judge arbitrator in the mixed court of commission and superintendent of liberated Africans in Havana from 1836 to 1839.

5. Madden's abridged translation is titled *Poems by a Slave in the Island of Cuba, Recently Liberated; Translated from the Spanish by R. R. Madden, M.D. with the History of the Early Life of the Negro Poet, Written by Himself; To which are Prefixed Two Pieces Descriptive of Cuban Slavery and the Slave-Traffic*.

6. See modernized editions by Schulman and Evelyn Picon Garfield's *Autobiography of a Slave/Autobiografía de un esclavo* (1996), and Abdeslam Azourgarh's *Juan Francisco Manzano: Esclavo poeta en la isla de Cuba* (2000). See the introduction to Luis's 2007 edition for a thorough history of the various editions of the text.

7. My citations are directly taken from Luis's transcription, including his system of marking. See Luis, ed., *Autobiografía del esclavo poeta*, 293–96, and especially 296, for clarification.

8. Luis argues for the reverse flow of influence: "Manzano's text influenced Suárez y Romero's [*Francisco: El ingenio o las delicias del campo*] and certainly the creation of his protagonist, Francisco, named after the slave he knew so well. It is also possible that Manzano was an inspiration for Tanco when he wrote his 'Historia de Francisco' even though it pertains to a twelve-year-old slave" (*Literary Bondage* 39).

9. An exception to this Gómez de Avellaneda's Sab, who is not the narrator but speaks extensively in the novel and writes a letter condemning slavery and misogyny (263–72). Sab is also one of very few literate enslaved characters in Cuban antislavery fiction.

10. See, for example, Jeffrey Gunn's "Literacy and the Humanizing Project in Olaudah Equiano's *The Interesting Narrative* and Ottobah Cugoano's *Thoughts and Sentiments*," and John Hansen's "Frederick Douglass's Journey from Slave to Freeman: An Acquisition and Mastery of Language, Rhetoric, and Power via the *Narrative*."

11. All translations are mine unless otherwise indicated. I do not attempt to replicate Manzano's spelling in my translations, but instead use standard English. Punctuation has not been standardized in English in an effort to capture the orality of Manzano's original narration. Honorifics remain in the original language. Ellipses are added unless otherwise indicated.

12. Manzano also remarks that his godparents did not want him to learn to write, so he worked by memory when composing his poems: "[C]uando yo tenia dose años ya abia compuesto muchas desimas de memorias causa p^r. q^e. mis padrinos no querian q^e. aprendiese a escribir" (When I was twelve years old I had already composed many *décimas* by memory because my godparents did not want me to learn how to write; 304). A *décima* is a poem consisting of a ten-line stanza.

13. I am connecting the terms *class* and *race* as *class/race* because they are intertwined in the social pyramid of colonial Cuba.

14. *Criado/a de razón* is a term for a domestic servant, such as a personal maid. Its use in the context of slavery is suggestive, however, as it implies that household servants have *razón* (reason) where agricultural workers do not.

15. The one instance in which Manzano becomes angry occurs under circumstances that are culturally permissible: He turns from a lamb into a lion when his mother is struck by the overseer (311–12).

16. The fact that Manzano primarily focuses on two female slaveholders was raised by a participant at the Calibans and Caribbeanisms: Spaces and Topographies Conference at Marquette University, April 2018, whom I would like to thank.

17. Robert Richmond Ellis reads some of the silences in Manzano's autobiography as episodes of sexual violence perpetrated by male overseers (423).

18. See also Lorna Valerie Williams, *The Representation of Slavery in Cuban Fiction* 42, and Ellis 431.

19. See, for example, Yolanda Pierce, "Redeeming Bondage: The Captivity Narrative and the Spiritual Autobiography in the African American Slave Narrative Tradition."

20. See chapters 2 and 4 of Pettway's *Cuban Literature in the Age of Black Insurrection*.

21. Pettway suggests that Manzano's experiences on the plantation would have exposed him to African and Afro-Cuban belief systems: "Manzano's life on a Matanzas plantation peopled with African labor, his frequent travels from Havana to Matanzas, strongly suggests that his ideas about the saints and their power to reward devotion and punish neglect were consistent with African ideas in circulation long before he was born" (143).

22. I found only one article on this topic, Julio Ramos's "The Law Is Other: Literature and the Constitution of the Juridical Subject in Nineteenth-Century Cuba."

23. All citations reproduce Luis's transcription, including his system of marking. See note 7 above.

24. See De la Fuente on the practice of *coartación* in Cuba from the late sixteenth through the nineteenth century (358, 365–66).

25. Pettway refers to the time after Manzano's mother's death as an existential crisis (133).

26. I opt to use the lowercase "b" in "black" in this translation to reflect more closely the sense of the Spanish citation.

27. See, for example, Schulman, Introduction 9 and Molloy 40–41. Branche counters this characterization by pointing out Manzano's escape attempts (81).

28. See Gema R. Guevara's "Inexacting Whiteness: *Blanqueamiento* as a Gender-Specific Trope in the Nineteenth Century" and Sara Rosell's "'Cecilia Valdés' de Villaverde a Arenas: La (re)creación del mito de la mulata."

29. Branche refers to the *Autobiografía* as "literary passing" ("'Mulato entre negros'" 83).

CHAPTER TWO: *COSTUMBRISMO CRIOLLO*: ENLIGHTENMENT IDEALS AND THE DISCOURSE OF COLONIALITY

1. *Costumbrismo* is a term that is not easily translated. "Local color writing" probably comes the closest to capturing the meaning of the term in Spanish, but it should also be understood to include satire and social criticism.

2. *Baile de cuna* literally means "cradle dance"; it figuratively means a ball for Afro-descendants from varying backgrounds and with varying skin tones.

3. *La tumba francesa* was proclaimed by UNESCO as an Intangible Cultural Heritage of Humanity in 2003 (*La tumba francesa*).

4. Méndez Rodenas refers to the concept outlined in Fernando Ortiz's well-known work, *Contrapunteo cubano del tabaco y el azúcar*.

5. For example, see Luis, *Literary Bondage* 43–58, and Claudette M. Williams's "Plumbing the Murky Depths: Anselmo Suárez y Romero's *Francisco*" for antislavery readings of *Francisco*.

6. See also Bueno, Prólogo xx–xxi, and Jorge Castellanos and Isabel Castellanos, *El negro en Cuba 1845–1959* 59–68.

7. I have translated "los cuartos de prima y de madrugada" literally to try to maintain the reference to canonical hours of prayer in Suárez y Romero's original text. Prime is around 6:00 a.m.

8. For more on the stereotyping of African groups by origin and characteristics as a means of controlling enslaved and colonial populations, see Guanche 48–60 and Ocasio 45.

9. "El cementerio del ingenio" was first published in the 1864 collection *Ofrenda al bazar de la Real Casa de Beneficencia* (*Offering at the Bazaar of the Royal House of Charity*; Ocasio 44).

10. Ocasio translates *carabelas* as "Africans of the same nation" (48).

11. See María Poumier Taquechel, "El suicidio esclavo en Cuba en los años 1840" for information on suicide among enslaved Afro-descendants, and Lisa Yun, *The Coolie Speaks*, for information on suicide among Chinese coolies.

12. Triay is briefly mentioned in Luis's *Literary Bondage* 44, and in Raquel Gutiérrez Sebastián's "Sabores, sones y trazos del costumbrismo cubano" 45.

13. See Rebecca Scott, *Slave Emancipation in Cuba*.

14. See José Martí, *Nuestra América, edición crítica*. Kevin Meehan and Paul B. Miller's "Martí, Schomburg y la cuestión racial en las Américas" addresses the marginalization of Blackness in Martí's raceless vision of Cuba and Latin America.

15. See Jill Lane's *Blackface Cuba, 1840–1895* for more on blackface in Cuban theater and in *teatro bufo*.

16. See Pilar Pérez-Fuentes and Lola Valverde, "La población de La Habana a mediados del siglo XIX: Relaciones sexuales y matrimonio" for a description of the divisions created by the city walls.

17. Ocasio translates *curro* as "thug," which is certainly how they are portrayed (132). However, *curro* also distinguishes this group as one that was first transculturated in Spain for generations and then in Cuba. See Alberto Yanuzzi, "Los negros curros del manglar según Fernando Ortiz," and Fernando Ortiz, *Los negros curros*, for more information on this sector of nineteenth-century Cuba's populace.

18. Triay uses the spelling *volante*, rather than *volanta*. The Real Academia Española accepts both spellings for this type of carriage. See *Diccionario*, under "volante."

CHAPTER THREE: THE TYRANNIES OF LIBERTY AND EQUALITY: THE CONDESA DE MERLIN'S COLONIALIST TRAVELS

1. For more on the accusations of plagiarism by nineteenth-century Cuban writers, see Salvador Bueno's "Un libro polémico: *El Viaje a la Habana* de la condesa de Merlin" and Adriana Méndez Rodenas's *Gender and Nationalism in Colonial Cuba: The Travels of Santa Cruz y Montalvo, Condesa de Merlin*" esp. 107–8.

2. All citations of Méndez Rodenas's scholarship in this chapter refer to *Gender and Nationalism in Colonial Cuba*.

3. Around the time of her husband's death, Merlin produced the Spanish-language translations *Mis doce primeros años* (1838) and *Historia de Sor Inés* (1839), which were each originally published in French in 1831.

4. See Paulk, "Representations of Slavery and Afro-Peruvians in Flora Tristán's Travel Narrative, *Peregrinations of a Pariah*," for more on Flora Tristán's work.

5. See Lawrence C. Jennings's *French Anti-Slavery: The Movement for the Abolition of Slavery in France, 1802–1848*.

6. An enormous body of scholarship is dedicated to Tocqueville in particular, and a complete review of the criticism is beyond the scope of this study. Among recent book-length studies of Tocqueville's thought are Matthew J. Mancini's *Alexis de Tocqueville and American Intellectuals*, Arthur Kaledin's *Tocqueville and His America*, and Olivier Zunz's *The Man Who Understood Democracy: The Life of Alexis de Tocqueville*. Jennifer A. Pitts's *A Turn to Empire* contextualizes Tocqueville's liberal thought and support of imperialism in the context of nineteenth-century British and French political theory.

7. See, for example, Louis J. Kern's "'Slavery Recedes but the Prejudice to Which It Has Given Birth Is Immovable': Beaumont and Tocqueville Confront Slavery and Racism," and Margaret Kohn's "The Other America: Tocqueville and Beaumont on Race and Slavery."

8. See Jane S. Cowden's "Charles Dickens in Pennsylvania in March 1842: Imagining America" for more on Dickens's visit.

9. See Leslie Patrick's "Ann Hinson: A Little-Known Woman in the Country's Premier Prison, Eastern State Penitentiary, 1831" for more on female prisoners at Eastern State Penitentiary.

10. See Méndez Rodenas for a discussion of the small differences between the published editions of "Lettre XX" as pamphlets in 1841 and as part of the complete *La Havane* in 1844 (149–50).

11. Figarola Caneda points out that it is possible that Merlin wrote her dedication to O'Donnell before news of the violence following the Conspiración de la Escalera had reached her (cited in Méndez Rodenas 145).

12. I cite the Spanish-language pamphlet rather than the French version of *La Havane* because it circulated first chronologically and would have been more accessible to Spanish speakers.

13. Some spellings and the use of accent marks are idiosyncratic in the 1841 edition of *Los esclavos en las colonias españolas*. I have not made changes or indicated these deviations from today's standard Spanish.

14. See Elizabeth Bohls's "Romantic Exploration and Atlantic Slavery: Mungo Park's Coffle" for more on Park's commentaries on Africa and enslavement.

15. Suárez y Romero's Ricardo appears in *Francisco* and Villaverde's Cándido y Leonardo Gamboa figure in *Cecilia Valdés*. See chapter 1 for a discussion of Manzano's legal case.

16. The footnote on p. 83 of *Los esclavos* is taken directly from Beaumont's *Marie* 377. In the original, French-language "Lettre XX" of *La Havane*, the author also includes an additional footnote about an interracial marriage in Utica, New York, that is worded similarly to Beaumont's description on p. 378 of *Marie*.

17. See chapter 16, titled "The Search for Freedom," of Daniel S. Levy's *Manhattan Phoenix* for more on the 1834 riots in New York City.

CHAPTER FOUR: MANIFEST COLONIALITY: MATURIN MURRAY BALLOU AND THE "AFRICANIZATION" OF CUBA

1. Ballou also wrote one additional text that included parts of Spanish America—*Equatorial America: Descriptive of a Visit to St. Thomas, Martinique, Barbadoes [sic], and the Principal Capitals of South America* (1892).

2. Some of Ballou's other travel narratives were given titles that more directly reflected their nature as travel narratives. For example, Ballou also wrote *Due West; or, Round the World in Ten Months* (1884), *Due North; or, Glimpses of Scandinavia and Russia* (1887), and *Foot-Prints of Travel; or, Journeyings in Many Lands* (1888).

3. In the US, this conflict is referred to as the Spanish-American War, meaning that the war was between Spain and the US. In Cuba, it is referred to as "La Guerra hispano-cubano-estadounidense," recognizing that it was a war that began in 1895 with Cuba's rebellion against Spain. The US entered the conflict following the explosion of the *Maine* in Havana's harbor in 1898. In Spain, the event is regularly referred to as either "La Guerra de Cuba" or "El Desastre del '98."

4. For more information on Mary Mann's *Juanita*, see my "Juanita Versus Cecilia: Competing Allegories of Cuba by Mary Peabody Mann and Cirilo Villaverde," in *Cosmic Wit: Essays in Honor of Edward H. Friedman*.

5. My discussion of efforts to purchase Cuba prior to the Pierce administration and the Narciso López expeditions is indebted to Tom Chaffin's "'Sons of Washington': Narciso López, Filibustering, and U.S. Nationalism, 1848–1851."

6. Like Cuban reformists who found enslavement of Africans and Afro-Cubans to be an impediment to the promotion of white labor, Barnburners like O'Sullivan opposed the spread of slavery because of their belief that white workers would not want to work beside slaves. As John Van Buren argued, "you cannot induce the white laboring man to work beside a black slave" (cited in Chaffin 97).

7. See "Africanization" in *The Oxford English Dictionary*, which identifies the nationalistic *John Bull* newspaper as the originator of this term.

8. For information on Del Monte's correspondence with Alexander Everett, see Francisco Morán's "Domingo del Monte, ¿'El más real y útil hombre de su tiempo'?"

9. See Edward W. Said's seminal work, *Orientalism*, for his elaboration of this concept.

10. The only source specifically named by Ballou in the preface is Ramón de la Sagra, a Spanish natural scientist.

11. See chapter 1 above for more on Manzano. Also see Manzano's *Autobiografía del esclavo poeta* and Montejo's *Biografía de un cimarrón*.

12. Juan Francisco Manzano's description of how he must rapidly and voraciously consume any food that comes his way in *Autobiografía* and the constant iteration of extreme hunger in the coolie testimonies in the *China Commission Report* provide counterarguments to Ballou's statements, if any are needed (Manzano, *Autobiografía* 305; Yun 160–62).

13. See, for example, Joseph Nevadomsky and Ekhaguosa Aisien's "The Clothing of Political Identity: Costume and Scarification in the Benin Kingdom."

14. The 1820 treaty signed by Spain and Britain outlawed the transatlantic slave trade to Cuba; people introduced into Cuba as forced laborers after that date were termed *emancipados* by the treaty.

15. See Havard 37–63, for a discussion of Joel Barlow's characterization of Colón as a New World visionary.

CHAPTER FIVE: BLACKFACE, PLANTATIONS, AND TROPICAL SPACES: JULIA WARD HOWE'S *A TRIP TO CUBA*

1. See María Lugones's "Heterosexualism and the Colonial / Modern Gender System" and Yuderkys Espinosa Miñoso's "De por qué es necesario un feminismo descolonial: Diferenciación, dominación co-constitutiva de la modernidad occidental y el fin de la política de identidad."

2. Showalter critiques racism in the suffragist movement and in Howe's *A Trip to Cuba* (153, 188).

3. See Edward J. Renehen's *The Secret Six: The True Tale of the Men Who Conspired with John Brown* for more information on Chev Howe's support for the raid.

4. Howe also notes that a friend entering Cuba years later had her copy of *A Trip to Cuba* confiscated by customs officials (236).

5. Howe specifically mentions Fredrika Bremer's visit to Cuba, William Henry Hurlbert's *Gan-Eden; or, Pictures of Cuba* (1854), and the work of Richard Henry Dana Jr. (37).

6. For additional information on yellowface performances, see for example Krystyn R. Moon's *Yellowface: Creating the Chinese in American Popular Music and Performance, 1850s–1920s*.

7. See also Kathleen López's *Chinese Cubans: A Transnational History*, Lisa Yun's *The Coolie Speaks: Chinese Indentured Laborers and African Slaves in Cuba*, and Ignacio López-Calvo's *Imaging the Chinese in Cuban Literature and Culture*.

8. The topic of indentured Chinese labor in Cuba is further explored in chapter 6 below.

9. Maria DeGuzman's term *off-white* is used here to reflect Howe's understanding of lighter-skinned Cubans as not white (4).

10. See, for example, Jen McDaneld's "Harper, Historiography, and the Race/Gender Opposition in Feminism."

CHAPTER SIX: LA GUERRA DE LOS DIEZ AÑOS AND THE LOST CAUSE: ELIZA RIPLEY'S DESENGAÑO

1. The University of Georgia's Hargrett Rare Books and Manuscripts Archive holds a collection of Ripley's personal papers, as well as documents related to her ownership of the Cuban plantation (Wong 36).

2. As Wong observes, *desengaño* is not easily translated into English (246n119). *El desengaño*, or the discovery of moral truth by way of disillusionment, is a major theme in baroque literature in Spanish. See, for example, José Antonio Maravall's *La cultura del barroco: Análisis de una estrutura histórica*.

3. See Andre M. Fleche's "The Last Filibuster: The Ten Years' War in Cuba and the Legacy of the American Civil War," and Gregg French's "Domestic Stability and Imperial Continuities: U.S.-Spanish Relations in the Reconstruction Era."

4. See Ada Ferrer's *Cuba: An American History* 119–20 for information on Cubans who fought in the US Civil War.

5. Examples of enslaved domestic workers presented as attractive in Cuban literature include Petrona and Rosalía of Félix Tanco y Bosmeniel's "Petrona y Rosalía" and Dorotea of Suárez y Romero's *Francisco. El ingenio o las delicias del campo*.

6. For more information on the different *colonos* brought to Cuba, see Ismael Sarmiento Ramírez's, "Cuba: Una sociedad formada por retazos. Composición y crecimiento de la población en los primeros 68 años del siglo XIX."

7. See also Evelyn Hu-DeHart's "Chinese Coolie Labor in Cuba and Peru in the Nineteenth Century: Free Labor or Neoslavery?"

8. See, for example, Richard Henry Dana's *To Cuba and Back* (1859), Julia Woodruff's *My Winter in Cuba* (1871), and James O'Kelly's *The Mambi-Land; or, Adventures of a Herald Correspondent in Cuba* (1874). These and other works are discussed in Edlie L. Wong's *Racial Reconstruction: Black Inclusion, Chinese Exclusion, and the Fictions of Citizenship*.

9. There were nineteen Chinese indentured workers and eighty-one African and Afro-Cuban slaves at Desengaño when the McHattons purchased it in 1866 (Wong 56).

10. At the same time that the McHattons employed Chinese contract labor on Desengaño, postwar Louisiana planters were doing the same (Wong 41).

11. See Evelyn Hu-DeHart's "From Slavery to Freedom: Chinese Coolies on the Sugar Plantations of Nineteenth Century Cuba" for a detailed study of indenture contracts and the divergences between the Chinese and Spanish versions. Wong also points out that the terms in the Chinese-language contract were slightly different from the terms in the Spanish-language version (60).

12. Ripley writes that Martha "collected a basketful of tightly-braided tails, and hired another darky to clean them. . . . [A]nd so I think she eventually made a pillow of it" (175).

13. See Rebecca J. Scott's *Slave Emancipation in Cuba* for a thorough history of the long process of the end of enslavement. Her book also references the end of Chinese indenture.

14. See Louis A. Pérez, "Toward Dependency and Revolution: The Political Economy of Cuba Between Wars, 1878–1895" for an account of the Cuban economy following La Guerra de los Diez Años.

CONCLUSION AND AN EPILOGUE: LEGACIES OF NINETEENTH-CENTURY COLONIALITY

1. See Doris Sommer, *Foundational Fictions: The National Romances of Latin America*.
2. For more on Ortiz, see also Miguel Arnedo-Gómez, Jorge Camacho, and Yairen Jerez Columbié.
3. See Erwan Dianteill and Martha Swearingen, Martin A. Tsang, and Emily Maguire for more on Cabrera.
4. The erasure of nonwhite identities inherent in the proposal of mestizo or *mulato* national identities by twentieth-century intellectuals in Latin America has been examined by a number of scholars. For more information, see especially Peter Wade's "Rethinking 'Mestizaje': Ideology and Lived Experience," and Antonio Cornejo Polar's "Mestizaje e hibridez: Los riesgos de las metáforas: Apuntes."
5. Barnet is normally listed as the sole author of *Biografía de un cimarrón*, which I argue diminishes Esteban Montejo's role as the source.
6. On the general absence and stereotyping of Black characters in Cuban literature after 1959, see also Odette Casamayor-Cisneros, Roberto Zurbano, Carlos Uxó González, and Julieta Karol Kabalin Campos.
7. See also "Race and Racism in Cuban Art" by Henry Louis Gates Jr., Elio Rodríguez Valdés, and Alejandro de la Fuente.
8. See the special issue of *Afro-Hispanic Review*, vol. 33, no. 1, 2014, for more on Zurbano's essay and the controversy surrounding his dismissal (Maddox and Steinkampf 82n13).
9. For more information on Moore's autobiography, see Trent Masiki's *The Afro-Latino Memoir* and Elio Bernardo Ruiz's "Tribulaciones de un pichón: (Recuento crítico de las memorias de Carlos Moore): Fragmento."
10. See Dunbar's "Where Diaspora Meets Disillusionment: Panther Politics in Castro's Cuba."
11. See Maddox and Steinkampf for information regarding differences between Gates's Cuba documentary and the book version.

WORKS CITED

Abbot, Abiel. *Letters Written in the Interior of Cuba*. Bowles and Dearborn, 1829.
"Africanization, N." *Oxford English Dictionary*, Oxford UP, 2023, https://0-doi-org.libus.csd.mu.edu/10.1093/OED/6778452987.
Aguilera Manzano, José M. "The Informal Communication Network Built by Domingo del Monte from Havana Between 1824 and 1845." *Caribbean Studies*, vol. 37, no. 1, 2009, pp. 67–96.
Aiken, Guy. "Educating Tocqueville: Jared Sparks, the Boston Whigs, and *Democracy in America*." *The Tocqueville Review/La Revue Tocqueville*, vol. 34, no. 1, 2013, pp. 169–92.
Allen, Jafari Sinclaire. "Looking Black at Revolutionary Cuba." *Latin American Perspectives*, vol. 36, no. 1, 2009, pp. 53–62.
Alvarado, Leonel. "Mrs. Howe in Havana: Activismo político y exploraciones sociales en *A Trip to Cuba*." *South Atlantic Modern Language Association*, vol. 81, no. 3, 2016, pp. 21–35.
Anderson, Katherine. "Female Pirates and Nationalism in Nineteenth-Century American Popular Fiction." *Pirates and Mutineers of the Nineteenth Century: Swashbucklers and Swindlers*, edited by Grace Moore, Ashgate, 2011, pp. 95–115.
Arnedo-Gómez, Miguel. "Fernando Ortiz's Transculturation: Applied Anthropology, Acculturation, and *Mestizaje*." *The Journal of Latin American and Caribbean Anthropology*, vol. 27, no. 1–2, 2022, pp. 123–45.
Avramenko, Richard, and Robert Gingerich. "Democratic Dystopia: Tocqueville and the American Penitentiary System." *Polity*, vol. 46, no. 1, 2014, pp. 56–80.
Bachiller y Morales, Antonio. *Tipos y costumbres de la isla de Cuba*. Miguel de Villa, 1881.
Badaracco, Claire M., editor. *The Cuba Journal by Sophia Peabody Hawthorne*. Rutgers UP, 1978.
Ballou, Maturin Murray. *Aztec Land: Central America, the West Indies and South America*. Houghton, Mifflin, 1890.
Ballou, Maturin Murray. *Due South; or, Cuba Past and Present*. Houghton, Mifflin, 1885.
Ballou, Maturin Murray. *Due West; or, Round the World in Ten Months*. Houghton, Mifflin, 1884.
Ballou, Maturin Murray. *Fanny Campbell, The Female Pirate Captain: A Tale of the Revolution*. E. D. Long, 1844.
Ballou, Maturin Murray. *History of Cuba; or, Notes of a Traveller in the Tropics. Being a Political, Historical, and Statistical Account of the Island, from Its First Discovery to the Present Time*. Phillips, Sampson, 1854.

Ballou, Maturin Murray. *The Naval Officer; or the Pirate's Cave*. F. A. Brady, 1845.
Ballou, Maturin Murray. *Red Rupert; or the American Buccaneer*. F. Gleason, 1848.
Ballou, Maturin Murray. *Under the Southern Cross; or, Travels in Australia, Tasmania, New Zealand, Samoa, and Other Pacific Islands*. Ticknor, 1888.
Baralt, Francisco. "Escenas campestres. Baile de los negros." *Costumbristas cubanos del siglo XIX*, edited by Salvador Bueno, pp. 151–60.
Barcía, Manuel. "'Going Back Home': Slave Suicide in Nineteenth-Century Cuba." *Millars: Espai i historia*, vol. 42, no. 1, 2017, pp. 49–73.
Barnet, Miguel. *Biografía de un cimarrón*. Ediciones Ariel, 1968.
Bartosik-Vélez, Elise. *The Legacy of Christopher Columbus in the Americas*. Vanderbilt UP, 2014.
Bauer, Ralph. "Hemispheric Studies." *PMLA*, vol. 124, no. 1, 2009, pp. 234–50.
Beaumont, Gustave de. *Marie, or Slavery in the United States: A Novel of Jacksonian America*. 1835. Translated by Barbara Chapman, Stanford UP, 1958.
Beaumont, Gustave de, and Alexander de Tocqueville. *On the Penitentiary System in the United States and Its Application in France*. Translated by Francis Lieber, Carey, Lea and Blanchard, 1833.
Benson, Devyn Spence. *Antiracism in Cuba: The Unfinished Revolution*. U of North Carolina P, 2016.
Benson, Peter. "Gleason's Publishing Hall." *Publishers for Mass Entertainment in Nineteenth-Century America*, edited by Madeleine B. Stern, G. K. Hall, 1980, pp. 137–45.
Benson, Sara M. "Democracy and Unfreedom: Revisiting Tocqueville and Beaumont in America." *Political Theory*, vol. 45, no. 4, pp. 466–94.
Bernardo Ruiz, Elio. "Tribulaciones de un pichón: (Recuento crítico de las memorias de Carlos Moore): Fragmento." *Afro-Hispanic Review*, vol. 34, no. 2, 2015, pp. 95–116.
Betancourt, José Victoriano. "Los curros del mangler. El triple velorio." *Costumbristas cubanos del siglo XIX*, edited by Salvador Bueno, pp. 261–68.
Bhambra, Gurminder, and John Holmwood. *Colonialism and Modern Social Theory*, Polity, 2021.
Bohls, Elizabeth. "Romantic Exploration and Atlantic Slavery: Mungo Park's Coffle." *Studies in Romanticism*, vol. 55, no. 3, 2016, pp. 347–445.
Borucki, Alex, David Eltis, and David Wheat. "Atlantic History and the Slave Trade to Spanish America." *The American Historical Review*, vol. 120, no. 2, 2015, pp. 433–61.
"Bozal, N." *Diccionario de la Real Academia Española*, 2023. https://dle.rae.es/bozal?m=form.
Branche, Jerome. "'Mulato entre negros' (y blancos): Writing, Race, the Antislavery Question, and Juan Francisco Manzano's *Autobiografía*." *Bulletin of Latin American Research*, vol. 20, no.1, 2001, pp. 63–87.
Bremer, Fredrika. *The Homes of the New World: Impressions of America*. Harper, 1853.
Brent, William Lee. *Long Time Gone: A Black Panther's True-Life Story of His Hijacking and Twenty-Five Years in Cuba*. ToExcel, 2000.
Briggs, Ronald. "US Travellers and the Poetics of the Cuban Aporia (1859)." *Studies in Travel Writing*, vol. 18, no. 1, 2014, pp. 18–33.
Bueno, Salvador, editor. *Costumbristas cubanos del siglo XIX*. Biblioteca Ayacucho, 1985.
Bueno, Salvador. "Un libro polémico: *El Viaje a la Habana* de la condesa de Merlin." *Cuadernos Americanos*, vol. 199, 1975, pp. 161–77.

Bueno, Salvador. Prólogo. *Costumbristas cubanos del siglo XIX*, edited by Salvador Bueno, pp. ix–xxix.

Cabañas, Miguel A. *The Cultural "Other" in Nineteenth-Century Travel Narratives: How the United States and Latin America Described Each Other.* Edwin Mellon P, 2008.

Cabrera, Lydia. *El monte: Notas sobre las religiones, la magia, las supersticiones y el folklore de los negros criollos y de los pueblos de Cuba.* 1954. Verbum, 2016.

Cabrera Saqui, Mario. "Vida, Pasión y Gloria de Anselmo Suárez y Romero." *Francisco: El ingenio o las delicias del campo. Novela cubana.* 1839. By Anselmo Suárez y Romero, Mnemosyne Publishing, 1969.

Camacho, Jorge. "*Los negros brujos* de Fernando Ortiz: Entre el atavismo de Lombroso y el evolucionismo sociocultural de John Lubbock y Edward Tylor." *Negritud*, vol. 1, no. 1, 2007, pp. 184–97.

Casamayor-Cisneros, Odette. "Negros de papel: Algunas apariciones del negro en la narrativa cubana después de 1959." *Artelogie*, vol. 17, 2021, pp. 1–25.

Castellanos, Jorge, and Isabel Castellanos. *Cultura Afrocubana, Tomo 2: El negro en Cuba 1845–1959.* Universal, 1990.

Castro-Gómez, Santiago. "(Post)Coloniality for Dummies: Latin American Perspectives on Modernity, Coloniality, and the Geopolitics of Knowledge." *Coloniality at Large: Latin America and the Postcolonial Debate.* Edited by Mabel Moraña, Enrique Dussel, and Carlos A. Jáuregui, Duke UP, 2008, pp. 260–85.

Cervantes Saavedra, Miguel de. *Don Quijote de la Mancha.* Edited by Martín de Riquer, Planeta, 2004.

Césaire, Aimé. *Discourse on Colonialism.* Translated by Joan Pinkham, Monthly Review, 2000.

Chaffin, Tom. "'Sons of Washington': Narciso López, Filibustering, and U.S. Nationalism, 1848–1851." *Journal of the Early Republic*, vol. 15, no. 1, 1995, pp. 79–108.

Chambers, Stephen. "At Home Among the Dead: North Americans and the 1825 Guamacaro Slave Insurrection." *Journal of the Early Republic*, vol. 33, no. 1, 2013, pp. 61–86.

Coca-Izaguirre, C. Manuel, Irma Pérez-Odio, and Greisy Pérez-Martínez. "Las sociedades de tumba francesa en Cuba: precedents investigativos." *Santiago*, vol. 140, 2016, pp. 339-355.

Corbitt, Duvon C. "Chinese Immigrants in Cuba." *Far Eastern Survey*, vol. 13, no. 14, 1944, pp. 130–32.

Cornejo Polar, Antonio. "Mestizaje e hibridez: Los riesgos de las metáforas." *Revista de crítica literaria Latinoamericana*, vol. 24, no. 47, 1998, pp. 7–11.

Cortijo Ocaña, Antonio, and Ricardo Fonseca. "Leyenda Negra y propaganda política: A propósito de la literature panfletaria." *Cincinnati Romance Review*, vol. 29, 2010, pp. 12–30.

Cowden, Jane S. "Charles Dickens in Pennsylvania in March 1842: Imagining America." *Pennsylvania History: A Journal of Mid-Atlantic Studies*, vol. 81, no. 1, 2014, pp. 51–87.

Crenshaw, Kimberlé. "Demarginalizing the Intersection of Race and Sex: A Black Feminist Critique of Antidiscrimination Doctrine, Feminist Theory." *University of Chicago Legal Review*, vol. 1989, no. 1, 1989, pp. 139–67.

The Cuba Commission Report: A Hidden History of the Chinese in Cuba. 1876. Johns Hopkins UP, 1993.

"Cuba: The Next Revolution." *Black in Latin America*, created by Henry Louis Gates Jr., season 1, episode 2, Public Broadcasting Service, 2011.
Cugoano, Ottobah. *Narrative of the Enslavement of Ottobah Cugoano, a Native of Africa*. 1787. Harchard and Company, 1825.
Dana, Richard Henry, Jr. *To Cuba and Back*. 1859. Edited by C. Harvey Gardiner, Southern Illinois UP, 1966.
DeGuzmán, María. *Spain's Long Shadow: The Black Legend, Off-Whiteness, and Anglo-American Empire*. U of Minnesota P, 2005.
Del Monte, Domingo. *Escritos de Domingo del Monte*. La Habana, Cultura, S.A., 1929.
Dianteill, Erwan, and Martha Swearingen. "From Hierography to Ethnography and Back: Lydia Cabrera's Texts and the Written Tradition in Afro-Cuban Religions." *Journal of American Folklore*, vol. 116, no. 461, 2003, pp. 273–92.
Domínguez, Daylet. "Alexander von Humboldt y Ramón de la Sagra: *Navegación* y el viaje al interior en la invención de Cuba en el siglo XIX." *Hispanic Review*, vol. 83, no. 2, 2015, pp. 143–64.
Domínguez, Daylet. "En los límites del discurso esclavista: Retórica abolicionista, afectos y sensibilidad en *Los esclavos en las colonias españolas* de la condesa de Merlin," *Cuban Studies*, no. 45, 2017, pp. 251–72.
Douglass, Frederick. *Narrative of the Life of Frederick Douglass*. 1845. Oxford UP, 1999.
Drescher, Seymour. *Abolition: A History of Slavery and Antislavery*. Cambridge UP, 2009.
Dunbar, Jessie Lafrance. "Where Diaspora Meets Disillusionment: Panther Politics in Castro's Cuba." *Interdisciplinary Literary Studies*, vol. 19, no. 3, 2017, pp. 299–319.
Duong, Kevin. "The Demands of Glory: Tocqueville and Terror in Algeria." *The Review of Politics*, vol. 80, no. 1, 2018, pp. 31–55.
Ellis, Robert Richmond. "Reading through the Veil of Juan Francisco Manzano: From Homoerotic Violence to the Dream of a Homoracial Bond." *PMLA*, vol. 113, no. 3 1998, pp. 422–35.
Equiano, Olaudah. *The Interesting Narrative of the Life of Olaudah Equiano*. 1789. Edited by Robert J. Allison, Palgrave MacMillan, 2007.
E. R. N. Biographical Note. *Social Life in Old New Orleans*, by Eliza Chinn McHatton Ripley, p. 331.
Espinosa Miñoso, Yuderkys. "De por qué es necesario un feminismo descolonial: Diferenciación, dominación co-constitutiva de la modernidad occidental y el fin de la política de identidad." *Solar*, vol. 12, no. 1, 2019, pp. 141–71.
Everett, George. "Maturin Murray Ballou (Lieutenant Murray)." *American Magazine Journalists, 1850–1900*, edited by Sam G. Riley, Thomson Gale, 1989, pp. 43–50.
Fanon, Frantz. *Black Skin, White Masks*. Translated by Richard Philcox, Grove Atlantic, 2008.
Fanon, Frantz. *The Wretched of the Earth*. Translated by Richard Philcox, Grove Atlantic, 2021.
Ferrell, Claudine L. *The Abolitionist Movement*. Greenwood, 2006.
Ferrer, Ada. *Cuba: An American History*. Scribner, 2021.
Ferrer, Ada. "Cuban Slavery and Atlantic Slavery." *Review (Fernand Braudel Center)*, vol. 31, no. 3, 2008, pp. 267–95.

Ferrer, Ada. *Insurgent Cuba: Race, Nation, and Revolution, 1868–1898*. U of North Carolina P, 1999.

Fleche, Andre M. "The Last Filibuster: The Ten Years' War in Cuba and the Legacy of the United States." *Reconstruction and Empire: The Legacies of Abolition and Union Victory for an Imperial Age*, edited by David Prior, Fordham UP, 2022, pp. 28–48.

French, Gregg. "Domestic Stability and Imperial Continuities: U.S.-Spanish Relations in the Reconstruction Era." *Reconstruction and Empire: The Legacies of Abolition and Union Victory for an Imperial Age*, edited by David Prior, Fordham UP, 2022, pp. 68–86.

Fuente, Alejandro de la. "Slave Law and Claims-Making in Cuba: The Tannenbaum Debate Revisited." *Law and History Review*, vol. 22, no. 2, 2004, pp. 339–69.

Gala, Marcial. *La catedral de los negros*. Corregidor, 2015.

Gates, Henry Louis, Jr., Elio Rodríguez Valdés, and Alejandro de la Fuente. "Race and Racism in Cuban Art." *Transition*, no. 108, 2021, pp. 33–51.

Gleijeses, Piero. "Clashing over Cuba: The United States, Spain and Britain, 1853–1855." *Journal of Latin American Studies*, vol. 49, no. 2, 2016, pp. 215–41.

Gómez de Avellaneda, Gertrudis. *Sab*. Edited by José Servera, 3rd edition, Ediciones Cátedra, 2001.

Gott, Richard. *Cuba: A New History*. Yale UP, 2005.

Grant, Mary H. *Private Woman, Public Person: An Account of the Life of Julia Ward Howe from 1819 to 1868*. Carlson Publishing, 1994.

Griffin, Eric. "From Ethos to Ethnos: Hispanizing 'the Spaniard' in the Old World and the New." *CR: The New Centennial Review*, vol. 2, no. 1, 2002, pp. 69–116.

Guanche, Jesús. *Componentes étnicos de la nación cubana*. Unión, 1996.

Guevara, Gema R. "Geographies of Travel and the Rhetoric of the Countryside: Mid-Nineteenth-Century North American and Cuban Travel Writing." *Bulletin of Spanish Studies*, vol. 85, no. 1, 2008, pp. 11–27.

Guevara, Gema R. "Inexacting Whiteness: *Blanqueamiento* as a Gender-Specific Trope in the Nineteenth Century." *Cuban Studies*, vol. 36, no. 1, 2005, pp. 105–28.

Gunn, Jeffrey. "Literacy and the Humanizing Project in Olaudah Equiano's *The Interesting Narrative* and Ottobah Cugoano's *Thoughts and Sentiments*." *eSharp*, vol. 10, 2007, pp. 1–19.

Gutierrez Sebastián, Raquel. "Sabores, sones y trazos del costumbrismo cubano." *La tribu liberal: el Romanticismo en las dos orillas del Atlántico*, edited by José María Ferri Coll and Enrique Rubio Cremades, Vervuert, 2016, pp. 37–50.

Hall, Stuart. "Cultural Identity and Diaspora." *Colonial Discourse and Post-Colonial Theory: A Reader*. Harvester Wheatsheaf, 1994, pp. 227–37.

Hansen, John. "Frederick Douglass's Journey from Slave to Freeman: An Acquisition and Mastery of Language, Rhetoric, and Power via the Narrative." *Griot: Official Journal of the Southern Conference on Afro-American Studies*, vol. 31, no. 2, 2012, pp. 14–23.

Harris, Joel Chandler. "Why the Negro Is Black." *Uncle Remus: His Songs and His Sayings*. 1880. Osgood, McIlvaine, 1895, pp. 163–65.

Havard, John C. *Hispanicism and Early US Literature: Spain, Mexico, Cuba, and the Origins of US National Identity*. U of Alabama P, 2018.

Hazard, Samuel. *Cuba with Pen and Pencil*. Hartford Publishing, 1871.

Heredia, José María. *Poesías completas.* Edited by Ángel Aparicio Laurencio, Ediciones Universal, 1970.

"Hispanism, N." *Merriam-Webster.com Dictionary,* Merriam-Webster, https://www.merriam-webster.com/dictionary/hispanism.

Horsman, Reginald. *Race and Manifest Destiny: The Origins of American Racial Anglo-Saxonism.* Harvard UP, 1981.

Howe, Julia Ward. "Battle Hymn of the Republic." Supervisory Committee for Recruiting Colored Regiments, 1863.

Howe, Julia Ward. *The Hermaphrodite.* Edited by Gary Williams, U of Nebraska P, 2009.

Howe, Julia Ward. *Passion-Flowers.* Ticknor and Fields, 1854.

Howe, Julia Ward. *Reminiscences, 1819–1899.* 1899. Negro Universities P, 1968.

Howe, Julia Ward. *A Trip to Cuba.* 1860. Negro Universities P, 1969.

Hu-DeHart, Evelyn. "Chinese Coolie Labor in Cuba and Peru in the Nineteenth Century: Free Labor or Neoslavery?" *Journal of Overseas Chinese Studies,* vol. 2, no. 2, 1992, 149–82.

Hu-DeHart, Evelyn. "From Slavery to Freedom: Chinese Coolies on the Sugar Plantations of Nineteenth Century Cuba." *Labour History,* no. 113, 2017, pp. 31–51.

Huberman, Ariana. "The Lure of the Exotic: The Travel Writings of María de las Mercedes Santa Cruz y Montalvo, Countess of Merlin." *Hispanic Journal,* vol. 29, no. 1, pp. 71–89.

Hughes, Langston, and Ben Frederic Carruthers, translators. *Cuba Libre: Poems by Nicolás Guillén,* by Nicolás Guillén, Ward Ritchie Press, 1948.

Humboldt, Alexander von. *Essai politique sur l'île de Cuba.* Gide Fils, 1826.

Hurlbert, William Henry. *Gan-Eden, or, Pictures of Cuba.* John P. Jewett, 1854.

Inikori, Joseph E. "Atlantic Enslavement and the Rise of the Capitalist Global Economy." *Current Anthropology,* vol. 61, no. S22, 2020, pp. S141–S339.

Irving, Washington. *A Chronicle of the Conquest of Granada.* 1829. Twayne, 1988.

Irving, Washington. *Tales of the Alhambra.* 1832. Editorial Padre Suárez, 1955.

Jackson, Richard L. *The Black Image in Latin American Literature.* U of New Mexico P, 1976.

Jennings, Lawrence C. *French Anti-Slavery: The Movement for the Abolition of Slavery in France, 1802–1848.* Cambridge UP, 2000.

Jerez Columbié, Yairen. "Sketches of Black People by White Intellectuals: Transculturation in Fernando Ortiz and Jaume Valls's *Afrocubanismo* in 1920s Havana." *Anthurium,* vol. 16, no. 2, 2020, pp. 1–11.

Johnson, Ollie. "Malcolm X and the Cuban Revolution." *Malcolm X's Michigan Worldview: An Exemplar for Contemporary Black Studies,* edited by Rita Kiki Edozie and Curtis Stokes, Michigan State UP, 2015, pp. 263–78.

Johnson, Wendy Dasler. "Male Sentimentalists Through the 'I's' of Julia Ward Howe's Poetry." *South Atlantic Review,* vol. 64, no. 4, 1999, pp. 16–35.

Juderías, Julián. *La leyenda negra: Estudios acerca del concepto de España en el extranjero.* 14th ed., Editora Nacional, 1960.

Kabalin Campos, Julieta Karol. "*Corazón mestizo* de Pedro Juan Gutiérrez y *La Catedral de los Negros* de Marcial Gala: Dos intervenciones de la narrativa cubana reciente en el debate racial." *Caracol,* no. 19, 2020, pp. 885–908.

Kagan, Richard L. *The Spanish Craze: America's Fascination with the Hispanic World, 1779–1939.* U of Nebraska P, 2019.

Kaledin, Arthur. *Tocqueville and His America: A Darker Horizon.* Yale UP, 2011.
Kelly, Patrick J. "The Cat's-Paw: Confederate Ambitions in Latin America." *American Civil Wars: The United States, Latin America, Europe, and the Crisis of the 1860s,* edited by Don H. Doyle, U of North Carolina P, 2017, pp. 58–81.
Kennedy, John Pendleton. *Swallow Barn; or, A Sojourn in the Old Dominion.* Carey and Lea, 1832.
Kerber, Linda K. "Abolitionists and Amalgamators: The New York City Race Riots of 1834." *New York History,* vol. 48, no. 1, 1967, pp. 28–39.
Kern, Louis J. "'Slavery Recedes but the Prejudice to Which It Has Given Birth Is Immovable': Beaumont and Tocqueville Confront Slavery and Racism." *National Stereotypes in Perspective: Americans in France, Frenchmen in America,* edited by William L. Chew III, Rodopi, 2001, pp. 143–85.
Kirk, Stephanie. "Mapping the Hemispheric Divide: The Colonial Americas in a Collaborative Context." *PMLA,* vol. 128, no. 4, 2013, pp. 976–82.
Kirkpatrick, Susan. "The Ideology of Costumbrismo." *Ideologies and Literature,* vol. 2, no. 7, 1978, pp. 28–44.
Kohn, Margaret. "The Other America: Tocqueville and Beaumont on Race and Slavery." *Polity,* vol. 35, no. 2, 2002, pp. 169–93.
Kutzinski, Vera M. "Fearful Asymmetries: Langston Hughes, Nicolás Guillén, and *Cuba Libre.*" *Diacritics,* vol. 34, no. 3/4, 2004, pp. 112–42.
Kynard, Carmen. "Writing While Black: The Colour Line, Black Discourses and Assessment in the Institutionalization of Writing Instruction." *English Teaching: Practice and Critique,* vol. 7, no. 2, 2008, pp. 4–34.
Landaluze, Víctor Patricio. *Los cubanos pintados por si mismos: Colección de tipos cubanos.* Imprenta de Barcina, 1852.
Lane, Jill. *Blackface Cuba, 1840–1895.* U of Pennsylvania P, 2005.
Leary, John Patrick. "Havana Reads the Harlem Renaissance: Langston Hughes, Nicolás Guillén, and the Dialectics of Transnational American Literature." *Comparative Literature Studies,* vol. 47, no. 2, 2010, pp. 133–58.
Levy, Daniel S. "The Search for Freedom." *Manhattan Phoenix: The Great Fire of 1835 and the Emergence of Modern New York.* Oxford UP, 2022, pp. 248–65.
López, Alfred J. "Intentions, Methods, and the Future of Global South Studies." *Comparative Literature Studies,* vol. 58, no. 3, 2021, pp. 485–508.
López, Kathleen. *Chinese Cubans: A Transnational History.* U of North Carolina P, 2013.
López-Calvo, Ignacio. *Imaging the Chinese in Cuban Literature and Culture.* UP of Florida, 2008.
Lugones, María. "Heterosexualism and the Colonial/Modern Gender System." *Hypatia,* vol. 22, no. 1, 2007, pp. 186–209.
Luis, William. Agradecimientos. *Autobiografía del esclavo poeta y otros escritos,* by Juan Francisco Manzano. Edited by William Luis, Iberoamericana, 2007, pp. 11–12.
Luis, William. *Culture and Customs of Cuba.* Peter Standish, 2001.
Luis, William. Introducción. *Autobiografía del esclavo poeta y otros escritos,* by Juan Francisco Manzano. Edited by William Luis, Iberoamericana, 2007, pp. 13–69.
Luis, William. *Literary Bondage: Slavery in Cuban Narrative.* U of Texas P, 1990.

Luis, William. "The Politics of Memory and Miguel Barnet's *The Autobiography of a Run Away Slave*." *MLN*, vol. 104, no. 2, 1989, pp. 475–91.

Madden, Richard Robert, translator and editor. *Poems by a Slave in the Island of Cuba, Recently Liberated; translated from the Spanish by R. R. Madden, M.D. with the History of the Early Life of the Negro Poet, written by Himself; To which are prefixed Two Pieces Descriptive of Cuban Slavery and the Slave-Traffic*, by Juan Francisco Manzano, London, T. Ward and Company, 1840.

Maddox, John, and Michael Steinkampf. "Continuing the Revolution: A Critical Analysis of Henry Louis Gates' Cuba: The Next Revolution." *Afro-Hispanic Review*, vol. 34, no. 1, 2015, pp. 71–85.

Maguire, Emily. *Racial Experiments in Cuban Literature and Ethnography*. UP of Florida, 2011.

Maldonado-Torres, Nelson. "El Caribe, la colonialidad, y el giro decolonial." *Latin American Research Review*, vol. 55, no. 3, 2020, pp. 560–73.

Maletz, Donald J. "Tocqueville's Tyranny of the Majority Reconsidered." *The Journal of Politics*, vol. 64, no. 3, 2002, pp. 741–63.

Mancini, Matthew J. *Alexis de Tocqueville and American Intellectuals: From His Times to Ours*. Rowan and Littlefield, 2006.

Mann, Mary. *Juanita: A Romance of Real Life in Cuba Fifty Years Ago*. 1887. UP of Virginia, 2000.

Manzano, Juan Francisco. *Autobiografía del esclavo poeta y otros escritos*. 1835. Edited by William Luis, Iberoamericana, 2007.

Manzano, Juan Francisco. *Autobiography of a Slave/Autobiografía de un esclavo*. Edited by Ivan A. Schulman and translated by Evelyn Picon Garfield, Wayne State UP, 1996.

Manzano, Juan Francisco. *Juan Francisco Manzano: Esclavo poeta en la isla de Cuba*. Edited by Abdeslam Azourgarh, Episteme, 2000.

Manzano, Juan Francisco. *Zafira: Tragedia en cinco actos*. Havana, 1842.

Maravall, José Antonio. *La cultura del barroco: Análisis de una estrutura histórica*. Ariel, 1975.

Martí, José. *Nuestra América, edición crítica*. Edited by Cintio Vitier, Centro de Estudios Martianos, 2005.

Martí, José. *Obras completas*. Editorial Nacional de Cuba, 1963–1973.

Martí, José, Salvador Bueno Menéndez, and Fredo Arias de la Canal. *Martí por Martí*. Frente de Afirmación Hispanista, 2003.

Martin, Claire Emily. "Colonizing the Self: Gender, Politics, and Race in the Countess of Merlin's *La Havane*." *Women at Sea: Travel Writing and the Margins of Caribbean Discourse*, edited by Lizabeth Paravisini-Gebert and Ivette Romero-Cesareo, Palgrave, 2001, pp. 183–201.

Martín, José Francisco. "El problema de España y el proyecto ilustrado en el costumbrismo de Larra." *Romanticismo, VI: El costumbrismo romántico*, Bulzoni Editore, 1996, pp. 223–29.

Masiello, Francine. "Diálogo sobre la lengua: Colonia, nación y género sexual en el siglo XIX." *Casa de las Américas*, vol. 34, no. 193, 1993, pp. 26–36.

Masiki, Trent. *The Afro-Latino Memoir: Race, Ethnicity, and Literary Interculturalism*. U of North Carolina P, 2023.

McBride, Dwight A., and Justin A. Joyce. "Reading Communities: Slave Narratives and the Discursive Reader." *The Oxford Handbook of the African American Slave Narrative*, Oxford UP, 2014, pp. 165–82.

McDaneld, Jen. "Harper, Historiography, and the Race/Gender Opposition in Feminism." *Signs: Journal of Women in Culture and Society*, vol. 40, no. 2, pp. 393–415.

Meade, Teresa, and Gregory Alonso Pirio. "In Search of the Afro-American 'Eldorado': Attempts by North American Blacks to Enter Brazil in the 1920s." *Luso-Brazilian Review*, vol. 25, no. 1, 1988, pp. 85–110.

Meehan, Kevin and Paul B. Miller. "Martí, Schomburg y la cuestión racial en las Américas." *Afro-Hispanic Review*, vol. 25, no. 2, 2006, 73–88.

Menchú, Rigoberta. *Me llamo Rigoberta Menchú y así me nació la conciencia*. 10th ed., Siglo Veintiuno Editores, 1994.

Méndez Rodenas, Adriana. *Gender and Nationalism in Colonial Cuba: The Travels of Santa Cruz y Montalvo, Condesa de Merlín*. Vanderbilt UP, 1998.

Méndez Rodenas, Adriana. "Poéticas de la transculturación: La tumba francesa y la etnografía de rescate." *Afro-Hispanic Review*, vol. 36, no. 2, 2017, 148–62.

Mignolo, Walter D. "*Islamophobia/Hispanophobia*: The (Re) Configuration of the Racial Imperial/Colonial Matrix." *Human Architecture: Journal of the Sociology of Self-Knowledge*, vol. 5, no. 1, 2007, pp. 13–28.

Mignolo, Walter D., and Caroline Levander. "The Global South and World Dis/Order." *The Global South*, vol. 5, no. 1, 2011, pp. 1–2.

Mignolo, Walter D., and Catherine E. Walsh. *On Decoloniality: Concepts, Analytics, Praxis*. Duke UP, 2018.

Molloy, Sylvia. *At Face Value: Autobiographical Writing in Spanish America*. Cambridge UP, 1991.

Montesinos, José F. *Costumbrismo y novela*. Editorial Castalia, 1960.

Moon, Krystyn R. *Yellowface: Creating the Chinese in American Popular Music and Performance, 1850s–1920s*. Rutgers UP, 2005.

Moore, Carlos. *Pichón: Race and Revolution in Castro's Cuba: A Memoir*. Lawrence Hill Books, 2008.

Mora, G. Cristina. *Making Hispanics: How Activists, Bureaucrats, and Media Constructed a New American*. U Chicago P, 2014.

Morán, Francisco. "Domingo del Monte, ¿'El más real y útil hombre de su tiempo'?" *Dirasat Hispanicas*, no. 3, 2016, pp. 39–65.

Moraña, Mabel, editor. *Ideologies of Hispanism*. Vanderbilt UP, 2005.

Moraña, Mabel, Enrique Dussel, and Carlos A. Jáuregui, editors. *Coloniality at Large: Latin America and the Postcolonial Debate*. Duke UP, 2008.

Murray, D. R. "Statistics of the Slave Trade to Cuba, 1790–1867." *Journal of Latin American Studies*, vol. 3, no. 2, 1971, pp. 131–49.

Nayar, Sheila J. "The Enslaved Narrative: White Overseers and the Ambiguity of the Story-Told Self in Early African American Autobiography." *Biography*, vol. 39, no. 2, 2016, pp. 197–227.

Nevadomsky, Joseph, and Ekhaguosa Aisien. "The Clothing of Political Identity: Costume and Scarification in the Benin Kingdom." *African Arts*, vol. 28, no. 1, 1995, pp. 62–73.

Nevaer, Louis. "In Cuba, Black Lives Matter to No One." *Medium*, 9 June 2020, https://medium.com/@nevaer1/in-cuba-black-lives-matter-to-no-one-d8cdee329ee1#_ftn26.

Nieto Soria, José Manuel. "Conceptos de España en tiempos de los Reyes Católicos." *Norba. Revista de Historia*, vol. 19, 2006, pp. 105–23.

Ocasio, Rafael. *Afro-Cuban Costumbrismo: From Plantations to the Slums*. UP of Florida, 2012.

O'Kelly, James J. *The Mambi-Land; or, Adventures of a Herald Correspondent in Cuba*. 1874. Edited by Jennifer Britain, U of Virginia P, 2022.

Olivera, Otto. *Viajeros en Cuba 1800–1850*. Ediciones Universal, 1997.

Ortiz, Fernando. *Contrapunteo cubano del tabaco y el azúcar: Advertencia de sus contrastes agrarios, económicos, históricos y sociales, su etnografía y su transculturación*. 1940. Cátedra, 2002.

Ortiz, Fernando. *Hampa afro-cubana: Los negros brujos (apuntes para un estudio de etnología criminal)*. 1906. Editorial América, 1917.

Ortiz, Fernando. *Los negros curros*. Edited by Diana Iznaga, Editorial de Ciencias Sociales, 1986.

El otro Francisco. Directed by Sergio Giral. 1975. Giral Media Productions, 2005.

Paquette, Robert L. *Sugar Is Made with Blood: The Conspiracy of La Escalera and the Conflict Between Empires over Slavery in Cuba*. Wesleyan UP, 1988.

Oyěwùmí, Oyèrónkẹ́. *The Invention of Women: Making an African Sense of Western Gender Discourses*. U of Minnesota P, 1997.

Patrick, Leslie. "Ann Hinson: A Little-Known Woman in the Country's Premier Prison, Eastern State Penitentiary, 1831." *Pennsylvania History: A Journal of Mid-Atlantic Studies*, vol. 67, no. 3, 2000, pp. 361–75.

Paulk, Julia C. "Juanita Versus Cecilia: Competing Allegories of Cuba by Mary Peabody Mann and Cirilo Villaverde." *Cosmic Wit: Essays in Honor of Edward H. Friedman*, edited by Vicente Pérez de León, Martha García, and G. Cory Duclós. Juan de la Cuesta, 2021, pp. 200–217.

Paulk, Julia C. "Representations of Slavery and Afro-Peruvians in Flora Tristán's Travel Narrative, *Peregrinations of a Pariah*," *Afro-Hispanic Review*, vol. 29, no. 1, 2010, pp. 117–34.

Pérez, Louis A., Jr. *On Becoming Cuban: Identity, Nationality, and Culture*. U of North Carolina P, 1999.

Pérez, Louis A., Jr. "The Nostalgia of Empire: Time Travel in Cuba." *International Journal of Cuban Studies*, vol. 10, no. 1, 2018, pp. 8–19.

Pérez, Louis A., Jr. *Slaves, Sugar, and Colonial Society: Travel Accounts of Cuba 1801–1899*. Scholarly Resources, 1992.

Pérez, Louis A., Jr. "Toward Dependency and Revolution: The Political Economy of Cuba Between Wars, 1878–1895." *Latin American Research Review*, vol. 18, no. 1, 1983, pp. 127–42.

Pérez-Fuentes, Pilar, and Lola Valverde. "La población de La Habana a mediados del siglo XIX: Relaciones sexuales y el matrimonio." *Historia Contemporánea*, vol. 19, 1999, pp. 155–79.

Pettway, Matthew. *Cuban Literature in the Age of Black Insurrection: Manzano, Plácido, and Afro-Latino Religion*. UP of Mississippi, 2020.

Pierce, Yolanda. "Redeeming Bondage: The Captivity Narrative and the Spiritual Autobiography in the African American Slave Narrative Tradition." *The Cambridge Companion to the African American Slave Narrative*, Cambridge UP, 2007, pp. 83–98.
Pitts, Jennifer A. *A Turn to Empire: The Rise of Imperial Liberalism in Britain and France*. Princeton UP, 2005.
Plasa, Carl. *Textual Politics from Slavery to Postcolonialism: Race and Identification*. MacMillan, 2000.
Poumier Taquechel, María. "El suicidio esclavo en Cuba en los años 1840." *Anuario de Estudios Americanos*, vol. 43, 1986, pp. 69–86.
Pratt, Mary Louise. *Imperial Eyes: Travel Writing and Transculturation*. Routledge, 1992.
Quijano, Aníbal. *Aníbal Quijano: Foundational Essays on the Coloniality of Power*. Edited by Walter D. Mignolo, Rita Segato, and Catherine E. Walsh, Duke UP, 2024.
Ramos, Julio. "The Law Is Other: Literature and the Constitution of the Juridical Subject in Nineteenth-Century Cuba." *Annals of Scholarship*, vol. 11, no. 1-2, 1996, pp. 1–35.
Regazzoni, Susana. *Entre dos mundos: la condesa de Merlin o de la retórica de la mediación*. Beatriz Viterbo, 2013.
Renehen, Edward J. *The Secret Six: The True Tale of the Men Who Conspired with John Brown*. Crown Publishers, 1995.
Ripley, Eliza McHatton. *From Flag to Flag: A Woman's Adventures and Experiences in the South During the War, in Mexico, and in Cuba*. D. Appleton and Company, 1889.
Ripley, Eliza McHatton. *Social Life in Old New Orleans: Being Recollections of My Girlhood*. D. Appleton and Company, 1912.
Ritterhouse, Jennifer. "Reading, Intimacy, and the Role of Uncle Remus in White Southern Social Memory." *The Journal of Southern History*, vol. 69, no. 3, 2003, pp. 585–622.
Rivas, Mercedes. *Literatura y la esclavitud en la novela cubana del siglo XIX*. Publicaciones de la Escuela de Estudios Hispano-Americanos de Sevilla, 1990.
Roberts, Brian. *Blackface Nation: Race, Reform, and Identity in American Popular Music, 1812-1925*. U of Chicago P, 2017.
Rodríguez, Raúl, and Harry Targ. "US Foreign Policy Towards Cuba: Historical Roots, Traditional Explanations and Alternative Perspectives." *International Journal of Cuban Studies*, vol. 7, no. 1, 2015, pp. 16–37.
Rodríguez-Mangual, Edna M. *Lydia Cabrera and the Construction of an Afro-Cuban Cultural Identity*. U of North Carolina P, 2004.
Rodríguez Pérez, Yolanda. *Literary Hispanophobia and Hispanophilia in Britain and the Low Countries (1550–1850)*. Amsterdam UP, 2020.
Rolle, Dominick D. "Marronage and Re-Creation in *Assata*." *CLA Journal*, vol. 61, no. 3, 2018, pp. 155–70.
Rosell, Sara. "'Cecilia Valdés' de Villaverde a Arenas: la (re)creación del mito de la mulata." *Afro-Hispanic Review*, vol. 18, no. 2, 1999, pp. 15–21.
Saco, José Antonio. *Papeles sobre Cuba*. 3 vols. Editora del Consejo Nacional de Cultura, 1963.
Saco, José Antonio. "Mi primera pregunta." Imprenta de Don Marcelino Calero, 1837.
Said, Edward W. *Orientalism*. Pantheon, 1978.
Salvatore, Ricardo D. "The Postcolonial in Latin America and the Concept of Coloniality: A Historian's Point of View." *A Contra Corriente*, vol. 8, no. 1, 2010, pp. 332–48.

Salvatore, Ricardo D. "On Knowledge Assymetries and Cognitive Maps: Reconsidering Hemispheric American Studies." *MLN*, vol. 130, no. 2, 2015, pp. 362–89.

San Millán, Blas. Introducción. *Los cubanos pintados por si mismos: Colección de tipos cubanos*, edited by Víctor Patricio de Landaluze, Imprenta de Barcina, 1852, pp. 3–5.

Santa Cruz y Montalvo, María de las Mercedes, Condesa de Merlin. *La Havane*. Vol. 1–2. Hauman, 1844.

Santa Cruz y Montalvo, María de las Mercedes, Condesa de Merlin. *Los esclavos en las colonias españolas*. Imprenta de Alegría y Charlain, 1841.

Santa Cruz y Montalvo, María de las Mercedes, Condesa de Merlin. *Mis doce primeros años e Historia de Sor Inés*. 1831. Imprenta El Siglo XX, 1922.

Sarmiento Ramírez, Ismael. "Cuba: Una sociedad formada por retazos. Composición y creciminto de la población en los primeros 68 años del siglo XIX." *Caravelle*, no. 81, 2003, pp. 111–46.

Schlesinger, Louis. "Personal Narrative of Louis Schlesinger, of Adventures in Cuba and Ceuta." *United States Democratic Review*, vol. 31, no. 171, 1852, pp. 210–25; vol. 31, no. 172, 1852, pp. 352–69; vol. 31, no. 173, 1852, pp. 553–92.

Schriber, Mary Suzanne. "Julia Ward Howe and the Travel Book." *New England Quarterly*, vol. 62, no. 2, 1989, pp. 264–79.

Schulman, Ivan A. Introduction. *Autobiography of a Slave/Autobiografía de un esclavo*, by Juan Francisco Manzano. Edited by Ivan A. Schulman and translated by Evelyn Picon Garfield, Wayne State UP, 1996, pp. 5–38.

Schulman, Ivan A. "Reflections on Cuba and Its Antislavery Literature." *Annals of the Southeastern Conference on Latin American Studies*, vol. 7, 1976, pp. 59–67.

Scott, Rebecca. *Slave Emancipation in Cuba: The Transition to Free Labor in Cuba, 1860–1899*. Princeton UP, 1985.

Shakur, Assata. *Assata: An autobiography*. L. Hill, 1987.

Showalter, Elaine. *The Civil Wars of Julia Ward Howe: A Biography*. Simon and Schuster, 2016.

Silverstein, Stephen. "The Cuban Anti-Antislavery Genre: Anselmo Suárez y Romero's *Colección de Artículos* and the Policy of *Buen Tratamiento*." *Revista Hispánica Moderna*, vol. 68, no. 1, 2015, pp. 59–75.

Sklodowska, Elzbieta. "Testimonio mediatizado: ¿Ventriloquia o heteroglossia? (Barnet/Montejo; Burgos/Menchú)." *Revista de Crítica Literaria Latinoamericana*, vol. 19, no. 38, 1993, pp. 81–90.

Sommer, Doris. *Foundational Fictions: The National Romances of Latin America*. U of California P, 1991.

Sousa Santos, Boaventura de. *Epistemologies of the South: Justice Against Epistemicide*. Routledge, 2014.

Suárez y Romero, Anselmo. Advertencia. *Francisco, El ingenio o las delicias del campo. Novela cubana*. 1839. Mnemosyne Publishing, 1969. 39–42.

Suárez y Romero, Anselmo. "El cementerio del ingenio." *Costumbristas cubanos del siglo XIX*, edited by Salvador Bueno, pp. 337–42.

Suárez y Romero, Anselmo. *Colección de artículos*. Establecimiento tip. La Antilla, 1859.

Suárez y Romero, Anselmo. "Los domingos en los ingenios." *Costumbristas cubanos del siglo XIX*, edited by Salvador Bueno, pp. 315–18.

Suárez y Romero, Anselmo. *Francisco, El ingenio o las delicias del campo. Novela cubana.* 1839. Mnemosyne Publishing, 1969.

Suárez y Romero, Anselmo. "Ingenios." *Costumbristas cubanos del siglo XIX*, edited by Salvador Bueno, pp. 309–14.

Suárez y Romero, Anselmo. *Ofrenda al bazar de la Real Casa de Beneficencia.* Imprenta del Tiempo, 1864.

Tanco y Bosmeniel, Félix. *Petrona y Rosalía.* 1838. Letras Cubanas, 1980.

Tillery, Alvin B. "Reading Tocqueville Behind the Veil: African American Receptions of *Democracy in America*, 1835–1900." *American Political Thought*, vol. 7, no. 1, 2018, pp. 1–25.

Tocqueville, Alexis de. *Democracy in America.* Translated and edited by Harvey C. Mansfield and Delba Winthrop, U of Chicago P, 2000.

Torre, Miguel A. de la. "Castro's Negra/os." *Black Theology*, vol. 16, no. 2, 2018, pp. 95–109.

Torres-Pou, Joan. "Nuevas consideraciones sobre La Havane de la condesa de Merlin: El viaje a los Estados Unidos." *Neophilologus*, vol. 100, 2016, pp. 63–79.

Triay, José E. "El calesero." *Costumbristas cubanos del siglo XIX*, edited by Salvador Bueno, pp. 417–24.

Tsang, Martin A. "Write Into Being: The Production of the Self and Circulation of Ritual Knowledge in Afro-Cuban Religious *Libretas*." *Material Religion*, vol. 17, no. 2, 2021, pp. 228–61

UNESCO. *La tumba francesa*, accessed 13 March 2023, https://ich.unesco.org/en/RL/la-tumba-francesa-00052.

Turnbull, David. *Travels in the West: Cuba—With Notices of Porto Rico, and the Slave Trade.* Longman, Orme, Brown, Green, and Longmans, 1840.

Urban, C. Stanley. "The Africanization of Cuba Scare, 1853–1855." *The Hispanic American Historical Review*, vol. 37, no. 1, 1957, pp. 29–45.

Uxó González, Carlos. *Representaciones del personaje negro en la literatura cubana: Una perspectiva desde lose studios subalternos.* Editorial Verbum, 2010.

Villaverde, Cirilo. *Cecilia Valdés; o, La Loma del Ángel.* 1882. Biblioteca Ayacucho, 1981.

"Volante, N." *Diccionario de la lengua española*, Real Academia Española, 2014, https://dle.rae.es/volante.

Wade, Peter. "Rethinking 'Mestizaje': Ideology and Lived Experience." *Journal of Latin American Studies*, vol. 37, no. 2, 2005, pp. 239–57.

Watson, Maida. "Viajes, bailes, romerías y ferias en el costumbrismo cubano del siglo XIX." *Reading Cuba: Discurso literario y geografía transcultural.* Advana Vieja, 2018, pp. 159–81.

Welch, Cheryl. "Out of Africa: Tocqueville's Imperial Voyages." *Review of Middle East Studies*, vol. 45, no. 1, 2011, pp. 53–61.

Wells, Jeremy. "Romances of the White Women's Burden: Chopin's *At Fault*, Faulkner's *Light in August*, and the Legacies of U.S. Plantation Fiction." *Faulkner and Chopin*, edited by Robert W. Hamblin and Christopher Rieger, Southern Missouri State UP, 2010, pp. 44–76.

Wexler, Alice R. "Sex, Race and Character in Nineteenth Century American Accounts of Cuba." *Caribbean Studies*, vol. 18, no. 3/4, 1978–1979, pp. 115–30.

Williams, Claudette M. "'Plumbing the Murky Depths': Anselmo Suárez y Romero's *Francisco*." *The Devil in the Details: Cuban Antislavery Narrative in the Postmodern Age*. U of the West Indies P, 2010, pp. 40–67.

Williams, Lorna Valerie. *The Representation of Slavery in Cuban Fiction*. U of Missouri P, 1994.

Wong, Edlie L. *Racial Reconstruction: Black Inclusion, Chinese Exclusion, and the Fictions of Citizenship*. New York UP, 2015.

Woodruff, Julia [W. M. L. Jay]. *My Winter in Cuba*. E. P. Dutton, 1871.

Wurdemann, John G. *Notes on Cuba: Containing an Account of Its Discovery and Early History*. J. Munroe, 1844.

Welch, Cheryl. "Out of Africa: Tocqueville's Imperial Voyages." *Review of Middle East Studies*, vol. 45, no. 1, 2011, pp. 53–61.

Yang, Caroline H. "Scenes of Slavery and the 'Chinee' in Uncle Remus and a Minstrel Picture Book." *Research on Diversity in Youth Literature*, vol. 3, no. 1, 2021, pp. 1–27.

Yanuzzi, Alberto. "Los negros curros del manglar según Fernado Ortiz." *Círculo*, vol. 37, 2008, pp. 94–101.

Yun, Lisa. *The Coolie Speaks: Chinese Indentured Laborers and African Slaves in Cuba*. Temple UP, 2008.

Zunz, Olivier. *The Man Who Understood Democracy: The Life of Alexis de Tocqueville*. Princeton UP, 2022.

Zurbano, Roberto. "For Blacks in Cuba, the Revolution Hasn't Begun." *The New York Times*, 23 March 2013, https://www.nytimes.com/2013/03/24/opinion/sunday/for-blacks-in-cuba-the-revolution-hasnt-begun.html.

Zurbano, Roberto. "El triángulo invisible de siglo XX cubano: raza, literatura y nación." *Temas*, no. 46, 2006, pp. 111–23.

INDEX

Abbot, Abiel, 102, 105, 109, 112, 113
abolition, 4, 30–31, 62, 71, 81, 83, 85, 89, 91, 94, 104, 114, 122, 128, 139, 145, 156, 158–59. *See also* antislavery
abyssal: line, 10–11, 23–25, 31, 43, 50–51, 70, 162; thinking, 10, 14, 17, 23–24, 163
Africa, 8, 14, 16, 21, 37, 50, 56, 59–60, 67–68, 71, 76, 88–93, 95, 96, 104, 113, 115, 134–35, 137, 143, 152, 167
African(s), 11, 14, 17, 22–23, 35, 40, 49–50, 68, 72, 90–91, 96, 106, 113–14, 118–19, 125, 127–28, 130, 149–51, 153; African-born, 14–16, 67, 112; culture, 16–17, 25, 43, 45, 54, 58, 60–63, 65–68, 71, 113, 128, 133, 163–64; diaspora, 7, 9, 76; ethnicity, 43, 50, 113; nationalities, 68–69, 113–14; religion, 43, 45, 52, 92
Afro-Cuban(s), 14, 17, 23, 46, 72, 119, 163, 166–67, 169–79; character types, 72, 76; culture, 17, 25, 52, 54, 58–60, 64–67, 71, 76, 113, 119, 133–34, 151, 164; religion, 44–45, 52, 66, 92, 164
Afro-descendant(s), 3–4, 11–12, 14–15, 17, 23, 25–27, 46, 58–59, 73–74, 76, 106–7, 111–12, 118–19, 129, 131–32, 134–35, 137, 139, 142, 150–51, 153, 158, 160, 170; characters, 54, 72, 74; culture, 59, 61–62, 66; US, 127–28, 145, 170; women, 129, 135, 170
American Hemisphere, 4, 8–9, 11–12, 14, 16, 19, 20, 22, 25, 46, 50, 51, 55, 105, 118, 146, 161, 170
Americas. *See* American Hemisphere
annexation, 3–4, 19, 101, 106, 110, 116–17, 145, 160

antislavery, 4, 33, 35–36, 39, 41, 43, 51, 63, 70, 75, 80, 88–90. *See also* abolition
Arango y Parreño, Francisco de, 26, 88, 91, 105
Autobiografía del esclavo poeta (Manzano), 16, 25, 31–52

Bahamas, 123–25, 127–28, 140
Ballou, Maturin Murray, 23, 26, 57, 99–119, 123, 129, 134, 142, 149, 161; *History of Cuba*, 26, 99–119
Baralt, Francisco, 17, 25, 54, 59–67, 71, 76, 133, 151; "Escenas campestres. Baile de los negros," 59–67
Barnet, Miguel, 31, 165, 173, 180; *Biografía de un cimarrón*, 31, 165
Beaumont, Gustave de, 17, 26, 77, 79–85, 87–89, 91–92, 94–96, 105–6, 111, 114, 118; *Marie, or Slavery in the United States*, 79–81, 83, 87, 89, 92, 94, 106
Benson, Sara M., 80, 100, 163–65
Bhambra, Gurminder K., 81–83, 89
Biografía de un cimarrón (Barnet), 31, 165
Black, 40, 67; abyssal representation of, 5, 11, 15–17, 26, 37, 41–42, 50–52, 59, 65–66, 72–73, 75–76, 81–83, 85–86, 89, 91, 93–95, 104, 111, 115, 122, 125–29, 131, 137, 144–47, 149–51, 162–64; activism, 28, 94, 115, 164, 166–68; in Hispanophobic discourse, 21–23, 99, 105–6, 140, 142, 145, 149–50; identity, 34, 50, 125; women, 38–39, 48, 69–70, 147–51, 159–60; writing, 36. *See also* Afro-descendant(s)
Black Legend. *See* Hispanophobia

Black Panthers, 167–68
Black US American(s), 23, 27, 82, 85–86, 149, 166–68; and Cuba, 166–68, 170
blackface, 23, 27, 72, 120, 125–27, 129–31, 134, 139–40, 144, 146, 149–50; minstrel, 125–26, 144
Blackness, 15–16, 50–52, 73, 83, 104, 126, 139, 163, 165; anti-Blackness, 99
blanqueamiento, 4, 16–17, 20, 23, 45, 51, 71, 76; whitening, 26, 85, 87, 99, 118, 128
bozal, 37–38, 49–50, 67–68, 90
Branche, Jerome, 33, 35, 37, 40, 42, 50–51
Bremer, Fredrika, 57, 102, 105, 129
Britain, 15, 18, 55, 104, 159
Bueno, Salvador, 17, 56–57, 78

Cabrera, Lydia, 164, 180
"calesero, El" (Triay), 17, 40, 71–76
Caribbean, 4, 7, 9, 13–15, 18, 23, 27, 45, 63, 76, 88, 102–4, 107, 116, 120, 124, 127–28, 139, 145, 150, 167
Castro, Fidel, 164–65, 167–68
Castro-Gómez, Santiago, 9, 26, 105, 110
Catholicism. *See* religion
Cecilia Valdés; o, La Loma del Ángel (Villaverde), 39, 59, 63, 132, 170
"cementerio del ingenio, El" (Suárez y Romero), 17, 68–71, 112, 175
Cervantes, Miguel de, 102; *Don Quijote de la Mancha*, 102, 124
Césaire, Aimé, 13
Chaffin, Tom, 103–4
China, 143–44, 152, 154–55, 159
Chinese: in Harris, 144–45; in Howe, 134, 138; indentured, 23, 27, 50, 134, 138, 142, 149, 152–55, 158–59, 161; in Ripley, 27, 142, 149, 151–56, 158–60; US exclusion, 142, 152. *See also* yellowface
Christianity. *See* religion
Christy's Minstrels, 125–26. *See also* blackface
Civil War, 3–4, 17–18, 23–24, 27, 72, 121–22, 139, 141–45, 147–48, 156–59
class/race, 39–41
coartación, 48, 74, 92

Colón, Cristóbal, 9, 14, 107, 117, 123
colonial matrix of power, 9, 24, 31, 34, 51, 55, 58–59, 82, 87, 96, 144, 163, 170
coloniality, 4–14, 16–22, 24–25, 27–28, 31–32, 34, 38, 43, 45, 51–53, 55, 57–59, 61–63, 65, 67, 69, 71, 73, 75, 77, 79, 81, 86–87, 90, 96, 99, 102, 104–6, 108–12, 115, 117–20, 124–28, 130, 134–35, 139–47, 149, 151–52, 155–56, 161–63, 165, 168, 170; of race and gender, 12, 27, 120, 128–29, 134–36, 139–40, 169–70. *See also* discourse of coloniality
colono, 152. *See also* coolie
Condesa de Merlin. *See* Merlin, Condesa de
Confederacy, 141, 143, 145–48, 156–59
Conspiración de la Escalera, 32, 167
contrapunteo, 62, 66, 164; counterpoint, 62, 76. *See also* Ortiz, Fernando
coolie, 134, 152, 154, 159
costumbrismo, 5, 17, 25, 53–59, 63–64, 69–72, 75–76
counterpoint. *See contrapunteo*
Cuba, 3–10, 12–16, 18, 22–28; language use, 14, 37; in US travel literature, 101–2. *See also* literature: Cuban
Cugoano, Ottobah, 36
curro, 73

Dana, Richard Henry, Jr., 57, 142
De la Fuente, Alejandro, 39, 44, 46–48, 52, 174
De la Torre, Miguel, 164–65
decoloniality, 4, 6, 8–9, 11, 13, 20, 36, 105, 162
DeGuzmán, María, 20, 22, 102, 105, 106, 108, 136
Del Monte, Domingo, 4, 15–16, 23, 31–33, 35–36, 51, 63–64, 77, 83, 85, 91, 111–13, 118, 130; *tertulia*, 16, 33, 35–36, 38, 42–43, 49, 51, 53, 63–64, 77
Democracy in America (Tocqueville), 79–83, 106, 111
discourse of coloniality, 4–5, 11, 18–22, 31, 34, 43, 45, 52, 61–62, 79, 86–87, 90, 96, 99, 102, 105–6, 108–9, 112, 115, 118–19, 124–26, 141, 144, 149, 151, 156,

161–62. *See also* Hispanophobic discourse of coloniality
discourse of empire building, 6, 9, 11–12, 15, 22–25
Domínguez, Daylet, 78, 88–92, 107
Don Quijote de la Mancha (Cervantes), 102, 124
Douglass, Frederick, 36, 111
Dussel, Enrique, 9

Eastern State Penitentiary, 79, 85
emancipation, 3–4, 10, 79, 83, 87, 89, 93–96, 99, 104, 111–12, 121, 137, 145, 158–59; self-emancipation, 17, 32, 44, 45, 74, 112, 146, 148, 158–59; self-purchase, 46, 74. See also *coartación*
England, 19, 21, 56, 101, 114
Enlightenment, 8, 23–26, 36, 43, 51, 53–56, 59, 67, 75–77, 79, 81, 84, 87, 93, 94, 96
enslavement: in Ballou, 99, 106, 111–13, 118–19; in Barnet, 165; in Beaumont and Tocqueville, 79–84; history of, 3–4, 7, 10, 14–16, 18, 46, 71, 104, 148; in Howe, 120, 122–23, 127–28, 130, 137–40; laws, 39, 44, 46–47, 49, 52, 91, 95, 112, 137–38, 154, 158–59; in literature, 3–7, 10, 16–18, 23–27, 36, 41–43, 54, 56, 58, 63–64, 71, 75, 142–44; in Manzano, 32, 36, 39–43, 46–47, 49–52; in Merlin, 77, 79, 87–96; in Ripley, 142–43, 146, 149, 152, 154, 158, 160–61; in Suárez y Romero, 63–64, 67–71; in Triay, 71–73, 76
Equiano, Olaudah, 36
"Escenas campestres. Baile de los negros" (Baralt), 59–67
esclavos en las colonias españolas, Los (Merlin), 77–96
Espinosa Miñoso, Yuderkys, 12, 128
Europe, 8, 11, 14–15, 19–20, 36, 55–56, 59–61, 67, 109, 128, 135, 144, 162
Everett, Alexander, 105, 110, 116–17
Everett, Edward, 105–7

Fanon, Frantz, 8, 13
Ferrer, Ada, 15, 146–49, 163

filibusters, 18, 101, 103, 116, 137
Fish, Hamilton, 145, 149–50
France, 17, 26, 55–56, 77, 79–80, 82, 84, 86, 93, 101, 104, 114, 132
Francisco. El ingenio o las delicias del campo (Suárez y Romero), 63–64, 66–67, 69–70, 72
freedom fighter. See *mambí*
French drum. See *tumba francesa*
From Flag to Flag (Ripley), 24, 27, 141–61

Gala, Marcial, 166
Garrison, William Lloyd, 123, 127
Gates, Henry Louis, Jr., 168, 170
gender, 12–13, 27, 42, 78, 87, 109–10, 120–23, 128–29, 134–35, 139–40
Giral, Sergio, 116
Gleason, Frederick, 100
Gleijeses, Piero, 103–4
godparenting. See *padrinazgo*
Gómez de Avellaneda, Gertrudis, 39, 49, 78
Gordon, Jane Anna, 6, 25, 35
Gordon, Lewis, 6, 35
Grant, Mary H., 122–23, 157
Grant, Ulysses S., 145, 158
Guerra de los Diez Años, 18, 24, 27, 71, 72, 101, 142, 145, 156–59, 161, 163–64
Guevara, Gema R., 16, 19, 26, 51, 101, 104, 110
Guillén, Nicolás, 166–67

Haiti, 15, 16, 86, 93; Revolution, 13, 16, 62, 78–79, 83, 86, 88–89, 91, 93, 104, 106, 111, 104
Harper, Frances Ellen Watkins, 139
Harris, Joel Chandler, 72, 144
Havana, 32–33, 36, 38, 43–44, 46, 49, 56, 63, 72–75, 78, 115–17, 129, 134, 136, 148, 168
Havard, John C., 14, 20–23, 102, 105, 108–9
Hawthorne, Sophia Peabody, 102
Hazard, Samuel, 102
Heredia, José María, 101
Hermaphrodite, The (Howe), 122
Hispanophilia, 22, 107, 172
Hispanophobia, 5, 11, 12, 15–16, 20–22, 105, 107, 109, 118, 124, 134, 141, 161

Hispanophobic discourse of coloniality, 5, 11, 20, 22, 27, 105–6, 109, 119–20, 124, 135, 138, 140, 142, 147, 161, 169; in Ballou, 99, 105–7, 109, 115, 118–19; in Howe, 120, 124, 135–36, 138–40; after nineteenth century, 162, 169; in Ripley, 142, 145, 147, 149, 152, 156–57, 159, 161
History of Cuba (Ballou), 26, 99–119
Howe, Julia Ward, 24, 26, 27, 57, 120–40, 145, 149–52, 161; *The Hermaphrodite*, 122; *Passion-Flowers*, 121; *Reminiscences, 1819–1899*, 121, 127–28, 140; *A Trip to Cuba*, 26–27, 120–40, 145, 152
Howe, Samuel "Chev" Gridley, 120–23, 140
Hughes, Langston, 166–67
Humboldt, Alexander von, 57, 102, 105, 107

identity: African, 4, 16–17, 34, 50, 52, 113; Afro-Cuban, 16, 32, 45, 52, 62, 66, 76, 113; Anglo-Saxon, 12, 19–20, 26–27, 99, 106, 108–9, 115, 117–20, 127, 142; Black, 34, 125; Cuban, 3–4, 15, 17, 23–25, 35, 38–39, 43, 51–52, 54, 57–58, 162–64; English, 19, 124–25; *mulato*, 35, 37, 45, 50–52, 164, 169; racial, 4–5, 17, 37, 50–52, 120, 125, 149, 162–63, 169; Spanish, 12, 21, 54, 71; US, 3, 5, 19, 20, 105, 120, 125, 141, 144, 149, 157, 163
indenture. *See* Chinese: indentured
Indigenous, 9, 11, 13–14, 82, 107, 109, 118, 162
"Ingenios" (Suárez y Romero), 64–67
Islam. *See* religion
Islamophobia, 5, 11, 21, 22, 105, 109. *See also* Orientalism

Jackson, Richard L., 50
Jáuregui, Carlos A., 9
Jefferson, Thomas, 4

Kennedy, John Pendleton, 143
Kirkpatrick, Susan, 55
Kohn, Margaret, 80–81
Kutzinski, Vera M., 167

Landaluze, Víctor Patricio de, 57
language use, 14

Larra, Mariano José de, 55
Latin America, 8–9, 13–14, 19–20, 22, 44–45, 57, 102, 148, 166–68
Lee, Robert E., 146
"Lettre XX" (Merlin), 77–96
Ley Moret, 158
literature: antislavery, 33, 35–36, 39, 41, 43, 51, 63, 70, 75, 80, 88–90; Cuban, 3–6, 17, 43, 91, 132, 150, 152, 166; nonfiction, 3–6, 10, 16–17, 63, 163; plantation narrative, 17, 27, 132, 141–44, 149–51, 159; travel narrative, 5–6, 18, 26, 101–2, 123, 135; US, 3–6, 18, 20–22, 102, 108–9, 143
López, Alfred J., 7
López, Narciso, 18, 101, 103
Lorde, Audre, 6, 25, 35
Louis Philippe I, 78
Lugones, María, 12, 121
Luis, William, 33–34, 46, 50, 71–72, 132, 165

Madden, Richard Robert, 33
Maldonado-Torres, Nelson, 4, 13
mambí, 158, 164; freedom fighter, 4, 28, 158, 163
Manifest Destiny, 18, 26, 99, 103, 105, 115–20, 138
Mann, Mary Peabody, 102
Manzano, Juan Francisco, 16–17, 25, 31–52, 64, 67, 74, 91–92, 112–13, 132; *Autobiografía del esclavo poeta*, 16, 25, 31–52
Marie, or Slavery in the United States (Beaumont), 79–81, 83, 87, 89, 92, 94, 106
maroon communities, 49, 158
Martí, José, 19, 31, 71, 163–64
McHatton, James Alexander, 143, 148, 151–54
Méndez Rodenas, Adriana, 62–63, 78, 87–88, 90
Merlin, Antoine Christophe, 78
Merlin, Condesa de, 17, 25–26, 77–96, 99, 102, 105–6, 111–12, 114–15, 118, 129–30; *Los esclavos en las colonias españolas*, 77–96; "Lettre XX," 77–96
Mesonero Romanos, Ramón de, 55
mestizo, 147, 166. *See also* race
Mexico, 27, 103, 107, 116–17, 141, 147–50, 157

Mignolo, Walter D., 4–7, 9, 11, 12, 15–16, 21, 22, 35, 43, 105, 109, 118, 162
modernity, 4, 7–12, 14, 17, 19, 23–24, 51, 53–56, 59, 73, 162; modernity/coloniality, 4, 7, 9–11
Molloy, Sylvia, 33–35, 40, 43, 67, 78
Montejo, Esteban, 31, 112, 165. *See also* Barnet, Miguel
Montesinos, José F., 54
mulato, 34, 36, 44, 48–50, 84, 134, 163, 165. *See also* race
mulata, 69, 173. *See also* race
multiracial population, 27, 144, 149, 158

Nayar, Sheila, 32, 36
North America, 19, 100, 107. *See also* United States

Ocasio, Rafael, 5, 55, 57–58, 63–64, 66–68, 70, 72–73, 113
O'Donnell, Leopoldo, 88
off-white, 20, 26, 106, 108–9, 111, 114, 116, 118, 135–36, 138. *See also* Hispanophobia
Orientalism, 22, 27, 99, 105, 108–10, 118, 120, 124, 128, 134, 136, 140, 147–48, 161, 169; Moorish, 22, 109, 148. *See also* Hispanophobia; Islamophobia
Oriente, 59, 62, 157–58
Ortiz, Fernando, 62, 164–65
Ostend Manifesto, 18, 103
O'Sullivan, John J., 103

padrinazgo, 44, 52
Palma, Ramón de, 33
Passion-Flowers (Howe), 121
patronato, 71, 159–60
penitentiary, 79–80, 84–85
Pérez, Louis A., Jr., 4, 169
Pettway, Matthew, 43–45
Pezuela, Juan Manuel González de la, 104, 115
Pierce, Franklin, 18, 103
Pizarro González, Francisco, 107, 135
Plácido. *See* Valdés, Gabriel de la Concepción
plantation narrative. *See* literature

Polk, James K., 18, 103
postcolonial theory, 8, 20, 67
Pratt, Mary Louise, 102, 130
pro-enslavement, 18, 23–24, 88, 94, 142; proslavery, 4, 88–89, 112, 123
Protestantism. *See* religion

Quijano, Aníbal, 4, 9, 12, 171–72

race, 4–5, 10, 12, 14, 16, 19–21, 23, 27; in Ballou, 99, 104, 111, 118; in Howe, 120–25, 127–29, 134–35, 137, 139–40; in Manzano, 35, 39, 40–41, 51; in Merlin, 79–80, 82–83, 86–88, 91, 94–95; mixed-race, 20, 51, 82–83, 86, 94, 135; race war, 16, 23, 79, 94–95, 99, 104, 111, 118, 137; in Ripley, 141–42, 149, 152, 155, 166–69
racelessness, 24, 71, 163, 164; myth of racial equality, 27, 163–66
racism, 22, 28, 50, 58, 79, 81–82, 85, 88, 113, 121–22, 127, 140, 164–68
Ramos, Julio, 47
Reconstruction, 141–43, 145, 152, 156
religion, 11, 31, 45, 92, 109, 162; African, 43, 45, 52, 92; Afro-Cuban, 44–45, 52, 66, 92, 164; Catholicism, 11, 19, 43–45, 92, 109, 126, 136; Christianity, 8–9, 11, 21, 19, 43–45, 52, 61, 67, 87, 91, 118, 136, 162; Islam, 11, 21–22, 118, 136, 162; Protestantism, 11, 19, 26, 43, 99, 100, 109, 147
Reminiscences, 1819–1899 (Howe), 121, 127–28, 140
resistance, 5–6, 8, 13, 17, 24–25, 32, 34–35, 43, 46, 67, 69, 71, 76, 99, 113–14, 119, 134, 148, 151, 158–59, 166
Ripley, Eliza Chinn McHatton, 23, 24, 27, 72, 132, 141–61; *From Flag to Flag*, 24, 27, 141–61; *Social Life in Old New Orleans*, 143
Rousseau, Jean-Jacques, 36, 39

Saco, José Antonio, 4, 15–16, 51, 64, 83, 85, 87, 88–90, 92, 95–96, 105, 111–12, 118
Sagra, Ramón de la, 105, 107
Said, Edward W., 8, 105

Salvatore, Ricardo D., 8
San Millán, Blas, 57–58
Santa Cruz y Montalvo, María de las Mercedes. *See* Merlin, Condesa de
Schulman, Ivan, 32–35, 41–42, 64, 171
Scott, Rebecca, 152, 158
self-emancipation. *See* emancipation
settlerism, 3, 16, 82, 85, 94, 100, 117–19, 137, 139
slavery. *See* enslavement
Social Life in Old New Orleans (Ripley), 143
solidarity, 5, 7, 17, 24–25, 46, 48–50, 52, 54, 59, 63–64, 67, 71, 76, 113–14, 119, 134, 151
Sommer, Doris, 163
Sousa Santos, Boaventura de, 10, 171. *See also* abyssal
Spain, 3–5, 8–11, 15–16, 19–23, 25–27, 32, 53–58, 73, 75–76, 78, 86, 99–109, 114–18, 120, 132, 134, 135, 138, 143, 145, 152, 157–59, 162–63
Spaniard: in Ballou, 105–8, 110–11, 116, 119; in Hispanophobic discourse, 11, 19, 20, 21, 23, 26, 102; in Howe, 134–35, 138
Steinkampf, Michael, 165–66, 168, 170
Suárez y Romero, Anselmo, 17, 25, 33, 39, 45, 49, 51, 54, 59, 63–72, 76, 91, 112–13, 130, 133, 173, 175, 177, 179; "El cementerio del ingenio," 17, 68–71, 112, 175; *Francisco. El ingenio o las delicias del campo*, 63–64, 66–67, 69–70, 72; "Ingenios," 64–67
suicide, 17, 69, 76, 114, 119, 131, 138
Sumner, Charles, 122

Tanco y Bosmeniel, Félix, 51
teatro bufo, 72–73
tertulia. *See* Del Monte, Domingo
Tocqueville, Alexis de, 17, 26, 77, 79–96, 105, 106, 111–12, 114, 117, 118, 130, 146; *Democracy in America*, 79–83, 106, 111
Torres-Pou, Joan, 78–79, 84–85
transculturation, 25, 45, 59, 62, 73, 76, 102, 164. *See also contrapunteo*; Ortíz, Francisco
travel narrative. *See* literature

Triay, José E., 17, 25, 40, 54, 71–76; "El calesero," 17, 40, 71–76
Trip to Cuba, A (Howe), 26–27, 120–40, 145, 152
Tristán, Flora, 78
tumba francesa, 59, 61–63, 76
Turnbull, David, 87, 102

United States, 3–8, 10, 12–15, 17–20, 22–27, 32, 63, 77–84, 86–87, 89, 92–96, 99–101, 103–4, 109, 114–20, 122, 125, 127–28, 130, 135, 137, 139–46, 149–50, 152–64, 166–70
US Americans, 14, 143, 147. *See also* Black US American(s)

Valdés, Gabriel de la Concepción (Plácido), 32
Villaverde, Cirilo, 39, 59, 91, 132; *Cecilia Valdés; o, La Loma del Ángel*, 39, 59, 63, 132, 170

Walker, William, 103
Walsh, Catherine E., 6–7, 35. *See also* Mignolo, Walter D.
Wexler, Alice R., 101–2, 104, 110
whiteness, 10, 12, 14–17, 23, 26–27, 34, 36–37, 43, 45, 50–52, 58, 70, 118, 135, 139, 142, 147, 150, 161–62
whitening. *See blanqueamiento*
Williams, Claudette M., 66–67, 70
Wong, Edlie, 142–43, 149, 152–56, 159–60

X, Malcolm, 167

yellowface, 134, 144–45. *See also* Chinese
Yun, Lisa, 134, 152–53

Zambrana, Antonio, 71
Zurbano, Roberto, 166

ABOUT THE AUTHOR

Photo courtesy of the author

JULIA C. PAULK is associate professor of Spanish at Marquette University in Milwaukee, Wisconsin. Specializing in nineteenth-century Cuban and comparative literature, Dr. Paulk has published scholarly articles in noteworthy academic journals such as *Afro-Hispanic Review*, *Latin American Literary Review*, *Hispanófila*, *Luso-Brazilian Review*, and *Revista Hispánica Moderna* and an edited volume of essays, *Dominant Culture and the Education of Women*. In a continuation of her scholarly interest in Cuba and decolonial approaches to literary studies, she is currently at work on a book-length study of the representation of indentured Chinese in nineteenth-century Cuban texts.

www.ingramcontent.com/pod-product-compliance
Lightning Source LLC
Chambersburg PA
CBHW022019220426
43663CB00007B/1147